Quicken 2002 Deluxe for Macintosh

THE OFFICIAL GUIDE

Maria Langer

Osborne/**McGraw-Hill**

New York   Chicago   San Francisco   Lisbon
London   Madrid   Mexico City   Milan   New Delhi
San Juan   Seoul   Singapore   Sydney   Toronto

Osborne/**McGraw-Hill**
2600 Tenth Street
Berkeley, California 94710
U.S.A.

To arrange bulk purchase discounts for sales promotions, premiums, or fund-raisers, please contact Osborne/**McGraw-Hill** at the above address. For information on translations or book distributors outside the U.S.A., please see the International Contact Information page immediately following the index.

Quicken 2002 Deluxe for Macintosh: The Official Guide

1234567890 FGR FGR 01987654321

ISBN 0-07-219389-1

Intuit P/N 247245

Publisher
Brandon A. Nordin

Vice President & Associate Publisher
Scott Rogers

Editorial Director
Roger Stewart

Acquisitions Editor
Megg Bonar

Project Manager
Deidre Dolce

Freelance Project Manager
Laurie Stewart

Acquisitions Coordinator
Alex Corona

Technical Editor
Leigh Chapman

Copy Editor
Lunaea Weatherstone

Proofreader
Kelly Marshall

Indexer
Jack Lewis

Computer Designer
Maureen Forys,
Happenstance Type-O-Rama

Series Design
Jill Weil, Peter F. Hancik

This book was composed with QuarkXPress 4.11 on a Macintosh G4.

To Jonathan Brubaker at Intuit, for his help
during the preparation of this book.

Contents

Part Seven   Appendices

Acknowledgments

This book, like any other, is the end product of a lot of imagination and hard work by many people. I'd like to take a moment to thank the people who were involved with the creation of this book.

First, thanks again to Joanne Cuthbertson who developed the Quicken Press series idea for Osborne/McGraw-Hill way back when we did the first *Official Guide* for Quicken. Although Joanne has moved on to other work, she should be glad to know that the series she developed is still going strong.

Next, thanks to Megg Bonar, acquisitions editor at Osborne/McGraw-Hill, for her guidance and support. Her patience, understanding, and support make her stand out among other editors.

Next, thanks to the folks at Intuit, starting with Adam Samuels, Leigh Chapman, and Jonathan Brubaker. These guys made sure I had everything I needed to write the book, and then made sure everything I wrote was correct. More thanks go out to Mike Barden, Linda Pan, Todd Santos, Theresa McGuinness, and Jeff Zimmerman. And a huge thanks go out to the Quicken 2002 development team for not only adding new features to the Mac version of Quicken, but rebuilding it for Mac OS X, so Mac users can take advantage of the latest version of Apple's new operating system. Finally, a big thanks to the Quicken 2002 beta support team for giving me quick answers to quick questions when I had them.

More thanks go to the production and editorial folks, including Alex Corona, Lunaea Weatherstone, Maureen Forys, and Laurie Stewart.

A huge thanks to Jeremy Judson at Osborne/McGraw-Hill for suggesting me for the Quicken Press projects. Four years and counting!

The last thanks goes to Mike for his continuing patience and support as I worked on this book—my 40th since 1992.

Introduction

Choosing Quicken to organize your finances was a great decision. Quicken has all the tools you need to manage your personal finances. Its well-designed, intuitive interface makes it easy to use. And its online and automation features make entering transactions and paying bills a snap. But if that isn't enough, Quicken also offers features that can help you learn more about financial opportunities that can save you time and money—two things there never seems to be enough of.

Choosing this book to learn Quicken was also a good decision. As the Official Guide, it has Intuit Corporation's "seal of approval"—which means that Intuit, the developer of Quicken, was involved throughout the book's planning, writing, and production stages. The book was even reviewed for accuracy by the folks at Intuit's Technical Support department.

This introduction tells you a little about the book and a little about me, so you know what to expect in the chapters to come.

About this Book

Throughout this book, I tell you how to get the most out of Quicken. I start by explaining the basics—the common, everyday tasks that you need to know just to use the program. Then I go beyond the basics to show you how to use Quicken to save time, save money, and make smart financial decisions. Along the way, I'll show you all of Quicken's features, including a bunch that you probably didn't even know existed. You'll find yourself using Quicken for far more than you ever dreamed you would.

Every book is based on certain assumptions, presents information in a certain order, and uses certain conventions to communicate information. This book is no different. Knowing the book's assumptions, organization, and conventions can help you understand how to use this book as a learning tool.

Assumptions

In writing this book, I had to make a few assumptions about your knowledge of your computer, Mac OS, Quicken, and financial management. These assumptions give me a starting point, making it possible for me to skip over the things that I assume you already know.

What You Should Know About Your Computer and Mac OS

To use this book (or Quicken 2002, for that matter), you should have a general understanding of how to use your computer and Mac OS. You don't need to be an expert. As you'll see, Quicken uses many standard and intuitive interface elements, making it easy to use even if you're a complete computer novice.

At a bare minimum, you should know how to turn your computer on and off and how to use your mouse. You should also know how to perform basic Mac OS tasks, such as launching and quitting programs, using menus and dialogs, and entering and editing text.

If you're not sure how to do these things, check the manual that came with your computer or consult Mac OS Help (for Mac OS X, choose Mac Help from the Help menu; for Mac OS 9, choose Help Center from the Help menu). These two resources can provide all the information you need to get started.

What You Should Know About Quicken and Financial Management

You don't need to know much about either Quicken or financial management to get the most out of this book: I assume that both are new to you.

This doesn't mean that this book is just for raw beginners. I provide plenty of useful information for seasoned Quicken users—especially those of you who have used previous versions of Quicken—and for people who have been managing their finances with other tools, such as other software (welcome to Quicken!) or pencil and paper (welcome to the new millennium!).

Because I assume that all this is new to you, I make a special effort to explain Quicken procedures, as well as the financial concepts and terms on which they depend. New concepts and terms first appear in italic type. By understanding these things, not only can you better understand how to use Quicken, you can communicate more effectively with finance professionals such as bankers, stock brokers, and financial advisors.

Organization

This book is logically organized into six parts, each with at least two chapters. It starts with the most basic concepts and procedures, most of which involve specific Quicken tasks, and then works its way up to more advanced topics, many of which are based on finance-related concepts that Quicken makes easy to master.

I want to stress one point here: it is not necessary to read this book from beginning to end. Skip around as desired. Although the book is organized for cover-to-cover reading, not all of its information may apply to you. For example, if you're not the least bit interested in investing, skip the chapters related to investing. It's as simple as that. When you're ready for the information that you skipped, it'll be waiting for you.

Now here's a brief summary of the book's organization and contents.

Part One: Quicken Setup and Basics

This part of the book introduces Quicken's interface and features and helps you set up Quicken for managing your finances. It also provides the information you need to set up and test Quicken's online features. If you're brand new to Quicken, I highly recommend reading at least the first two chapters in this part of the book.

Part One has three chapters:

- Chapter 1: Getting to Know Quicken
- Chapter 2: Setting Up Accounts and Categories
- Chapter 3: Going Online with Quicken and Quicken.com

Part Two: Managing Your Bank and Credit Card Accounts

This part of the book is primarily how-to information about using Quicken to record financial transactions in bank and credit card accounts. One chapter concentrates on the basics while the other chapter goes beyond the basics to discuss online features available within Quicken and on Quicken.com.

There are two chapters in Part Two:

- Chapter 4: Recording Your Bank and Credit Card Transactions
- Chapter 5: Online Banking with Quicken

Part Three: Tracking Your Investments

This part of the book explains how you can use Quicken and Quicken.com to keep track of your investment portfolio and get information to help you make smart investment decisions. The first chapter covers the basics of Quicken's investment tracking features while the other two chapters provide information about other tools within Quicken and on Quicken.com for entering investment transactions and researching investment opportunities.

There are three chapters in Part Three:

- Chapter 6: Investment Tracking Basics
- Chapter 7: Using Online Investment Tracking Tools
- Chapter 8: Maximizing Investment Returns

Part Four: Managing Your Assets and Debt

This part of the book concentrates on assets and liabilities, including your home- and car-related loans. It starts by explaining how you can track these items in Quicken, then goes on to explain how you can minimize expenses with research features on Quicken and Quicken.com.

There are two chapters in Part Four:

- Chapter 9: Monitoring Assets and Loans
- Chapter 10: Minimizing Home, Car, and Insurance Expenses

Part Five: Saving Money and Achieving Your Goals

This part of the book helps you save money by minimizing your income taxes and using Quicken's built-in and Web-based saving tools. This part also shows you how you can use Quicken to help achieve your goals through the use of Quicken and Quicken.com's thorough and well thought-out planning features. Whether you want to have financial security in your retirement years or save up for the down payment on a house or college education for your children, Quicken can help you.

Part Five has three chapters:

- Chapter 11: Saving Money at Tax Time
- Chapter 12: Reducing Debt and Saving Money
- Chapter 13: Planning for the Future

Part Six: Working with Quicken Data

Once you've entered data into Quicken, you can use that information to manage and analyze your finances. That's what this part of the book is all about. It explains how to reconcile accounts and generate reports and graphs. But it starts with a useful topic for any Quicken user: automation.

There are three chapters in Part Six:

- Chapter 14: Automating Your Quicken Transactions
- Chapter 15: Reconciling Accounts
- Chapter 16: Insights, Reports, and Graphs

Part Seven: Appendices

If 16 chapters aren't enough for you, there's more. Two appendices provide additional information about working with Quicken:

- Appendix A: Managing Quicken Files
- Appendix B: Customizing Quicken

Conventions

All how-to books—especially computer books—have certain conventions for communicating information. The following sections outline the conventions I use throughout this book.

Menu Commands

Quicken, like other Mac OS programs, makes commands accessible on the menu bar at the top of screen. Throughout this book, I tell you which menu commands to choose to open a window or dialog or to complete a task. I use the following format to indicate menu commands: Menu | Submenu (if applicable) | Command.

So, for example, if I wanted you to choose the Bills command under the Lists menu, I'd tell you to choose Lists | Bills. If I wanted you to choose the Budget Setup command from the Budgeting submenu under the Activities menu, I'd tell you to choose Activities | Budgeting | Budget Setup.

Keystrokes

Keystrokes are the keys you must press to complete a task. There are two kinds of keystrokes.

Keyboard Shortcuts   Keyboard shortcuts are combinations of keys you press to complete a task more quickly. For example, the shortcut for "clicking" a Cancel button may be to press the ESC key. When instructing you to press a key, I provide the name of the key in small caps, like this: ESC. If you must press two or more keys simultaneously, I separate them with a hyphen, like this: COMMAND-P.

Literal Text   Literal text is text that you must type in exactly as it appears in the book. Although there aren't many instances of literal text in this book, there are a few. I display literal text in bold type, like this: **Checking Acct**. If literal text includes a variable—text you must substitute when you type—I include the variable in bold italic type, like this: ***Payee Name.***

Icons

I use icons to indicate a wide variety of useful information.

Shortcut | *Like most other Mac OS programs, Quicken frequently offers more than one way to complete a task. The Shortcut icon identifies a method for completing a Quicken task more quickly than other methods.*

Tip | *A Tip is a little something extra that you don't really need to know. Tips help you get more out of Quicken when you're ready to go beyond the basics.*

Note   *A Note provides more information to explain how Quicken works or how a Quicken feature can help you manage your finances.*

Caution   *A Caution is vitally important information that can protect you from data loss or other serious consequences. Don't skip the Cautions!*

New In Quicken 2002   In addition to extensive interface changes, the folks at Intuit made plenty of changes to Quicken's feature set. The New In Quicken 2002 icon identifies many new features.

About the Author

Finally, let me tell you a little bit about me.

I graduated from Hofstra University with a BBA in Accounting in—well, you don't really need to know *when*. I worked as an accountant, auditor, and financial analyst over the next eight years. Then I realized that I really didn't like what I was doing every day and took the necessary steps to change careers. This is the 40th computer book I've written since the change; many of the others are about business and productivity software such as Word, Excel, and FileMaker Pro. Although some of my books are for Windows users, I'm a Mac person at heart, so most of my books are for the Mac OS platform.

I use Quicken. I've been using it for years. I use it to manage five bank accounts and four credit card accounts, to track three mortgages, and to pay all my bills (online, of course). I also use its investment features to track my portfolio and research the companies in which I invest. While I don't use all Quicken features regularly, I've used them all at least once to save time, save money, make important financial decisions, or help me plan for my future.

Frankly, I can't imagine not using Quicken. And I'm glad to have the opportunity to show you why you should agree.

Quicken Setup and Basics

This part introduces Quicken's interface and features. It begins by explaining how to install Quicken and showing you the elements of its user interface. It tells you all about Quicken's accounts and categories, and explains how you can modify the default setup to add your own accounts and categories. Finally, it tells you why you should be interested in online access and how you can set up your computer to access the Internet and Quicken.com. The three chapters are:

Chapter 1: *Getting to Know Quicken*

Chapter 2: *Setting Up Accounts and Categories*

Chapter 3: *Going Online with Quicken and Quicken.com*

Getting to Know Quicken

In this Chapter:

- *An overview of Quicken*

- *Installing Quicken*

- *Launching and quitting Quicken*

- *The Quicken interface*

- *Onscreen help*

If you're brand new to Quicken, get your relationship with Quicken off to a good start by properly installing it and learning a little more about how you can interact with it.

In this chapter, I provide a brief overview of Quicken, explain how to install and launch it, take you on a tour of its interface, tell you how to customize it, and show you how to use its extensive onscreen Help features. Although the information I provide in this chapter is especially useful to new Quicken users, some of it also applies to upgrading users.

What Is Quicken?

On the surface, Quicken is a computerized checkbook. It enables you to balance your accounts and organize, manage, and generate reports for your finances. But as you explore Quicken, you'll learn that it's much more than just a computerized checkbook. It's a complete personal finance software package—a tool for taking control of your finances and making your money work harder for you.

What Quicken Can Help You Do

At the very least, Quicken can help you manage your bank and credit card accounts. You can enter transactions and have Quicken generate reports and graphs that show where your money went and how much is left.

Quicken can also help you manage investment accounts. You can enter transactions and have Quicken tell you the market value of your investments. Quicken can also help you organize other data, such as the purchase price and current worth information for your possessions.

With all financial information stored in Quicken's database, you can generate net worth reports to see where you stand today. You can also use a variety of planning calculators to make financial decisions for the future. And Quicken's Deduction Finder helps you find deductible expenses for tax time.

With Quicken's online features, you can automate much of your data entry. Online banking enables you to keep track of bank account transactions and balances and to pay bills without writing checks or sticking on stamps. You can also explore a whole world of up-to-date information that you can use to shop for the best bank accounts, credit card accounts, loans, and insurance. You can read news and information about investment opportunities and advice offered by financial experts. You can get in touch with other Quicken users to see how they use Quicken to manage their money.

Now tell me, can the paper check register that came with your checks do all that?

Save Time, Save Money, Get Smarter

This book has an underlying theme: save time, save money, and make informed financial decisions. You'll see plenty of examples of how Quicken can do this throughout this book, but here are a few simple examples to whet your appetite:

Save Time   Entering transactions into registers can be tedious. But Quicken offers several features for speeding up this process, including memorized transactions, QuickFill, and the ability to download transactions from financial institutions.

Save Money   Many of the organizations you pay every month—credit card companies, banks, and utilities—charge a late fee when payment is received after the due date. Quicken's Billminder feature helps you remember when payments are due. Its online payment and scheduling features can work together to automatically pay bills when they are due. Making timely payments saves money.

Get Smarter   Buying a home is a big purchase decision that is based on many smaller decisions. How much can you afford to spend on a home? What are the current interest rates and other loan terms? What will your monthly payments be? Which loan is right for you? Quicken can help answer all of these questions by providing access to up-to-date information via Quicken Loans and a variety of planning tools, such as the Loan Calculator.

These are just a few examples. Quicken is full of smart features like these. It takes the drudgery out of organizing and managing your finances and rewards you by helping you make the most of your money.

Quicken 2002 Is Built for Mac OS X

For 2002, Quicken was rewritten to take advantage of many of Mac OS X's new features, including the Aqua interface. You'll see how Quicken looks on Mac OS X in screen shots throughout this book.

Don't think you need to upgrade to Mac OS X to use Quicken 2002. The so-called "Classic Mac" version of Quicken 2002 will work on systems running Mac OS 9.0.4 or later. Although this book illustrates Quicken on Mac OS X, if instructions vary between the Mac OS X and Classic Mac versions of Quicken, they'll be provided in the text.

Getting Started

Ready to get started? This section explains how to install, launch, and register Quicken. It also explains how to prepare a new data file or update an existing data file for use with Quicken 2002.

Installing Quicken

Quicken uses a basic Mac OS installer that should be familiar to you if you've installed other Mac programs. It installs the software in the Applications folder of your hard disk.

Insert the Quicken CD into your CD-ROM drive. If necessary, double-click the Quicken 2002 Deluxe CD icon that appears on your Desktop to open its window. Double-click the Install Quicken 2002 icon. The installer's splash screen with general information about Quicken appears. Click Continue.

The installer displays a software license agreement. Read the agreement. To continue the installation, you'll have to click Accept.

Next, the installer displays some important information about installing Quicken. Read the information and click Continue.

Finally, the main Install Quicken 2002 window appears:

Tip   *By default, the installer installs Quicken's files in the Applications folder on your startup disk, which is normally your internal hard disk. You can select a different location from the Install Location pop-up menu at the bottom of the window. If you choose Select Folder, a standard Open dialog appears. Use it to locate and select the folder you want to install the Quicken 2002 Deluxe folder into. Then click Select.*

Click Install. The installer begins the installation process. It displays a progress dialog and information about Quicken's features while it works. When it's finished, it displays a dialog telling you that the software was successfully installed. Click Quit or Restart—whichever appears.

Tip   *If you're upgrading from a previous version of Quicken, you can delete the old Quicken folder once you've begun using your data file with Quicken 2002. Make sure your Quicken data file is not in the old Quicken folder, and then drag the folder to the Trash and empty the Trash.*

Quicken 2002 Deluxe Components

A default installation of Quicken places the Quicken 2002 Deluxe folder in the Applications folder on your hard disk. Open the folder to access Quicken's files:

- **Quicken 2002 Deluxe** is the main Quicken program I discuss throughout this book.
- **Installation Guide.pdf** and **User Guide.pdf** are two documentation files you can open to learn more about installing and using Quicken.

Other items in the Quicken 2002 Deluxe folder include information and support files that work with Quicken.

QuickEntry and Billminder, which were part of previous versions of Quicken, are no longer supported by Intuit so they are not installed with Quicken 2002. You can find them, however, in the Unsupported Applications folder on the Quicken 2002 Deluxe CD.

Launching Quicken

You can launch Quicken components two different ways:

Open the Quicken application icon   To open Quicken, double-click its icon in the Quicken 2002 Deluxe folder window.

Open a Quicken data file icon   You can launch Quicken and open a specific Quicken data file by double-clicking the data file icon. I tell you more about data files later in this chapter.

Tip   *If you use Quicken often, you can add it to the Dock (Mac OS X) or Favorites submenu on the Apple menu (Mac OS 9) so it's quicker and easier to open. On Mac OS X, drag the Quicken 2002 Deluxe icon to the Dock to add the Quicken application icon to the Dock. On Mac OS 9, select the Quicken 2002 Deluxe icon and choose File | Add To Favorites to add it to the Favorites submenu.*

Personalizing and Registering Quicken

The first time you launch Quicken, a personalization dialog appears. Enter your name in the edit box and click OK.

Next, a registration dialog appears. You have three options:

- **Remind Later** tells Quicken to remind you to register the next time you launch Quicken. Quicken will keep reminding you until you register.

- **Don't Register** dismisses the dialog without giving you a chance to register. The dialog will not appear again.

- **Register Online** uses your Internet connection to exchange information with the folks at Intuit. When you click this button, Quicken launches your default Web browser—Netscape Navigator (or Communicator) or Microsoft Internet Explorer—connects to the Internet, and displays a Product Registration form on Quicken.com. Follow the instructions that appear onscreen to complete the registration process and set up a Quicken.com account if you don't already have one. Then click the Quicken 2002 Deluxe icon in the Dock (Mac OS X) or choose Quicken 2002 Deluxe from the application menu in the upper-right corner of the screen (Mac OS 9) to return to Quicken.

Preparing a Data File

Quicken stores all of your financial information in a Quicken data file. Before you can use Quicken, you must either create a new data file or convert an existing data file for use with Quicken 2002.

The first time you launch Quicken 2002, a dialog asks whether you are an upgrading user or a new user. Click the appropriate button.

Upgrading User Setup

When you click Upgrading User, Quicken displays a series of dialogs with information about Quicken's new features. Click Continue in each dialog to learn about these features.

Next, Quicken displays a standard Open dialog you can use to locate, select, and open your existing data file:

When you click Open, Quicken makes a copy of the data file and puts it into a folder called Old Quicken Data. It then updates the data file, which may take a few minutes; a progress bar appears as Quicken works. When it's finished, it opens the updated data file and displays the Quicken Insights window in the Services tab (see Figure 1-1).

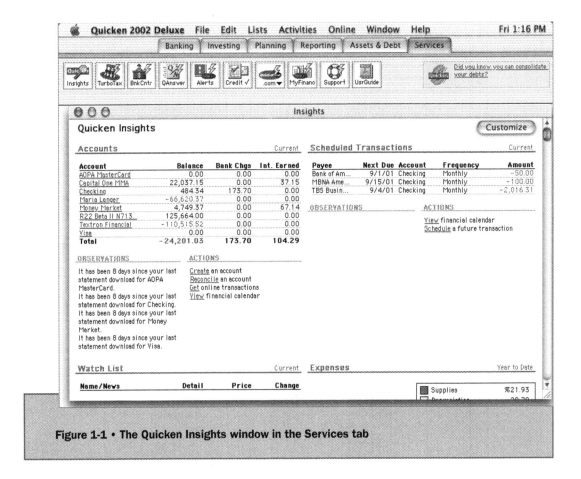

Figure 1-1 • The Quicken Insights window in the Services tab

Note   *If your Quicken data file included a customized toolbar, before updating it, Quicken displays a dialog telling you that it must overwrite previous settings. Click Yes to continue.*

New User Setup

When you click New User, Quicken displays the Quicken Assistant, a series of dialogs you can use to set up a new Quicken data file. The first dialog, which is shown next, asks what you plan to use Quicken for: household use, business use, or both. Click to place check marks beside each use; the options you check will determine which categories are included in your Quicken data file. (I tell you more about categories in Chapter 2, so don't worry if the term doesn't mean much to you now.) Then click Continue.

Quicken creates a data file named Quicken Data. It displays the next dialog of the Quicken Assistant, which tells you a little about the types of accounts you can create. (I tell you more about accounts in Chapter 2, also.) Click Next to continue. The next dialog provides some more information about accounts. Click Next.

In the next dialog, you can use a pop-up menu to select the type of account you want to create. Normally, the first account you create will be a bank account, so choose Bank from the pop-up menu and click Next.

Next, Quicken asks you to enter a name for the account. Enter a descriptive account name in the edit box, such as Checking or Savings, and click Next. The next thing Quicken wants to know is the date and balance on your last bank statement. If your bank statement is handy, enter this information in the edit boxes, as shown next. Otherwise, you can enter today's date and 0 for the balance. Click Next.

A summary dialog appears next. It summarizes the information you entered in the previous steps. If the information is correct, click Go Ahead. If an item in the summary is not correct, click it to display a Quicken Assistant dialog where you can change it. Then click Return to Summary to return to the corrected summary, and click Go Ahead.

Quicken creates the new account and displays a Conclusion dialog. Click OK to dismiss the Quicken Assistant.

Note | *I explain the options in the Conclusion dialog of the Quicken Assistant in Chapter 2.*

Quicken displays the new data file's Quicken Insights and Accounts windows in its Services tab (see Figure 1-2).

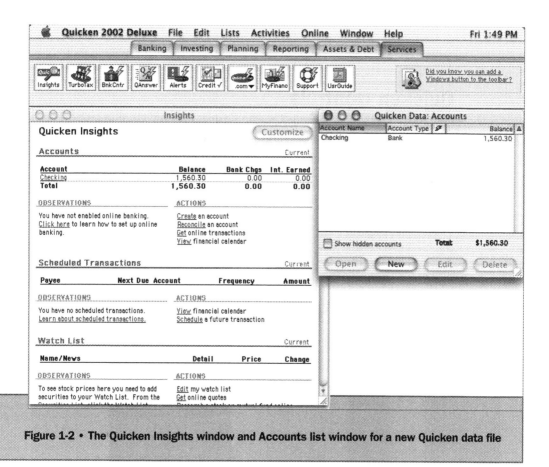

Figure 1-2 • The Quicken Insights window and Accounts list window for a new Quicken data file

Quitting Quicken

When you've finished using Quicken, choose Quicken 2002 Deluxe | Quit Quicken 2002 Deluxe (Mac OS X) or File | Quit (Mac OS 9) or press COMMAND-Q. This saves your data file and closes the Quicken application.

The Quicken Interface

Quicken's interface is designed to be intuitive and easy to use. It puts the tools you need to manage your finances right within mouse pointer reach. You never have to dig through multiple dialogs and menus to get to the commands you need most.

In this section, I tell you about the components of the Quicken interface and explain how you can use them to make your work with Quicken easy.

Quicken Controls

Like most Mac OS programs, Quicken utilizes a number of menus and other controls to access information and features. Figures 1-1, 1-2, and 1-3 show some of these elements. Here's a quick look at each of them.

Menu bar   Quicken displays a number of menus in a menu bar at the top of the screen. You can choose commands from the menus in two ways:

- Click the menu name to display the menu. If necessary, click the name of the submenu you want (as shown next), and then click the name of the command you want.

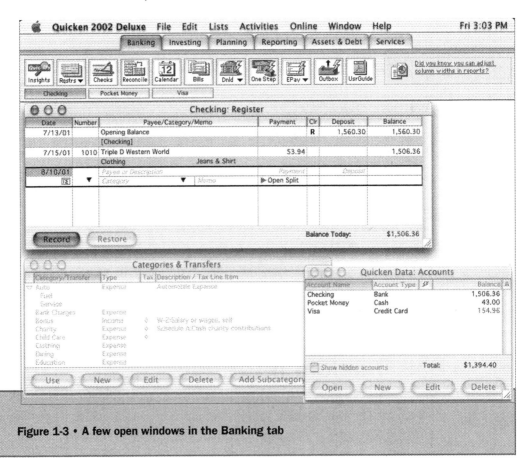

Figure 1-3 • A few open windows in the Banking tab

- Press the shortcut key combination for the menu command you want. A command's shortcut key, if it has one, is displayed to the right of the command name on the menu.

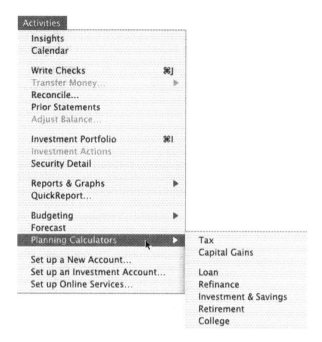

Contextual menus   Quicken fully supports Apple's contextual menus feature, which enables you to display a menu of commands for specific items on your screen. To use this feature, hold down the CONTROL key while clicking on an item. The following illustration, for example, shows the contextual menu that appears when you CONTROL-click on a register transaction. To access a command, click it. To close the contextual menu without selecting a command, click elsewhere on the screen.

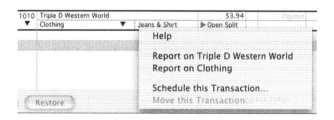

Tabs   Tabs are used to switch from one set of open Quicken windows and command buttons to another set. When you switch to a different tab, Quicken saves the open windows in the current tab. Thus, when you return to that tab, the windows appear just as you left them, enabling you to continue working where you left off.

Here's an example of how you can use tabs. You can use the Banking tab to pay some bills, then click the Investing tab to check your investments, and then click the Reporting tab to create a report. When you click the Banking tab, the windows are exactly the same as they were when you left them—set up for your banking tasks.

> **Tip**   *You can create new tabs for additional custom window configurations. I tell you how in Appendix B.*

Command buttons   Command buttons offer access to frequently used Quicken features. The command buttons that appear in the toolbar vary depending on the currently displayed tab. For example, the Banking tab displays command buttons for banking features, while the Investing tab displays command buttons for investing features. Buttons that include tiny black triangles (such as the Rgstrs button in Figure 1-3) are menus; choose an option from the button's menu to access its feature.

> **Tip**   *You can customize each set of command buttons by adding or removing buttons as desired. I tell you how in Appendix B.*

Account buttons   Account buttons (see Figure 1-3) offer one-click access to account registers.

> **Tip**   *You can specify which account buttons appear in each tab. I explain how in Chapter 2 and Appendix B.*

Tip Area   The Tip Area offers tips and other information about getting the most out of Quicken. Click an underlined link to learn more about a tip topic.

Windows

Quicken displays information in windows. It has different types of windows for the different types of information it displays. Here are some of the windows you'll work with as you use Quicken.

Insights   The Insights window (see Figures 1-1 and 1-2) provides information about your financial status, as well as clickable links to work with Quicken features and get information from the Internet.

Tip   *You can customize the Insights window so it shows the things that interest you most. I tell you how in Chapter 16.*

List windows   A list window shows a list of information about related things, such as accounts, categories, classes, or scheduled transactions. You can use a list window to perform tasks with items in the list. The Accounts window shown in Figures 1-2 and 1-3 and the Categories & Transfers window shown in Figure 1-1 and 1-3 are two examples of list windows.

Register windows   You use a register window to enter and edit transactions for a specific account. Each account has its own register. The Checking: Register window shown in Figure 1-3 is an example of a register window. I tell you more about using registers in Chapter 4.

Dialogs

Like other Mac OS applications, Quicken uses dialogs to communicate with you. Some dialogs display a simple message, while others include edit boxes, radio buttons, check boxes, and pop-up menus you can use to enter information. When a dialog appears, you must dismiss it before you can continue working with Quicken.

Quicken's Onscreen Help

Quicken includes a number of onscreen Help features that can you can use to learn more about using Quicken. This section takes a closer look at each of them.

Quicken Help

Quicken's primary onscreen Help feature uses the Mac OS Help Viewer engine to display Help topics and information for using Quicken. To access this feature, choose Help | Quicken Help. The Quicken Help window appears. Here's what it looks like with the Accounts topic selected:

Browsing Help

You can browse through Quicken Help topics by clicking a topic link on the left side of the window to display a list of subtopics on the right side of the window. Then click a link for a subtopic to display Help information or instructions for completing a task. Here's an example of the step-by-step instructions for setting up an account:

Searching Help

You can also search Quicken Help for specific topics. Simply enter a search word or phrase in the edit box at the top of the Quicken Help window and click Ask. A list of search results appears, as shown next. Click a topic's link to display information or instructions for that topic.

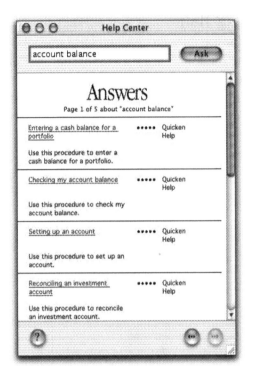

Tip   *The bullets to the left of each Help topic indicate how closely the topic matches the word or phrase you entered; the more bullets, the closer the match.*

User Guide

As discussed near the beginning of this chapter, a standard installation of Quicken places a file called User Guide.pdf in the Quicken 2002 Deluxe folder. This file is the Quicken 2002 User Guide in Adobe Acrobat PDF format. To display this document, click the User Guide button in the toolbar or double-click the document's icon in the Finder. Preview (Mac OS X) or Adobe Acrobat Reader (Mac OS 9) launches and the User Guide appears (see Figure 1-4).

Note   *Preview (Mac OS X) or Adobe Acrobat Reader (Mac OS 9) must be installed on your computer to use this feature. Preview is part of Mac OS X. The Adobe Acrobat Reader Installer is included on the Quicken 2002 Deluxe CD. If Acrobat is not already installed on your Mac OS 9 computer, you can use this installer to install it.*

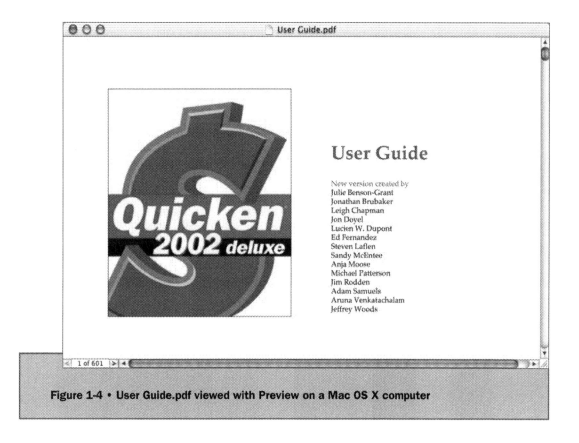

Figure 1-4 • User Guide.pdf viewed with Preview on a Mac OS X computer

Tip   *Clicking the User Guide button on Quicken's toolbar on a Mac OS X system may cause Quicken to launch the Classic environment to display the User Guide.pdf file. Although this is not a problem, it isn't the fastest way to open the file. To force your computer to open the file with Preview under Mac OS X, drag the User Guide.pdf file icon on top of the Preview icon in the Applications folder.*

You can use the page navigation buttons within the document window to move from one page to another. If desired, you can even use the Print command (File | Print or COMMAND-P) to print all 600 or so pages of the manual for reference.

Setting Up Accounts and Categories

In this Chapter:

- *Overview of data files, accounts, and categories*

- *Setting up accounts*

- *Working with the Accounts list*

- *Setting up categories and subcategories*

- *Working with the Categories & Transfers list*

To make the most of Quicken, you must properly set it up for your particular financial situation. This means adding accounts and categories as necessary to meet your specific needs. It takes only a minute or two to add each account or category. You'll probably want to do this when you first start using Quicken, but you can do it any time you like.

In this chapter, I explain how to set up the Quicken accounts and categories you'll use to organize your finances.

Before You Begin

Before you start the setup process, it's a good idea to have an understanding of how data files, accounts, and categories work. You should also gather together a few documents to help you properly set up your accounts.

Data Files

All the transactions you record with Quicken are stored in a *data file* on your hard disk. This file includes all the components—accounts, categories, and transactions—that make up your Quicken accounting system.

Although it's possible to have more than one Quicken data file, it isn't usually necessary. One file can hold all of your data. In fact, it's difficult (if not downright impossible) to use more than one Quicken file to track a single account, such as a checking or credit card account. And splitting your financial records among multiple data files makes it impossible to generate reports that consolidate all the information.

When would you want more than one data file? Well, you could use two data files if you wanted to use Quicken to organize your personal finances and the finances of your business, which have entirely separate bank, credit, and asset accounts. Multiple data files would also come in handy if you're using Quicken to track the separate finances of multiple individuals.

Accounts and Categories

There are two primary components to every transaction you record in Quicken: account and category.

An *account* is a record of what you either own or owe. For example, your checking account is a record of cash on deposit in the bank that is available for writing checks. A credit card account is a record of money you owe to the credit card company or bank for the use of your credit card. All transactions either increase or decrease the balance in one or more accounts.

A *category* is a record of where your money comes from or goes. For example, Salary is an income category for recording the money you earn from your job. Dining is an expense category you might use to record the cost of eating out. Categories make it possible to track how you earn and spend money.

If you know anything about accounting, these concepts should sound familiar, even if the names don't match what you learned in school or on the job. Accounts are what you'd find on a *balance sheet*; categories are what you'd find on an *income statement*. Quicken can produce reports like these; I tell you how in Chapter 16.

What You Need

To properly set up accounts, you should have balance information for the accounts that you want to monitor with Quicken. You can get this information from your most recent bank, investment, and credit card statements. It's a good idea to gather these documents before you start the setup process so they're on hand when you need them.

If you plan to use Quicken to replace an existing accounting system—whether it's paper-based or prepared with a different computer program—you may also find it helpful to have a *chart of accounts* (a list of account names) or a recent income statement. This way, when you set up Quicken accounts and categories, you can use familiar names.

Accounts

While the majority of your expenditures may come from your checking account, you probably have more than one account that Quicken can track for you. By setting up all of your accounts in Quicken, you can keep track of balances and activity to get a full picture of what you own and what you owe.

Types of Accounts

Quicken Deluxe offers seven different kinds of accounts for tracking what you own and what you owe.

What You Own

In accounting jargon, what you own are *assets*. In Quicken, an asset is one type of account, but there are several others:

Bank   Bank accounts are for tracking money in the bank. You can use bank accounts for checking, savings, and money market accounts.

Cash   Cash is for tracking cash inflows and expenditures—pocket money, so to speak.

Asset   Asset accounts are for tracking items that you own, such as your home, car, or recreational vehicle.

Portfolio   Portfolio accounts are for tracking the stocks, bonds, and groups of mutual funds in your portfolio.

Mutual Fund   Mutual fund accounts are for tracking individual mutual funds.

What You Owe

The accounting term for what you owe is *liabilities*. Quicken offers two kinds of accounts for amounts you owe:

Credit Card   Credit Card is for tracking credit card transactions and balances.

Liability   Liability is for tracking loans, such as a mortgage or car loan, and other liabilities.

Displaying the Accounts List Window

You can view a list of your accounts at any time. Choose Lists | Accounts, or press COMMAND-A. The Accounts list window, which is shown next, appears. For each account, it displays the account name, account type, and balance.

Tip *You can change the sort order of items in the Accounts list window by clicking the heading for the column you want to sort by. To reverse the sort order, click the Reverse Sort Order button above the vertical scroll bar.*

Setting Up Accounts

You create new accounts by entering basic information into the Set Up Account dialog, and then entering starting balances for most types of accounts in the account's register.

Entering Account Information

Click the New button at the bottom of the Accounts list window or, with the Accounts list window active, choose Edit | New Account, or press COMMAND-N. The Set Up Account dialog shown next appears:

Enter information about the account in the appropriate areas of the dialog. Here's the information you'll have to provide:

Account Type The account type is one of the seven account types. Select a radio button to specify the type.

Account Name The account name is the name of the account. Account names should be short yet descriptive, so they're not confused with other accounts. For example, rather than name your two checking accounts Checking 1 and Checking 2, give them names that are based on their purposes, like Primary Checking and House Checking.

Description   Although a description is optional, you may want to use it to provide additional information about the account, such as the financial institution name or the account number.

Credit Limit   For credit card accounts, Quicken prompts you to enter the credit limit for the account. This is the amount of credit you're allowed to accumulate on the credit card.

Hide In Lists   The Hide In Lists check box enables you to create an account that does not appear in the Accounts list window. With this option turned on, you would not be able to use the account. Why would you want to create an account and hide it at the same time? Well, you probably wouldn't. But this option also appears in the Edit Account dialog, so you can use it to hide an account you no longer use.

Add Account To Toolbar   You can turn on the Add Account To Toolbar check box to automatically add an account button for the account to the toolbar of the currently displayed tab.

Taxable   For portfolio and mutual fund accounts, Quicken provides a check box you can use to specify whether the account is taxable. For example, the account for an IRA would not be taxable, so you can turn off the check box for this type of account.

Notes   To enter more information about the account, such as the contact information for the financial institution or a complete description of the account's purpose, click the Notes button. Enter information in the Notes dialog and click OK.

When you've finished entering account information, click Create to create the account.

Entering Account Balances

When you click Create in the Set Up Account dialog, the account is created and its register window, which is shown next, appears. If you created any account other than a portfolio or mutual fund account, you can enter opening balance information for the account right in the register window. The best place to get opening balance information is from your most recent account statement—a bank statement, credit card bill, or similar document for the account.

Date	Number	Payee/Category/Memo	Payment	Clr	Deposit	Balance
8/10/01		Opening Balance	Payment	R		0.00
	▼	[Money Market] ▼ Memo	▶ Open Split			
8/10/01						

Money Market: Register

Record   Restore   Balance Today: $0.00

Note *I tell you more about using register windows in Chapter 4 and elsewhere in this book.*

Where you enter the opening balance depends on the type of account:

Type of Account	Enter Opening Balance in First Row of this Column:
Bank	Deposit
Cash	Receive
Asset	Increase
Credit Card	Charge
Liability	Increase

You should also enter the statement date for the account. This defines your starting date—you will only enter new transactions for the account if they occurred *after* that date.

After entering the opening balance and date, click Record to save the entry.

Note *You enter balances for portfolio and mutual fund accounts by entering security transactions. I explain how to do this in Chapter 6.*

Managing Accounts

The Accounts list window offers a quick and easy way to manage your accounts. You can use buttons at the bottom of the window to open, add, remove, or modify accounts and you can edit accounts to hide or display them in lists. Here's a quick rundown of the things you can do.

Working with Accounts

The buttons at the bottom of the Accounts list window perform specific account management tasks:

Open   Open opens the register for the selected account. I explain how to use registers in Chapter 4.

Shortcut   *You can also open an account by double-clicking its name in the Accounts list window or by clicking its button in the toolbar.*

New   New displays the Set Up Account dialog (illustrated earlier in this chapter) so you can create a new account.

Edit   Edit displays the Edit Account dialog for the selected account. This dialog looks and works just like the Set Up Account dialog. You can use it to change the name and description of the account or hide the account. For some types of accounts, you can also change the account type. Just make the desired changes and click Change.

Delete   Delete enables you to delete the selected account. It displays a dialog you can use to confirm that you want to delete the account. You must click Yes in the dialog to delete the account.

Caution   *When you delete an account, you permanently remove all of its transactions—including associated transfer transactions—from your Quicken data file. To get the account out of sight without actually deleting it and its data, consider hiding it instead.*

Hiding Accounts

You can use the Hide feature to remove an account from view so it does not appear in lists and cannot be used in transactions. This is a good way to get an inactive account out of the way without deleting it and its transactions.

In the Set Up Account or Edit Account dialog, turn on the Hide In Lists check box. When you click Create or Change, the account is hidden.

You can display hidden accounts in the Accounts list window by turning on the Show Hidden Accounts check box. The information for a hidden account appears in italics, like this:

To unhide an account, turn off the check box for the account in the Edit Account dialog. The account appears in lists and can be used in transactions again.

Categories

When you create a data file, Quicken automatically creates dozens of commonly used categories based on options you set. Although these categories might completely meet your needs, there may be times when you'll want to add, remove, or modify a category to fine-tune Quicken for your use.

Types of Categories

There are basically two types of categories:

Income   *Income* is incoming money. It includes things such as your salary, commissions, interest income, dividend income, child support, gifts received, and tips.

Expense   An *expense* is outgoing money. It includes things such as insurance, groceries, rent, interest expense, bank fees, finance charges, charitable donations, and clothing.

Subcategories

A *subcategory* is a subset or part of a category. It must be the same type of category as its primary category. For example, the Auto category may be used to track expenses to operate your car. Within that category, however, you may want subcategories to record specific expenses, such as fuel and repairs. Subcategories make it easy to keep income and expenses organized into manageable categories, while providing the transaction detail you might want or need.

Displaying the Categories & Transfers List Window

You can view a list of your categories at any time. Choose Lists | Categories & Transfers or press COMMAND-L. The Categories & Transfers list window appears. For each category, it displays the category name, type, tax status, and description or tax line item:

> **Tip**   *You can change the sort order of items in the Categories & Transfers list window by clicking the heading for the column you want to sort by. To reverse the sort order, click the Reverse Sort Order button above the vertical scroll bar.*

Creating a New Category

Click New at the bottom of the Categories & Transfers list window or, with the Categories & Transfers list window active, choose Edit | New Category, or press COMMAND-N. The Set Up Category dialog appears:

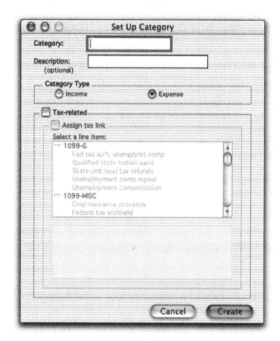

Enter information about the category in the appropriate areas of the dialog and click Create to add the category to the list. Here's the information you'll have to provide:

Category Name   Make sure the category name you enter here is descriptive enough that you won't confuse it with other categories.

Description   The Description field allows you to enter an optional description for the category.

Type   Type is the type of category: Income or Expense. Select one of the radio buttons.

Tax-Related   If the category can be included on your tax returns, turn on the Tax-Related check box. The category will then appear on tax reports you generate with Quicken. I explain how to use the tax link feature to set the category's line item in Chapter 14 and how to create reports in Chapter 16.

Creating a Subcategory

You create a subcategory almost the same way you create a category. Start by selecting the category under which you want to create the subcategory. Then click Add Subcategory. The Set Up Category dialog that appears looks and works just like the one shown previously, but you cannot select a category type—remember, a subcategory must be the same type as its parent category. Enter information about the subcategory and click Create. It's added to the Categories & Transfers list window, indented beneath the parent category, like this:

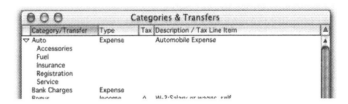

Tip   You can collapse or expand the list of subcategories beneath a category by clicking the triangle to the left of the category name.

Tip   You can turn a category into a subcategory by dragging its name onto the name of another category. When you release the mouse button, the category you dragged becomes a subcategory. Likewise, you can "promote" a subcategory to a category by dragging its name to the left. When a tiny box appears to the left of the subcategory name, release the mouse button. The subcategory turns into a category.

Managing Categories

You can use buttons at the bottom of the Categories & Transfers list window to work with the list.

Use   The Use button enables you to use the selected category in a transaction. I explain how to enter transactions in Chapter 4.

New   The New button displays the Set Up Category dialog illustrated earlier in this chapter. Use it to create a new category.

Edit   The Edit button displays the Edit Category dialog for the selected category or subcategory. This dialog looks and works just like the Set Up Category dialog. You can use it to make just about any change to a category.

Delete   The Delete button enables you to delete the selected category or subcategory. If you click this button, a dialog appears asking you to confirm that you really do want to delete the category. You must click Yes to delete it. If the category is referenced by transactions, the category is removed from those transactions, thus resulting in uncategorized transactions.

Caution   *If you delete a category that has subcategories, the category and all of its subcategories are removed.*

Add Subcategory   The Add Subcategory button enables you to create a subcategory for the selected category, as discussed earlier in this chapter.

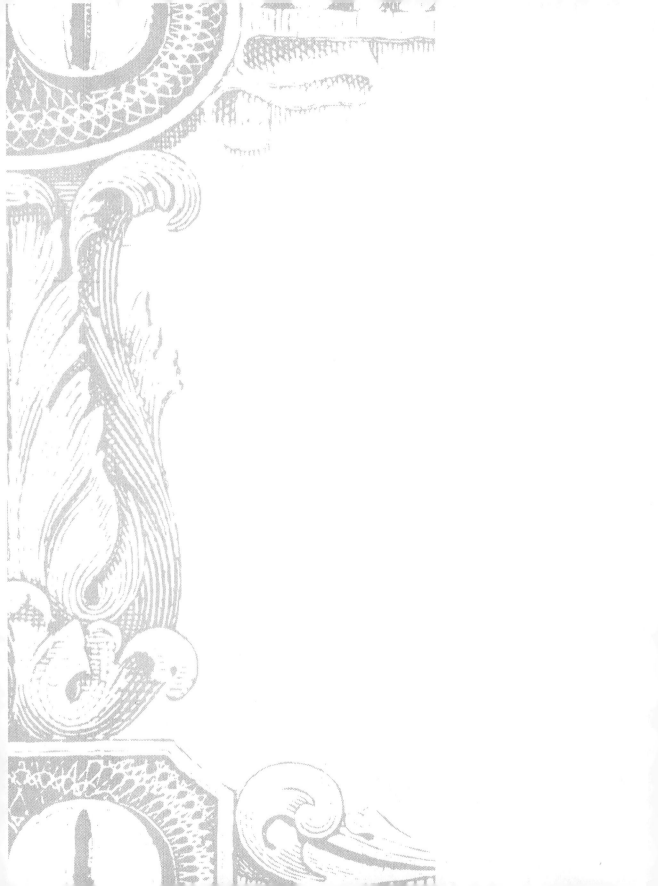

Going Online with Quicken and Quicken.com

In this Chapter:

- *Benefits of going online with Quicken*

- *Setting up, testing, and troubleshooting an Internet connection*

- *Accessing Quicken on the Web*

- *Quicken.com and other Web-based features*

- *Quicken financial partners*

- *Applying for Online Financial Services*

M any of Quicken's features work seamlessly with the Internet. If you have access to the Internet, either through a connection to an Internet service provider (ISP) or through a connection to an online service such as America Online, you can take advantage of these online features to get up-to-date information, automate data entry, pay bills, and obtain Quicken maintenance updates.

In this chapter, I tell you why you might want to take advantage of Quicken's online features. Then I explain how to set up Quicken to go online. Finally, I tell you a little about surfing the Web and introduce you to Quicken.com, Intuit's excellent financial information Web site.

Tip   *If you don't already have access to the Internet but think you may want to get it, be sure to read this chapter. It will convince you that now's the time to go online.*

Going Online

If you're already using your computer to access the features of the Internet or online services such as America Online, you probably already know a lot about it. In this part of the chapter, I fill in any gaps in your knowledge by telling you about the benefits of going online with Quicken and addressing any security concerns you might have. Finally, for the folks who aren't already online, I explain how to take the first steps for going online.

Why Go Online?

Before I go any further, I want to remind you that you don't have to go online to use Quicken. Quicken is a good financial management software package, even without its online features. But Quicken's online features make it a great financial management software package. As you'll see in this section and throughout this book, Quicken 2002 uses the Internet to help you make better financial decisions by bringing you information and resources relevant to your personal financial situation.

The best way to explain the benefits of going online is to list a few of the features online users can take advantage of.

If You Have a Bank Account, You Can Benefit

Throughout the month, you write checks and mail them to individuals and organizations. You enter these transactions in your checking account register. At month's end, you reconcile the account. You can do all this without going online. I tell you how in Chapters 4 and 15.

But if you register for Online Account Access with your bank, you can download all bank account activity on a daily basis so you know exactly when the transactions hit your account—even the ATM and debit card transactions you always forget to enter. If you register for Online Payment, you can pay your bills without licking another envelope or pasting on another stamp. I explain how all this works in Chapter 5.

If You Have Credit Cards, You Can Benefit

Do you have credit cards? Then you may take advantage of Quicken's credit card tracking features, which I cover in Chapter 4, to keep track of your charges, payments, and balances. You don't need to go online.

But if you sign up for Online Account Access, all your credit card charges can be downloaded directly into Quicken, eliminating the need for time-consuming data entry, while giving you an up-to-date summary of your debt and how you spent your money. Online Account Access can even prepare bill payment transactions. I tell you more about this in Chapter 5.

If You Invest, You Can Benefit

Quicken can keep track of your investments, whether they are 401(k) accounts, mutual funds, or stocks. You can enter share, price, and transaction information into Quicken and it will summarize portfolio value, gains, and losses. It'll even keep track of securities by lot. You don't need to go online to track your investments. I explain how in Chapter 6.

But with Online Investment Tracking, Quicken can automatically obtain quotes on all the securities in your portfolio and update its market value. Depending on your brokerage firm, you may also be able to download transactions and other account information directly into Quicken. You can use its online features to obtain valuable, up-to-date research information about securities that interest you. You can share opinions with other investors to learn what's hot—and what's not. These online features help you make informed investment decisions. I tell you about all this in Chapters 7 and 8.

If You Want to Save Money, You Can Benefit

Car insurance. Mortgages. Car loans. Bank accounts. All of these things have one thing in common: their rates vary from one provider to another. Shopping for the best deal can be a lot of time-consuming work—wading through newspaper and magazine ads, making calls, visiting banks. Quicken's planners can help you evaluate the deals you learn about, without going online.

But with the help of Quicken's built-in Internet links, you can shop for the best deal online, without leaving the comfort of your desk, getting newspaper ink all over your hands, or spending an afternoon listening to music while on hold. Up-to-date rates are only a mouse click away with an Internet connection and Quicken to guide you.

Enough Already!

If all this doesn't convince you that going online with Quicken can help you save time, save money, and get smarter, stop reading and move on to the next chapter. You'll probably never be convinced. I will say one more thing, however: after using Quicken's online features for more than five years now, I can't imagine using Quicken any other way.

Security Features

Perhaps you're already convinced that the online features can benefit you. Maybe you're worried about security, concerned that a stranger will be able to access your accounts or steal your credit card numbers.

You can stop worrying. The folks at Intuit and the participating banks and credit card companies have done all the worrying for you. They've come up with a secure system that protects your information and accounts.

PINs

A *PIN*, or *personal identification number*, is a secret password you must use to access your accounts online. If you have an ATM card or cash advance capabilities through your credit card, you probably already have at least one PIN, so the idea shouldn't be new to you. It simply prevents anyone from accessing the account for any reason without first entering the correct PIN.

An account's PIN is initially assigned by the bank, credit card company, or brokerage firm. Some companies, like American Express, require that your PIN consist of a mixture of letters and numbers for additional security. You can change your PINs to make them easier to remember—just don't use something obvious like your birthday or telephone number. And don't write it on a sticky note and attach it to your monitor! If you think someone might have guessed your PIN, you can change it.

Tip   *It's a good idea to regularly change all your PINs and passwords—not just the ones you use in Quicken.*

Encryption

Once you've correctly entered your PIN, the instructions that flow from your computer to the bank, credit card company, or brokerage firm are *encrypted*. This means they are encoded in such a way that anyone able to "tap in" to the transactions would "hear" only gibberish. Quicken does the encryption using, at a minimum, the 56-bit single Data Encryption Standard (DES). Quicken is also capable of encrypting data with stronger methods, including the 128-bit RC4 or 168-bit triple DES. Once the encrypted information reaches the computer at the bank, credit card company, or brokerage firm, it is unencrypted, and then validated and processed.

Encryption makes it virtually impossible for any unauthorized party to "listen in" on your transaction. It also makes it impossible for someone to alter a transaction between the moment it leaves your computer and the moment it arrives at your bank or credit card company for processing.

Other Security Methods

Quicken also takes advantage of other security methods for online communications, including Secure Sockets Layer (SSL) encryption, digital signatures, and digital certificates. Together, all of these security methods make online financial transactions secure—even more secure than telephone banking, which you may already use!

Getting Connected

To take advantage of Quicken's online features, you need a connection to the Internet. You get that through an ISP. An *ISP* is an organization that provides access to the Internet, usually for a monthly fee. These days, there are literally thousands of ISPs that can provide the access you need for Quicken's online features. America Online, CompuServe, and Earthlink Network are just three of them.

Note   *America Online (AOL), Microsoft Network (MSN) and CompuServe are ISPs that provide an Internet connection as well as additional information and online services.*

If you don't already have an account with an ISP, you must set one up before you can configure Quicken to use its online features. Consult the information that came with your copy of Quicken for special deals on Internet accounts through Quicken-preferred ISPs. Or check your local phone book for an ISP near you. Your ISP can explain everything you need to know to get connected and help you set up your computer to go online.

Setting Up, Testing, and Troubleshooting Your Connection

Before you can use Quicken's online features, you need to set up and test your Internet connection. You set up the connection within your Mac OS system software and then test the connection by using Quicken (or another application) to display Internet content. In this section I explain how to do both of these things. I also explain how to troubleshoot problems you may encounter during the testing process.

Setting Up an Internet Connection

How you set up an Internet connection depends on the answers to two questions:

Which version of the System software are you using?   If you are using Mac OS X, you set up an Internet connection with the Setup Assistant that runs automatically when you install Mac OS X or by setting options in Network preferences. If you are using Mac OS 9, you set up an Internet connection with Apple's Internet Setup Assistant.

Are you setting up the Internet connection as part of a Mac OS installation or afterwards?   If you are setting up the cohnection as part of the installation of your System software, the appropriate assistant will run automatically as part of the installation procedure. If you are setting up the connection after your System software has been installed and used, you may have to set options in Network preferences or various control panels.

Fortunately, Apple makes it easy to set up an Internet connection. Here's the information you need to get started. Only one of the following four sections will apply to you.

Tip   *If you've already gone through the process of setting up an Internet connection and can successfully connect to the Internet, you can skip this section— you're all ready to connect with Quicken, too.*

Note   *If you are connecting to the Internet via a direct or network connection, you may have to set proxy server information within Quicken. Ask your network administrator. I explain how to set Proxy Server Preferences in Appendix B.*

Setting Up an Internet Connection When Installing Mac OS X

When you first install Mac OS X, it displays a series of Setup Assistant dialogs that you use to configure your system—including its connection to the Internet. Each dialog explains exactly what you need to enter. Just enter the information provided by your ISP or network administrator. When you're finished, the Assistant sets all preferences so you're ready to connect.

Setting Up an Internet Connection After Installing Mac OS X

If you didn't set up an Internet connection when you first installed Mac OS X, things won't be quite as easy. Instead, you'll need to enter information into the Network preferences window. Choose Apple | System Preferences to display the System Preferences window. Then click the Network icon to display its options. You'll need to set options in one or more of the window's tabs. I'll provide instructions here for a dial-up connection, since that's what most readers will have. If you have a network connection, consult your network administrator for assistance.

The TCP/IP tab, shown next, is for setting IP addresses and domain name server information for your connection. This information should be provided by your ISP or network administrator. Choose a modem option from the Configure pop-up menu above the tabs. Then choose an option from the Configure menu below the tabs—in most cases, this will be Using PPP. Enter the domain name

server (DNS) and search domains information provided by your ISP in the
appropriate boxes.

Next, click the PPP tab, which is shown next. Enter the appropriate
information provided by your ISP into each of the edit boxes.

Finally, click the Modem tab to check its settings, shown next. The most important setting is Modem—make sure the correct modem is selected from the pop-up menu. Then check and, if necessary, change the other settings.

When you're finished, click Save. Then choose System Prefs | Quit System Prefs, or press COMMAND-Q. You're now ready to connect.

Using Apple's Internet Setup Assistant on Mac OS 9

Apple's Internet Setup Assistant, which is part of the Mac OS 9 System software, walks you step by step through the process of setting up an Internet connection. It prompts you for information you should have received from your ISP or network administrator when you opened your Internet access account. When it's finished, it sets all TCP/IP and Remote Access (if applicable) control panel options and offers to connect you to the Internet so you can test your setup.

Apple's Internet Setup Assistant launches automatically at the end of the Mac OS 9 setup process, so you can enter information about your ISP then. But if you didn't set up your Internet connection when you installed and configured Mac OS 9, you can launch the Internet Setup Assistant by double-clicking its icon. You should find it in the Assistants folder inside the Utilities folder, which may be inside the Applications (Mac OS 9) folder.

Testing Your Connection

Once you've set up your computer for an Internet connection, you're ready to test it with Quicken. Here are three simple tasks to get you started.

Visiting Quicken.com

A good connection test is a visit to Quicken.com, Intuit's feature-packed financial Web site for Quicken users and other visitors. I tell you more about Quicken.com later in this chapter and elsewhere throughout this book, but for now, let's just connect to it to make sure your Internet connection works.

Choose Online | To the Web | Quicken.com. Quicken launches your Web browser and attempts to connect to the Internet. What you see during the connection process will vary depending on your ISP. If you use an online service such as America Online, the service's access software may start automatically to make the connection. You may be prompted to enter a username or password. Other dialogs may appear. Provide any requested information.

When the connection is complete, your Web browser requests the Quicken.com home page. After a few moments, it appears in the Web browser window. Figure 3-1 shows what the Quicken.com home page looked like on August 11, 2001.

Tip   *If you were already connected to the Internet when you accessed one of Quicken's online features or you have a direct connection to the Internet, you won't see the connection happening. Instead, the Quicken.com home page will simply appear in your Web browser window.*

Note   *If you're using Mac OS X, you may have to use the Internet Connect application to initiate an Internet connection. If your computer does not automatically connect to the Internet when you choose the Quicken.com command within Quicken, switch to the Finder and double-click the Internet Connect icon in the Applications folder. Then click Connect in the window that appears to connect to the Internet.*

Switching Back to Quicken

When you accessed the Quicken.com home page from within Quicken, the Quicken application remained open but moved to the background. You can switch back to Quicken at any time:

- In Mac OS X, click the Quicken 2002 Deluxe icon in the Dock.
- In Mac OS 9, choose Quicken 2002 Deluxe from the Application menu in the top-right corner of the screen.

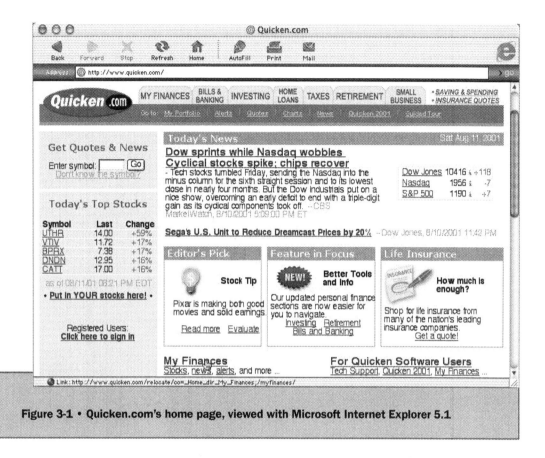

Figure 3-1 • Quicken.com's home page, viewed with Microsoft Internet Explorer 5.1

Quicken 2002 moves back into the foreground so you can continue working with it.

Disconnecting from the Internet

If you are using a dial-up connection to the Internet, it's a good idea to disconnect from the Internet when you have finished using Quicken's online features. How you do this depends on your Internet service provider:

- If you are connected via an online service such as America Online, switch to the online service's access software by clicking its icon in the Dock (Mac OS X) or by choosing its name from the Application menu (Mac OS 9). Then choose the Quit command or press COMMAND-Q to quit the online service's software, thus disconnecting from the Internet.

- If you are connected via another ISP, click the Internet Connect icon in the Dock (Mac OS X) or choose Remote Access Status from the Apple menu (Mac OS X). Then click Disconnect in the window that appears.

 Note   *If you have a direct connection to the Internet, you can't disconnect.*

Troubleshooting

If you followed the instructions I provided throughout the chapter, you shouldn't have any trouble connecting to the Internet from Quicken. But things aren't always as easy as they should be. Sometimes even the tiniest problems can prevent you from successfully connecting and exchanging data.

In this section, I provide some troubleshooting advice to help you with connection problems you may experience. Check this section before you start pulling out your hair and cursing the day computers were invented.

Setup Problems

To determine whether the problem is a Quicken setup problem or a general Internet setup problem, quit Quicken and try connecting to the Internet from another program, such as your Web browser or e-mail program:

- If you have a direct or network connection and can connect to the Internet from another program but not from within Quicken, the problem may be with Quicken's Proxy Server preferences. Check with your network administrator to make sure you have the correct settings. I discuss Proxy Server preferences in Appendix B.
- If you have a dial-up connection and you can't connect to the Internet from any other program or with Internet Connect (Mac OS X) or Remote Access (Mac OS 9), the problem is probably with one of the following: your Network preferences settings (Mac OS X), your TCP/IP or Remote Access control panel settings (Mac OS 9), or your modem.
- If you have a direct or network connection and you can't display Internet content from any program, the problem is probably with one of the following: your Network preferences settings (Mac OS X), your TCP/IP control panel settings (Mac OS 9), or your network.

Modem Problems

Problems with a dial-up connection may be related to your modem. Try each of the following, attempting a connection after each one:

- Check all cables between your computer and your modem (if you have an external modem), and between your modem and the telephone outlet.
- Check the telephone line to make sure it has a dial tone and that it is not being used by someone else or another program.
- If you have an internal modem, restart your computer. This resets the modem and may resolve the problem. Or, if you have an external modem, turn off your modem, and then turn it back on.

If you can connect but have trouble staying connected, try the following:

- Make sure no one is picking up an extension of the phone line while you are online.
- Make sure call waiting is disabled by entering the appropriate codes for the dial-up connection.
- Have the phone company check the line for noise. If noise is detected, ask the phone company to fix the problem. (It shouldn't cost you anything if the line noise is the result of a problem outside your premises.)

Network Problems

Problems with a direct connection may be related to your network. Try these things, attempting a connection after each one:

- Check all cables between your computer and the network hub or router.
- Restart your computer. Sometimes resetting your computer's system software can clear network problems.
- Ask your network administrator to check your network setup, including Proxy Server settings.

Introducing Quicken.com

The World Wide Web has had a greater impact on the distribution of information than any innovation since the invention of moveable type hundreds of years ago. The Web makes it possible to publish information almost instantly, as it becomes available. Accessible by anyone with a computer, an Internet connection, and Web browsing software, it gives individuals and organizations the power to reach millions of people worldwide without the delays and costs of traditional print and broadcast media.

While this power to publish has flooded the Internet with plenty of useless and trivial information, it has also given birth to exceptional Web sites, full of useful, timely, and accurate information that can make a difference in your life. Quicken.com, Intuit's site, is one of the best financial information sites around.

In this part of the chapter, I'll lead you on a short tour of Quicken.com and other Quicken features on the Web. My goal is to introduce you to what's out there so you can explore the areas that interest you most.

Keep one thing in mind as you read through this information: Quicken.com is an incredibly dynamic Web site that changes frequently. The screen illustrations and features I tell you about will probably appear differently when you connect. In addition, brand-new features might be added after the publication of this book. That's why I won't go into too much detail in this chapter. The best way to learn about all the features of Quicken.com when you're ready for them is to check them out for yourself.

An Introduction to Web Surfing

Before I start my overview of Quicken on the Web, let me take a moment to explain exactly what you're doing when you connect to Quicken.com and the other Quicken features on the Web. If you're brand-new to Web surfing—that is, exploring Web sites—be sure to read this section. But if you're a seasoned surfer, you probably already know all this stuff and can skip it.

One more thing: This section is not designed to explain everything you'll ever need to know about browsing the World Wide Web. It provides the basic information you need to use the Web to get the information you need.

Going Online

When you access Quicken's online features, you do so by connecting to the Internet through your ISP. It doesn't matter whether you connect via a modem or a network, or whether your ISP is America Online or Joe's Dial-up Internet Service. The main thing is having a connection or a conduit for information.

Think of an Internet connection as some PVC piping running from your computer to your ISP's, with a valve to control the flow of information. Once the valve is open (you're connected), any information can flow through the pipe in either direction. You can even exchange information through that pipe in both directions at the same time. This makes it possible to download (or retrieve) a Web page with your Web browser while you upload (or send) e-mail with your e-mail program.

Quicken's online features use the pipe (or connection) in two ways:

- Your Web browser—typically Netscape Navigator (or Communicator) or Microsoft Internet Explorer—sends your requests for information and displays the information in its browser window (see Figure 3-1). It's live and interactive— click a link and a moment later new information starts to appear.
- The Online Account Access, Online Payment, and Online Quotes features, as well as similar features, work in the background to communicate with financial institutions with which you have accounts. Quicken sends information you prepared in advance and retrieves the information the financial institution has waiting for you.

There's one important thing to remember when using Quicken's online features to browse the Web: You browse Web pages with your Web browser, not with Quicken software. Although selecting certain options within Quicken will display Web pages, those Web pages appear in your Web browser window, not within Quicken. To go back to Quicken when you've finished browsing the Web, click the Quicken 2002 Deluxe icon in the Dock (Mac OS X) or choose Quicken 2002 Deluxe from the Application menu at the top-right corner of your screen (Mac OS 9), as discussed in the section titled "Switching Back to Quicken" earlier in this chapter.

This chapter concentrates on Web browsing—the interactive features of Quicken.com. But it also provides some information to help you find financial institutions that work with Quicken for the Online Account Access and Online Payment features.

Navigating

The main thing to remember about the Web is that it's interactive. Every time a Web page appears on your screen, it'll offer a number of options for viewing other information. This is known as "navigating the Web."

Hyperlinks and Forms

You can move from page to page on the Web in two ways, both of which are illustrated in Figure 3-1:

- **Hyperlinks** (or **links**) are text or graphics that, when clicked, display another page. Hypertext links are usually underlined, colored text. Graphic links sometimes have a colored border around them. You can always identify a link by pointing to it—your mouse pointer will turn into a hand with a pointing finger.

- **Forms** offer options for going to another page or searching for information. Options can appear in pop-up menus, text boxes that you fill in, check boxes that you turn on, or radio buttons that you select. Often there are multiple options. You enter or select the options you want and click a button to send your request to the Web site. The information you requested appears a moment later.

Other Navigation Techniques

The toolbar at the top of your Web browser window (refer to Figure 3-1) includes a number of buttons you might find handy for navigating the Web and working with Web pages. Here are the ones I think you'll use most with Quicken:

- **Back** displays the previously viewed page.
- **Forward** displays the page you viewed after the current page. This button is only available after you have used the Back button.
- **Stop** stops the loading of the current page. This may result in incomplete pages or error messages on the page. You might use this button if you click a link and then realize that you don't really want to view the information you requested.
- **Reload** (in Netscape Navigator or Communicator) or **Refresh** (in Microsoft Internet Explorer) refreshes the information on the page by loading a new copy from the Web site's server. This button is handy for updating stock quotes or news that appears on a page.
- **Print** prints the currently displayed Web page.

Working Offline

When you've finished working with online features, if you have a dial-up connection, you may want to disconnect. This frees up your telephone line for incoming calls. You can continue working offline with Quicken features that don't require Internet access.

To work offline, disconnect from the Internet as discussed earlier in this chapter.

Accessing Quicken on the Web

You can access Quicken's online features using commands on its Online menu. One of these commands, To The Web, is really a submenu full of options for Quicken Web features, as shown next:

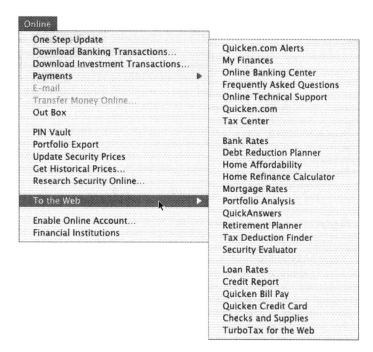

Here's a quick overview of some of these options.

Quicken.com Features and Support

The first group of commands offers access to Quicken.com pages that extend Quicken's basic financial features with Web-based features and information:

Quicken.com Alerts   The Quicken.com Alerts command displays the Quicken.com Customize Alerts page where you can set up alerts for your stock portfolio.

My Finances   The My Finances command displays the Quicken.com My Finances page, which you can customize to display the financial information that interests you, including your account balances, alerts, bills, portfolio, and more.

Online Banking Center   The Online Banking Center command displays the Online Banking page of Quicken.com's Bills & Banking channel. This is where you can learn all about online banking and find banks that offer online features.

It's also a great place to start searching for a credit card, loan, or bank account online.

Frequently Asked Questions   The Frequently Asked Questions command displays a page with frequently asked questions about Quicken; click a question link to learn its answer.

Online Technical Support   The Online Technical Support command takes you to the Quicken Support page. This is where you can find answers to frequently asked questions, information about solving problems with Quicken, and program updates. Use this command when you can't find the information you need in this book or with Quicken's Onscreen Help features.

Quicken.com   The Quicken.com command takes you to the home page for Quicken.com, Intuit's financial Web site, which is illustrated in Figure 3-1. Although designed to be of most use to Quicken users, most of its features are accessible to anyone. (Tell your friends about it!)

Note   *Quicken.com is divided into different channels. You can go to a channel by clicking its tab near the top of the Quicken.com home page (refer to Figure 3-1). Some Quicken.com channels are also accessible directly from the To The Web submenu shown previously.*

Tax Center   The Tax Center command is a shortcut to Quicken.com's Taxes channel, which provides information you can use to prepare and file your tax returns, including federal tax forms, IRS publications, and state tax forms. News, articles, and advice offer additional insight into the world of taxation, to help you understand and minimize your tax burden.

Planners and Calculators

The next group of commands extends Quicken by offering access to interactive, Web-based planners and calculators. Use these features to perform all kinds of complex planning and calculation tasks for your finances:

Bank Rates   The Bank Rates command displays the home page for Quicken.com's Bills & Banking channel. That's where you can find rates for bank, credit card accounts, and loans, and learn more about banking.

Debt Reduction Planner   The Debt Reduction Planner command displays the first page of Quicken.com's Debt Reduction Planner, an interactive tool you can use to save money while reducing your debt.

Home Affordability   This command displays the Home Affordability page of the Home Loans channel on Quicken.com. Use the form on this page to determine how much you can afford to spend on a home.

 Note   *The Home Loans channel is also referred to on Quicken.com as Quicken Loans.*

Home Refinance Calculator   The Home Refinance Calculator command displays the Refinance Calculator page of the Home Loans channel on Quicken.com. Use this interactive tool to determine whether it is a good time to refinance your home.

Mortgage Rates   The Mortgage Rates command displays the Quick Rates page of the Home Loans channel on Quicken.com. Use the form on this page to learn about mortgages and rates in your area.

Portfolio Analysis   The Portfolio Analysis command takes you to the Portfolio Analysis feature of Quicken.com, where you can check the asset allocation, and security and sector diversification for Quicken portfolio accounts that you export to the Web. This feature helps you maintain a more balanced and diversified portfolio.

QuickAnswers   The QuickAnswers command displays the Quick Answer Calculators page on Quicken.com (see Figure 3-2). This page is full of questions; click a question to display an interactive calculator to get the answer.

Retirement Planner   The Retirement Planner command takes you to the first page of the Retirement Planner in Quicken.com's Retirement channel. Use this interactive tool to plan for your retirement.

Tax Deduction Finder   The Tax Deduction Finder command takes you to the first page of the Deduction Finder feature on Quicken.com's Taxes channel. You can use this interactive tool to find expenses that you can deduct from your income tax.

Security Evaluator   The Security Evaluator command displays the first page of the Security Evaluator feature on Quicken.com's Investing channel. Simply enter the ticker symbol for a security and click a button to learn all about it.

Intuit Services

The last batch of commands on the To The Web submenu offers access to services provided by Intuit, Inc., makers of Quicken:

Loan Rates   The Loan Rates command takes you to the home page of Quicken Loans (Quicken.com's Home Loans channel), where you can research mortgages and other loans online.

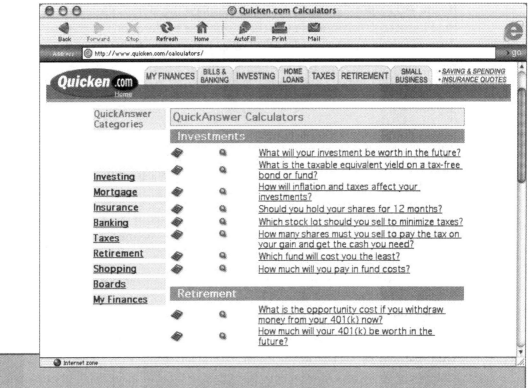

Figure 3-2 • The Quick Answer Calculators page on Quicken.com provides links to calculators you can use to answer a variety of questions about your finances.

Credit Report   The Credit Report command takes you to a page on Quicken.com's Bills & Banking channel where you can order a credit report and sign up for a credit monitoring service. You might find these features useful if you're not sure about your credit history and want to make sure all your credit records are correct.

Quicken Bill Pay   The Quicken Bill Pay command takes you to the Quicken Bill Pay page of the Intuit Web site. That's where you can learn how the Quicken Bill Pay feature of Quicken makes it possible to pay your bills online even if your bank does not directly support Quicken's online banking features.

Quicken Credit Card   The Quicken Credit Card Link displays the Quicken MasterCard Platinum Card home page. You can use links on this page to learn all about the features and benefits of the Quicken MasterCard and apply for a card.

Checks and Supplies   The Checks and Supplies command displays the home page for IntuitMarket, your source for software, Quicken-compatible checks, and other supplies. Use links on this page to order products online via a secure server.

TurboTax for the Web   This command displays information about TurboTax for the Web. You can use this Intuit service to file your tax returns online, right from your Web browser, without purchasing special tax-preparation software.

Quicken Financial Partners

If you're interested in keeping track of your finances with the least amount of data entry, you should be considering Quicken's online features for bank account access and payment, credit card account access, and investment tracking. Earlier in this chapter, in the section titled "Why Go Online?" I tell you about the benefits of these features. Chapters 5 and 7 tell you how to use them. But you can't use them until you've set up an account with a Quicken financial partner and have applied for the online financial services you want to use.

Finding a Quicken Partner

Finding a Quicken financial partner is easy. Choose Online | Financial Institutions. The Financial Institutions window, shown next, appears. This window, which can be updated to add new partners that come on board, provides the name and contact information for each financial institution that directly supports Quicken 2002 software.

Buttons along the bottom of the Financial Institutions window enable you to work with items in the list:

- **Update List** connects to the Internet to update the list of Quicken partner institutions.

Tip *Click the Update List button if your financial institution does not appear on the list and you want to see if it has been added since the last time the list was updated.*

- **Update Item** connects to the Internet to update the information about the selected financial institution.

Tip *It's a good idea to use the Update Item button to update the information for your financial institution before you set up for Online Account Access or Online Payment.*

- **Apply** displays a Web page with information about how you can apply for Online Account Access or Online Payment with the selected financial institution. (You may have to click Update Item to update information about the financial institution before you can click Apply.)
- **Use** copies the financial institution's name into the Enable Online Banking window, which you use to set up Online Account Access and Online Payment. (I explain how to use this window in Chapter 5.)

Types of Services

Quicken partner institutions offer two types of services:

- **Account Access** enables you to download bank or credit card account transactions directly into your Quicken data file. In Quicken 2002, you can now use the account access feature to download investment transactions from certain brokerage firms into your Quicken data file, too.
- **Online Payment** enables you to send payment instructions from within Quicken. This makes it possible to pay bills and send payments to anyone without writing a check.

If Your Financial Institution Is Not on the List

If your bank or credit card company is not on the list, you have four options:

Change financial institutions.   I know it sounds harsh, but if your bank or credit card company doesn't support online banking with Quicken and you really want to use this feature, you can find a financial institution that does support it and open an account there.

Wait until your financial institution appears on the list.   The list of partner institutions is updated quite often. If your bank or credit card company doesn't appear there today, it may appear next month. Or next year. You can hurry things along by asking your financial institution to become a Quicken partner institution. If enough customers ask for it, they might add this feature. (My bank did.)

Check to see if your financial institution supports Quicken Web Connect.   This feature enables you to download transactions from your financial institution in a specially formatted, Quicken-compatible .QFX file, which are then automatically imported into your Quicken data file. This method limits your online activities to Online Account Access; Online Payment is not supported.

Use Quicken Bill Pay.   If all you're interested in is the Online Payment feature, you can use Quicken Bill Pay. This enables you to process online payments via CheckFree Corporation, which can prepare checks from your existing bank accounts. There's no need to change banks or wait until your bank signs on as a Quicken partner. Quicken Bill Pay is listed as one of the Quicken partners in the Financial Institutions window.

Applying for Online Financial Services

To apply for online financial services, click to select the financial institution's name in the Financial Institutions window. Then click Apply. Follow the instructions on the Web page that appears to apply by phone or online. This gets the wheels turning to put you online. It may take a few days to get the necessary access information, so apply as soon as you're sure you want to take advantage of the online financial services features.

Managing Your Bank and Credit Card Accounts

This part of the book explains how to use Quicken to keep track of your bank and credit card accounts. It starts by explaining the basics of manually recording bank and credit card transactions, then goes on to tell you how you can take advantage of Quicken's online account access and payment features to automate much of the data entry. This part has two chapters:

Chapter 4: *Recording Bank and Credit Card Transactions*

Chapter 5: *Online Banking with Quicken*

Part Two

Recording Bank and Credit Card Transactions

In this Chapter:

- *Entering payments and other transactions*

- *Using splits and classes*

- *Writing and printing checks*

- *Entering credit card transactions*

- *Transferring money*

- *Working with existing transactions*

At Quicken's core is its ability to manage your bank accounts. This is probably Quicken's most-used feature. You enter the transactions and Quicken keeps track of account balances and the source and destination of the money you spend. You can even have Quicken print checks for you.

Using similar transaction entry techniques, Quicken can also keep track of credit card accounts. You enter transactions as you make them or at month's end when you receive your statement and pay your bill. Quicken keeps track of balances and offers you an easy way to monitor what you used your credit card to buy. It also enables you to keep an eye on how much your credit cards cost you in terms of finance charges and other fees.

Tip   *Quicken's Online Account Access and Online Payment features can save you time and money. Once you understand the basics of entering transactions as discussed in this chapter, be sure to consult Chapter 5 to see how Quicken's online features can make transaction entry easier.*

Overview of Accounts and Transactions

Most of the transactions you track with Quicken will involve one or more of its bank, cash, or credit card accounts. Before you can use Quicken to track bank and credit card transactions, you should prepare by creating the necessary accounts and having a good idea of how recording transactions works.

Here's a closer look at each account type, along with some transaction examples. As you read about these accounts, imagine how they might apply to your financial situation.

Note   *I explain how to use the Set Up Account window to create new Quicken accounts in Chapter 2.*

Bank Accounts

Bank accounts are for tracking the money you have in checking, savings, or money market accounts in a bank or similar financial institution. Generally speaking, bank account transactions can be broken down into three broad categories: payments, deposits, and transfers.

Payments   *Payments* are cash outflows. Here are some examples:

- You write a check to pay your electric bill.
- You withdraw money from your savings account to buy a gift for your mother.
- You use your ATM card to withdraw spending money from a bank account.
- You use your debit card to buy groceries.
- You pay a monthly checking account fee.

Tip   *Quicken's Online Payment feature enables you to send a check to anyone, without actually writing or mailing the check. I tell you about this feature in Chapter 5.*

Deposits   *Deposits* are cash inflows. Here are some examples:

- You deposit your paycheck in your checking account.
- You sell your old computer and deposit the proceeds in your savings account.
- Your paycheck or Social Security check is deposited into your bank account as a direct deposit.
- You earn interest on your savings account.

Transfers   A *transfer* is a movement of funds from one account to another. Here are some examples:

- You transfer money from an interest-bearing savings account to your checking account when you're ready to pay your bills.
- You transfer money from a money market account to your home equity line of credit account to reduce its balance.

Cash Accounts

Quicken offers cash accounts for tracking cash expenditures. For example, you might create an account called My Wallet or Spending Money and use it to keep track of the cash you have on hand. Cash accounts are like bank accounts, but there's no bank. The money is in your wallet or your pocket or the old coffee can on the windowsill.

Cash accounts have two types of transactions: receive and spend.

Receive   When you receive cash, you increase the amount of cash you have on hand. Here are some examples:

- You withdraw cash from the bank for weekly spending money.
- You sell your *National Geographic* magazine collection for cash at a garage sale.
- You get a $20 bill in a birthday card from your grandmother.

Spend   When you spend cash, you reduce your cash balance. Here are some examples:

- You buy coffee and a newspaper and pay a bridge toll on your way to work.
- You give your son his allowance.
- You put a $20 bill in the birthday card you send to your granddaughter.

Tip   *Tracking every penny you spend, from the cup of coffee you buy at work in the morning to the quart of milk you pick up on your way home that evening, isn't for everyone. You may prefer to track only large cash inflows or outflows and record the rest as Miscellaneous expenses.*

Credit Card Accounts

Credit card accounts track money you owe, not money you own. Some credit cards, such as MasterCard, Visa, American Express, and Discover, can be used in most stores that accept credit cards. Other credit cards, such as Macy's, Dillard's, and Texaco, can only be used in certain stores. But they all have one thing in common: if there's a balance, it's usually because you owe the credit card company money.

Credit card account transactions can also be broken down into two categories: charges and payments.

Charges   Charges result when you use your credit card to buy something or the credit card company charges a fee for services. Here are some examples:

- You use your Visa card to buy a new computer.
- You use your Discover card to pay for a hotel stay.
- You use your Texaco card to fill the gas tank on your boat at the marina.
- A finance charge based on your account balance is added to your Macy's bill at month's end.

- A late fee is added to your MasterCard bill because you didn't pay the previous month's bill on time.
- A fee is added to your American Express bill for annual membership dues.

The opposite of a charge is a *credit*. Think of it as a negative charge; don't confuse it with a payment. Here are two examples:

- You return the sweater you bought with your American Express card to the store you bought it from.
- In reviewing your MasterCard bill, you discover that a merchant charged you in error and you arrange to have the incorrect charge removed.

Payments   Payments are amounts you send to a credit card company to reduce your balance. Here are three examples:

- You pay the minimum amount due on your Visa card.
- You pay $150 toward the balance on your Macy's card.
- You pay the balance on your American Express card.

Credit Card Tracking Techniques

You can use either of two techniques for paying credit card bills and monitoring credit card balances:

- Simply record amounts paid to each credit card company in your checking account. Although this does track the amounts you pay, it doesn't track how much you owe or the individual charges.
- Record each individual credit card expenditure and payment in the appropriate credit card account. This takes a bit more effort on your part, but it tracks how much you owe and what you bought.

Tip   *Knowing how much you owe on your credit cards helps you maintain a clear picture of your financial situation. In my opinion, it's worth the extra effort to track your credit card expenditures and balances in individual credit card accounts.*

Credit Card Transaction Recording Strategies

There are two strategies you can use to record transactions in credit card accounts. Choosing the strategy that's right for you makes the job easier to handle.

Enter as You Spend   One strategy is to enter transactions as you spend. To do this, you must collect all the credit card receipts that are handed to you when you use your credit cards—which might be something you already do. Don't forget to jot down the totals for any telephone and online shopping you do. Then, every day or every few days, sit down with Quicken and enter the transactions.

While this strategy requires you to stay on top of things, it offers two main benefits:

- Your Quicken credit card registers always indicate what you owe to credit card companies. This prevents unpleasant surprises at month-end, or at the check-out counter when you're told you've reached your limit.

- At month-end, you don't have to spend a lot of time entering big batches of transactions. All (or at least most) of them should already be entered.

I'll be the first to admit that I have never been able to use this strategy. I just don't like holding on to all those pieces of paper. (Of course, since signing up for Online Account Access, all this information is entered regularly for me.)

Enter When You Pay   The other strategy, which you may find better for you, is to enter transactions when you get your monthly statement. With this strategy, when you open your credit card statement, you'll spend some time sitting in front of your computer with Quicken to enter each and every transaction. If there aren't many, this isn't a big deal. But if there are many transactions, this could take some time.

Of course, the main benefit of this strategy is that you don't have to collect credit card receipts and spend time throughout the month entering your transactions. But you still have to enter them! This is the method I use for the one credit card I have that I cannot access online yet.

Entering Transactions

To make the most of Quicken, you must be willing to spend a little time entering transactions for the accounts you want to track. There are different ways to enter transactions, based on the type of transaction you want to enter:

- Use registers to record virtually any type of transaction, including checks, bank account payments and deposits, credit card charges and payments, and cash receipts and spending.

- Use the Write Checks window to record checks to be printed by Quicken.
- Enter transfers to transfer money from one account to another.

In this section, I cover all of these techniques.

Tip   *You may prefer to work with bank, cash, and credit card accounts while in the Banking tab's work environment. By default, this tab has buttons commonly used for banking-related transactions. I tell you how to work with Quicken's tabs in Chapter 1 and customize tabs in Appendix B.*

Note   *QuickEntry, a companion program to Quicken Deluxe in previous versions of Quicken, is no longer supported by Intuit so it is not covered in this book.*

Using Account Registers

Quicken's account registers offer a standard way to enter all kinds of transactions. As the name suggests, these electronic account registers are very similar to the paper checking account register that comes with your checks.

Tip   *You can customize the way the account register window looks and works by setting Register options in the Preferences dialog. I tell you how in Appendix B.*

There are several ways to open an account register. Here are three of them:

- Choose Lists | Accounts or press COMMAND-A to display the Accounts list window, shown next. Then double-click the name of the account for which you want to use the register.

- Choose the name of the register from the Rgstrs button menu at the top of the Banking tab:

> **Tip** | *The Current Register is the register in the active window or, if no register windows are open, the register window that was open last.*

- Click the button for the account near the top of the Banking tab:

The account's register window appears (see Figure 4-1). Use it to enter and record transactions.

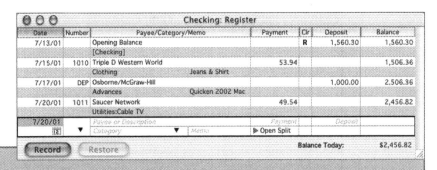

Figure 4-1 • The account register window for a checking account

Basic Entry Techniques

You enter transactions into the account register by filling in a two-line form. A blank transaction, which is shown in Figure 4-1 with a black box around its two lines, includes a default date and gray italic text that identifies each field. Your job is to fill in the appropriate fields with information about your transaction. When you're finished, click Record or press RETURN.

Here's some additional information about entering transactions.

Advancing from Field to Field   To move from one edit box to another when entering transactions, you can either click in the edit box or press the TAB key. Pressing TAB is usually quicker.

Entering the Transaction Date   The Date field automatically displays a default date, which is either today's date or the date of the last transaction you entered during this Quicken session. You can overwrite the date by entering a new one. If you click the calendar icon in the Date field, a tiny calendar appears, as shown next. You can click the arrow buttons at the top of the calendar to change the month displayed. Then click a date to select and enter it in the Date field.

Entering a Transaction Number or Type   The Number field is where you enter a transaction number or type. You can enter any number you like or use the pop-up menu to display a list of standard entries:

- **Next # [+]** automatically increments the most recently entered check number and enters the resulting number in the Number field.
- **– None –** leaves the Number field blank. This is the default selection.
- **ATM** is for ATM transactions.
- **Deposit** is for deposits.
- **EFT**, which stands for *Electronic Funds Transfer*, is for direct deposits and similar transactions.
- **Print Check** is for transactions for which you want Quicken to print a check. Quicken automatically records the check number when the check is printed.
- **Send** is for online payments. This option is only available when Online Payment is enabled for the account. I tell you about paying bills online in Chapter 5.
- **Transfer** is for a transfer of funds from one account to another.
- **Withdrawal** is for withdrawals and direct debit transactions.

 Tip   *You can press the + or – key on the keyboard to increment or decrement the check number while the Number field is active.*

Note   *The Number field is not required. You can leave it blank if you like.*

Entering a Payee or Description   The Payee or Description field can be used to enter any kind of descriptive information about the destination of funds (the payee) or the source of funds (a payer). Do not leave this field blank.

Using QuickFill   As you start to enter the name of a payee or payer that is already in Quicken's data file, Quicken may fill in the entire name and most recent transaction for you. This is Quicken's QuickFill feature, which I tell you more about in Chapter 14.

Entering the Amount   Enter the amount in only one of the amount fields (for example, Payment or Deposit in Figure 4-1). The field you enter the amount into will determine whether the amount is subtracted from or added to the account balance.

Using a Calculator   When an Amount field is active, you can display a calculator (like the one shown next) by entering a number and then pressing any standard mathematical operator, such as +, –, * (for multiplication), or / (for division). Complete the calculation and click Total or press RETURN to enter the result in the field.

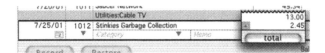

Entering a Category   When you enter the name of a category in the Category field, Quicken attempts to match the characters to entries in the Categories & Transfers list and complete the entry for you. If you prefer, you can click the triangle in the category field to display and choose from a pop-up menu of categories and transfer accounts.

Entering New Categories   If you enter a category that does not exist in the Categories & Transfers list, Quicken displays a dialog that offers to create the category for you. Click Set Up to create a new category; click Select to display the Categories & Transfers list window to select an existing category. (I explain how to create categories in Chapter 2.)

Entering Multiple Categories   To enter more than one category for a transaction, click the triangle beside Open Split. This enables you to enter multiple categories for the transaction.

Using Splits

A *split* is a transaction with more than one category. For example, suppose you pay one utility bill for two categories of utilities, electric and water. If you want to track each of these two expenses separately, you can use a split to record each category's portion of the payment you make. This enables you to keep good records without writing multiple checks to the same payee.

To record a transaction with a split, click the triangle beside Open Split in the account register window (refer to Figure 4-1) or Write Checks window (see Figure 4-5 later in this chapter) when entering the transaction. The entry area expands to include multiple category lines. Figure 4-2 shows what it might look like for an account register window with two categories entered.

Figure 4-2 • Opening a split enables you to enter more than one category for a transaction.

Enter the category name and amount for each category that you want to include in the transaction, one per line. Quicken automatically totals the amounts you enter for the transaction. You can use buttons beneath the split area to work with the split:

- **Close Split** closes the split.
- **Clear Split** clears all lines from the split, permanently removing them.
- **Adjust Total** adjusts the transaction total, if necessary, to match the total of all amounts entered for the split.

When you click Record, the transaction is recorded. When the split is closed, the word "split" appears in the Category field of the transaction:

Using Classes

A class is an optional identifier for specifying what a transaction applies to. For example, if you have two cars for which you track expenses, you can create a class for each car—say, Jeep and Toyota. Then, when you record a transaction for one of the cars, you can include the appropriate class with the category for the transaction. Because Quicken can produce reports based on categories, classes, or both, classes offer an additional dimension for tracking and reporting information.

Working with the Class List Window   Quicken maintains a list of all the classes you create. You can display the Classes list by choosing Lists | Classes, or by pressing COMMAND-K. Here's an example with some classes I created:

You can use buttons in the Classes list window to work with the class list or a selected class:

- **Use** uses the class in the current transaction.
- **New** enables you to create a new class.
- **Edit** enables you to modify the currently selected class name or other information.
- **Delete** enables you to delete the currently selected class.
- **Add Subclass** enables you to create a subclass for the currently selected class.

Creating a New Class   Click New in the Classes list window. The Set Up Class window, which is shown next, appears. Use it to enter a name and description for the class and click Create.

Only one piece of information is really necessary: the class name. You may want to make it short so it's easy to remember and enter. The description can be used to provide additional information on what the class is used for. The Assign Tax Copy area enables you to set the tax copy number for the class, which can be used to help you prepare your taxes; I tell you how to take advantage of this feature in Chapter 11. When you click Create, the new class is added to the Classes list.

Including a Class in a Transaction   To include a class in a transaction, enter a slash (/) followed by the class name after the category. Here's an example in the register window:

8/1/01	1013	Drive Safe Insurance Co		234.55		2,099.70
		Insurance/Jeep	Auto Insurance			

> **Tip**   *If you enter a class name that is not on the Classes list, Quicken displays a dialog offering to set up or select the class.*

Entering Cash Transactions

Although Quicken enables you to keep track of cash transactions through the use of a cash account, not everyone does. The reason: most people make many small cash transactions every day. Is it worth tracking every penny you spend? That's something you need to decide.

Personally, I don't track all cash transactions. I only track expenditures that are large or tax-deductible. You may want to do the same. If so, you still need to set up a cash account, but you don't need to record every transaction. Figure 4-3 shows an example.

Figure 4-3 • Typical cash account transactions

Cash Receipts   Cash receipts may come from using your ATM card, cashing a check, or getting cash from some other source. If the cash comes from one of your other accounts through an ATM or check transaction, when you record that transaction, use your cash account as the transfer in the Category edit box (refer to item A in Figure 4-3). That increases your cash balance. Here's what the transaction might look like in your checking account:

8/10/01	ATM	Withdrawal		50.00		2,049.70
		[Pocket Money]	ATM Withdrawal			

Important Cash Expenditures   In your cash account, record large, tax-deductible, or other important cash expenditures like any other transaction. Be sure to assign the correct category. The two items marked B in Figure 4-3 are examples.

Other Cash Expenditures   Throughout the week, you may spend fifty cents for a newspaper, a dollar for a cup of coffee, and about seven dollars for lunch at your favorite sushi restaurant. Recording transactions like these can be tedious, so don't bother if you don't want to. Instead, at the end of the week, compare your cash on hand to the balance in your cash account register. Then enter a transaction to record the difference as an expenditure. You can use the Miscellaneous category—it's for miscellaneous expenditures—and put anything you like in the Payee or Description edit box (refer to item C in Figure 4-3).

Entering Credit Card Transactions

Entering credit card transactions works very much like entering banking transactions. Check Figure 4-1 for step-by-step instructions. Here are a few additional tips; Figure 4-4 illustrates some examples.

	Date	Ref #	Payee/Category/Memo		Charge	Clr	Payment	Balance
A	8/11/01		Triple D Western World		145.16			1,300.12
			Horse Expenses	Feed				
B	8/11/01		Deuce Hardware				15.87	1,284.25
			Home Repair	Return Air Filter				
C	8/15/01		Bank of America		15.15			1,299.40
			Interest Paid	Finance Charge				
D	8/20/01		Bank of America				100.00	1,199.40
			[Checking]	Payment on Acct				
	8/20/01	▼	Payee or Description		Charge		Payment	
			Category ▼	Memo	▶ Open Split			

Balance 8/20/01: $1,199.40
Credit Remaining: $9,800.60

[Record]   [Restore]

Figure 4-4 • Typical credit card account transactions

Entering Individual Charges   Open the account register for the credit card account. Then enter the charge transaction, using the name of the merchant that accepted the charge as the payee name; you can leave the Ref edit box empty (refer to item A in Figure 4-4).

Entering Credits   Enter the transaction just as if it were a charge, but put the amount of the credit in the Payment edit box (refer to Item B in Figure 4-4). This subtracts it from your account balance.

Entering Finance Charges   In the credit card account register, enter the name of the credit card company as the payee and the amount of the finance charge as a charge (refer to Item C in Figure 4-4).

Entering Payments   In the account register for your checking account or in the Write Checks window, enter a payment transaction with the credit card company name in the Payee or Description edit box. Enter the credit card account name in the Category edit box; you should find it as a transfer account at the bottom of the Category pop-up menu that appears when you activate the field. The checking account register transaction should look like the one shown next; item D in Figure 4-4 shows what this transaction looks like in the credit card account register.

8/20/01	1020	Bank of America		100.00		1,949.70
		[Visa]	Payment on Acct			

Writing Checks

Quicken's Write Checks window uses a basic check-like interface to record checks. You enter the same information that you would write on an actual check. You then tell Quicken to print the check based on the information you entered.

Tip   *You can customize the way the Write Checks window looks and works by setting Register options in the Preferences dialog. I explain how in Appendix A.*

Note   *To use this feature, you must order compatible check stock from Intuit or another check printer. I tell you how and explain how to print checks later in this chapter.*

To begin, open or activate the register window for the account from which you want to write checks. Then open the Write Checks window using one of these techniques:

- Choose Activities | Write Checks or press COMMAND-J.
- Click the Checks button near the top of the Banking tab.

The Write Checks window, which is shown in Figure 4-5, appears. Use it to enter the necessary information for a check and record the transaction. As you can imagine, the Write Checks window works a lot like the account register window discussed earlier in this chapter—consult that section for more information. Here are a few additional things to consider when entering transactions in the Write Checks window.

Addresses on Checks   If you enter an address on the check, you can mail the check using a window envelope. Quicken will remember the address and automatically enter it in the Write Checks window the next time you enter the payee's name.

Check Memos   If you enter a note on the memo field of the check form, it might be visible if you mail the check in a window envelope.

Recording a Check   When you click Record to accept the information entered for a check, Quicken automatically displays a blank Write Checks window so you can record another check.

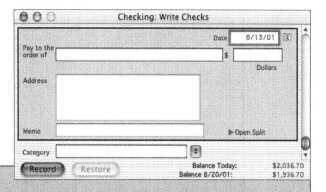

Figure 4-5 • The Write Checks window offers a familiar form for entering transactions.

Viewing Other Checks   You can use the scroll bar along the right side of the Write Checks window to scroll through checks you have written. Click the up arrow to see the previous check; click the down arrow to see the next check. In addition, the checks you write with the Write Checks window appear in the account's register window. As shown next, the word "PRINT" appears in the Number edit box until the check is printed.

8/13/01	PRINT	Stinkies Garbage Service		13.00		2,036.70
		Household				

Transferring Money

You can also record the transfer of funds from one account to another. You might find this feature especially useful for recording telephone or ATM transfers.

Tip   *Online Account Access enables you to transfer money from one account to another by simply entering the transaction and sending it to your bank via the Internet. There's no need to call or visit your bank or submit any paper forms. I tell you more about this feature in Chapter 7.*

Using the Transfer Window

One way to record a transfer is with the Transfer window. Choose Activities | Transfer Money | Between Registers. The Transfer Money Between Quicken Registers window appears:

This window is a simple form for providing information about the transfer. Enter the transfer date and amount in the top two edit boxes. Then choose the source and destination accounts for the money from the two pop-up menus. If desired, you can edit or enter information in the Payee and Memo fields. When you're finished, click Transfer to enter the transaction.

Recording a Transfer in the Account Register Window

The Transfer window isn't the only way to record a transfer. You can also record a transfer in the account register window of either the source or destination account. Choose Transfer from the Number pop-up menu, choose the other transfer account from the pop-up menu in the Category field, and click Record to complete the transaction.

The following illustrations show a transfer of $500 from a money market account to a checking account. Here's what the money market account transaction looks like:

8/13/01	TXFR	Transfer	500.00		4,736.97
		[Checking]			

And here's what the corresponding checking account transaction looks like:

8/13/01		Transfer		500.00	2,536.70
		[Money Market]			

Working with Existing Transactions

So far, this chapter has concentrated on entering transactions. What do you do when you need to modify a transaction you already recorded? That's what this section is all about.

Searching for Transactions

Quicken's Find and Replace features enable you to search for transactions and to replace information within found transactions. In this section, I explain how they work and how you can use them to locate and modify transactions.

Tip   *You might also find it helpful to sort a register window's transactions by clicking the Date or Number column heading. For example, clicking the Number heading to sort by check number groups the transactions by the Number field, making it easy to find transactions by number or type. You can quickly move to a specific date or transaction number by dragging the register window's scroll box. The QuickScroll feature displays the date and number of the transaction that will appear when you release the mouse button.*

Using the Find Command

To use the Find command, choose Edit | Find, or press COMMAND-F. The Find tab of the Find and Replace window appears:

Enter the text you want to search for in the Find box. Then set other search criteria as desired:

- **Searching** enables you to specify the fields in which Quicken should look for the Find text.

Note   *The Searching pop-up menu includes all possible fields for a transaction, including fields that only appear in portfolio account transactions. I tell you more about portfolio transactions in Chapter 6.*

- **Matching if** enables you to specify how the Find text should match a field's contents. This pop-up menu includes options such as Contains (the default selection), Exact, Starts With, Equal, and Less.
- **In Account** enables you to specify the account Quicken should search.
- **Search Direction** enables you to specify whether Quicken should search Backward, from the last (or currently selected) transaction to the first one or Forward, from the first (or currently selected) transaction to the last one.

When you click Find, Quicken begins searching for matches. It activates the first match it finds in the register window. You can then click Find again to find the next match.

When Quicken is finished searching, it may display a dialog that offers to continue the search at the beginning of the account register. Click Yes to continue searching; click No to stop searching.

Tip   *Once you've set up criteria in the Find tab of the Find and Replace window, you can choose Edit | Find Again or press COMMAND-G at any time to search for the same information again.*

Using the Replace Command

To use the Replace command, choose Edit | Replace or press COMMAND-R. The Replace tab of the Find and Replace window, which is shown next, appears. It looks and works very much like the Find tab, but it includes a Replace With edit box you can use to enter replacement information. In addition, it only works with one transaction field at a time, so be sure to choose the appropriate field from the Searching pop-up menu before you begin a search.

When you set up the search and click Find, Quicken displays the first match for the search criteria. You can then click one of the four buttons at the bottom of the window to continue:

- **Replace All** replaces all occurrences.

Caution   *Use the Replace All option with care! You will not get a chance to review each change before you make it.*

- **Replace & Find** replaces the currently found occurrence and finds the next occurrence.
- **Replace** replaces the currently found occurrence. You'll have to click Find again to continue searching for other occurrences.
- **Find** finds the next occurrence without changing the currently found occurrence.

Changing Transactions

Quicken enables you to change a transaction at any time—even after it has been reconciled. This makes it possible to correct errors in any transaction you have entered.

Making Minor Changes

If all you want to do is change one of the fields in the transaction—such as the category, date, or number—simply find the transaction in the appropriate account register, make changes as desired, and click Record to record them.

Using Edit Menu Commands

The Edit menu offers other options for working with a selected transaction:

Edit	
Undo	⌘Z
Cut	⌘X
Copy	⌘C
Paste	⌘V
Clear	
New Transaction	⌘N
Split Transaction	⌘E
Delete Transaction	⌘D
Memorize	⌘Y
Void Transaction	
Schedule Transaction...	
Move Transaction...	
Go To Transfer	⌘[
Find...	⌘F
Find Again	⌘G
Replace...	⌘R

- **New Transaction** (COMMAND-N) enables you to create a new transaction for the account. This does not affect the currently selected transaction.
- **Split Transaction** (COMMAND-E) enables you to enter multiple categories for an account. I tell you more about splits earlier in this chapter.
- **Delete Transaction** (COMMAND-D) deletes the selected transaction.

Caution *Deleting a transaction removes the transaction from the Quicken data file, thus changing the account balance and category activity.*

- **Memorize** (COMMAND-Y) tells Quicken to add the selected transaction to its list of memorized transactions. I tell you more about memorized transactions in Chapter 14.
- **Void Transaction** marks the selected transaction as void. This reverses the effect of the transaction on the account balance and category activity without actually deleting the transaction.
- **Move Transaction** displays the Move Transaction dialog, shown next, which enables you to move the transaction to another account. Simply choose a new account from the pop-up menu and click Move.

Tip   *Don't forget Quicken's contextual menus, which I discuss in Chapter 1. Hold down the CONTROL key while clicking a register entry to display a short list of commands you can use to work with the entry.*

Printing Checks

Quicken's ability to print checks enables you to create accurate, legible, professional-looking checks without picking up a pen. In this section, I explain how to print the checks you enter in the Write Checks window, discussed earlier in this chapter.

Getting the Right Checks

Before you can print checks from Quicken, you must obtain compatible check stock. Intuit offers checks in a number of different styles:

- **Standard checks** print just checks. There's no voucher or stub.

- **Voucher checks** pair each check with a similarly sized voucher form. When you print on a voucher check, the transaction category information, including splits and classes, can be printed on the voucher part.
- **Wallet checks** pair each check with a stub. When you print on a wallet check, the transaction information is printed on the stub.

In addition to these styles, you can get the checks in two different formats for your printer:

- **Sheet-fed** or **page-oriented** checks are for laser and inkjet printers.
- **Continuous** checks are for pin-feed printers.

A catalog and order form for checks came with your copy of Quicken. You can use it to order checks. If you have an Internet connection, you can order checks from Intuit by visiting the IntuitMarket Web site (www.intuitmarketplace.com); just choose Online | To the Web | Checks and Supplies. Or you can order checks by phone by calling (800) 433-8810.

Setting Up

Quicken must also be set up to print the kind of checks you purchased. You do this once and Quicken remembers the settings.

Choose Quicken 2002 Deluxe | Preferences (Mac OS X) or Edit | Preferences (Mac OS 9) to display the Preferences window. Click Print under Checks on the left side of the window to display Print Checks preferences:

Three of these options must be set correctly for checks to print properly:

- **Account** is the account for which you want to print checks.
- **Check Style** is the type of check stock you will print on, as discussed earlier.
- **Alignment when printing one or two checks** is the location and orientation of the check when printing fewer than all three checks on a sheet.

Tip   *If you're not sure how to set these options, follow the instructions below to print checks on a blank sheet of paper, then compare the results to what you expected to see. Make changes to the Preference settings as necessary and try again.*

Note   *I explain Print Checks preferences options in detail in Appendix B. Consult that appendix if you need additional information about check printing options.*

Printing Checks

Once setup is complete, you're ready to print checks. Insert the check stock in your printer. Then choose File | Print Checks or press COMMAND-P. The Print Checks dialog, which is shown next, appears. Use it to set printing options.

Note   *The options in the Print Checks dialog can vary depending on your printer and the type of checks you selected in the Preferences window.*

In the Starting Check Number edit box, enter the number that appears on the first check you inserted in your printer. Then select a Print option. If you select the Selected Checks option, the Select Checks to Print dialog, shown next, appears.

Click to place a check mark beside each check you want to print and click OK to return to the Print Checks dialog.

When you click Print, a standard Mac OS Print dialog, similar to the one shown next, appears. Check the settings in the dialog and click Print to send the print job to your printer.

Note | *The options in the Print dialog vary depending on your printer and the version of Mac OS running on your computer. (The dialog illustrated here is for a Hewlett-Packard LaserJet 2100TN printer on Mac OS X.) If you need assistance using this dialog, consult your Mac OS documentation or the manual that came with your printer.*

Quicken then displays a dialog asking if the checks printed correctly. You have two options:

- If all checks printed fine, click Yes.
- If there was a problem printing the checks, click No. If you attempted to print more than one check, the Incorrectly Printed Checks dialog, shown next, appears. Enter the number of the first incorrectly printed check and click OK. Then use the Print Checks command to try printing the incorrectly printed check(s) again.

Online Banking
with Quicken

In this Chapter:

- *Benefits and costs of online financial services*

- *Setting up online financial services*

- *Downloading transactions*

- *Comparing downloaded transactions to register transactions*

- *Setting up payees*

- *Entering online payments*

- *Exchanging e-mail with your financial institution*

- *Transferring money online*

Quicken's Online Account Access and Online Payment features enable you to do most (if not all) of your banking from the comfort of your own home. These two individual features can be used separately or together:

- **Online Account Access** enables you to download bank and credit card account activity and transfer money online between accounts.
- **Online Payment** enables you to pay bills online, without manually writing or mailing a single check.

If your financial institution does not directly support Quicken's online banking features, you have two other options for online banking:

- **Quicken Bill Pay** offers the features of Online Payment with payment processing by CheckFree Corporation.
- **Web Connect** automatically imports downloaded data from your financial institution's Web site to your Quicken data file.

In this chapter, I explain how these features work and how you can use them to save time and money.

> **Note** *The instructions in this chapter assume that you have already configured your computer for an Internet connection. If you have not done so, do it now. Chapter 3 provides the instructions you need to set up and test an Internet connection. This chapter also assumes that you understand the topics and procedures discussed in Chapters 2 and 4. This chapter builds on many of the basic concepts discussed in those chapters.*

Why Do Your Banking Online?

Consider the following scenario: every week (or two), you go to the bank to deposit your paycheck. (If you're lucky, you can use an ATM or drive-up window where you don't have to wait in line.) Throughout the month, you stop at ATMs and withdraw cash. You use your debit card at the pharmacy. You write checks for groceries, dentist visits, and car repairs. Periodically, you sit down to pay your bills. You write checks, insert them with statement stubs in window envelopes, put your return address on the envelopes, and stick on stamps. Once in a while, you call your bank to transfer money from one account to another. At month-end, you get a bank statement full of surprises: ATM withdrawals, debit card transactions, and checks you neglected to enter. Your bank balance may be dangerously close to zero because of these omissions. Or maybe you even bounced a few checks. And what about late payments (and fees) for the bills that sat on a table by the door, waiting for days to be mailed?

Sound familiar? At least some of it should. Life can be pretty hectic sometimes—too hectic to keep track of your bank accounts, pay bills before they're overdue, and buy stamps. But with Online Account Access and Online Payment, banking can be a lot less of a chore.

Benefits

The benefits of online financial services vary depending on the services you use. I've been doing my banking online for years. Here are some of the benefits I've seen.

Online Account Access

Online Account Access performs three primary tasks:

Download transactions that have cleared your account   Bank account transaction downloads include all deposits, checks, interest payments, bank fees, transfers, ATM transactions, and debit card transactions. Credit card transaction downloads include all charges, credits (for returns), payments, fees, and finance charges. Quicken displays all the transactions, including the ones you have not yet entered in your account register, as well as the current balance of the account. A few clicks and keystrokes is all it takes to enter the transactions you missed. This feature makes it virtually impossible to omit entries, while telling you exactly how much money is available in a bank account or how much money you owe on your credit card account. No more surprises in that monthly statement.

Transfer money between accounts   If you have more than one bank account at the same financial institution, you can use Online Account Access to transfer money between accounts. Although many banks offer this feature by phone, it usually requires dialing a phone number and entering an account number and PIN while navigating through voice prompts. Even if you get a real person on the phone, you still have to provide the same information every time you call. With Online Account Access, you merely enter a transfer transaction and let Quicken do the rest.

Send e-mail messages to your financial institution   Ever call the customer service center at your bank or credit card company to ask a question? If you're lucky, real people are waiting to answer the phone. But if you're like most people, your financial institution uses a call routing system that requires you to listen to voice prompts and press telephone keypad keys to communicate with a machine. Either way, when a real person gets on the line, you have to provide all kinds of information about yourself just to prove that you are who you say you are. Then you can ask your question. But the e-mail feature that's part of Online Account Access makes communicating with your bank or credit card company's customer service department easy. You normally get a response within one business day.

Online Payment

Online Payment enables you to send a check to anyone without physically writing, printing, or mailing a check. You enter and store information about the payee within Quicken. You then create a transaction for the payee that includes the payment date and amount. You can enter the transaction weeks or months in advance if desired—the payee receives payment on the date you specify.

Online Payment is one of the least understood Quicken features. Many folks think it can only be used to pay big companies like the phone company or credit card companies. That just isn't true. You can use Online Payment to pay any bill, fund your IRA, donate money to a charity, or send your niece a graduation gift.

How It Works   Suppose you use Quicken to send Online Payment instructions to pay your monthly bill at Joe's Hardware Store. You've already set up Joe as a payee by entering the name, address, and phone number of his store, as well as your account number there. Quicken sends your payment instructions to your bank, which stores it in its computer with a bunch of other Online Payment instructions. When the payment date nears, the bank's computer looks through its big database of payees that it can pay by wire transfer. It sees phone companies and credit card companies and other banks. But because Joe's store is small, it's probably not one of the wire transfer payees. So the bank's computer prepares a check using all the information you provided. It mails the check along with thousands of others due to be paid that day.

Joe's wife, who does the accounting for the store, gets the check a few days later. Although it doesn't look like a regular check, when she deposits it with the other checks she gets that day, it clears just like any other check. The amount of the check is deducted from your bank account and your account balance at Joe's. If you use Online Account Access, the check appears as a transaction. It also appears on your bank statement. If your bank returns canceled checks to you, you'll get the check along with all your others.

Tip   *If your bank doesn't return canceled checks, you can see for yourself what an Online Payment check looks like. Just use the Online Payment feature to write a check to yourself. It'll arrive in the mail on or before the date you specified. Although the check looks different, it works like any other check.*

When the Money Leaves Your Account   The date the money is actually withdrawn from your account to cover the payment varies depending on your bank. There are four possibilities:

- One to four days before the payment is processed for delivery
- The day the payment is processed for delivery
- The day the payment is delivered
- The day the paper check or electronic funds transfer clears your bank

You can find out when funds are withdrawn from your account for online payments by contacting your bank.

The Benefits of Online Payment   Online Payment can benefit you in several ways. You can pay your bills as they arrive, without paying them early—the payee never receives payment before the payment date you specify. You don't have to buy stamps and the bank never forgets to mail the checks.

Tip   *If your bank does not support Online Payment with Quicken, you can still take advantage of this feature by signing up for Quicken Bill Pay. This service works with your checking account like Online Payment does.*

Costs

The cost of Online Account Access and Online Payment varies from bank to bank. Check with your bank to see what the exact fees are. Here's what you can expect:

- Online Account Access is often free to all customers or to customers who maintain a certain minimum account balance. Otherwise, you could pay up to $5 for this service.

- Online Payment is sometimes free, but more often it costs from $5 to $10 per month for 20 to 25 payments per month. Each additional payment usually costs 40¢ to 60¢. Again, some banks waive this fee if you maintain a certain minimum balance. Quicken Bill Pay is $9.95 for up to 20 payments and $2.49 foe each set of five payments after that.

If you think this sounds expensive, do the math for your bank's deal. Here's an example: I get 25 payments per month for $5. If I had to mail 25 checks, it would cost me $8.50. So I'd actually save $3.50 per month if I made 25 online payments. Even if I don't make 25 payments a month, I also don't have to stuff envelopes, apply return address labels, stick on stamps, or wait in line at the post office. My bills get paid right on time, I earn more interest income, and I haven't bounced a check in over five years.

Does it sound like I'm sold on this feature? You bet I am!

Security

If you're worried about security, you must have skipped over the security information in Chapter 3. Go back and read that now. It explains how Quicken and financial institution security works to make Online Account Access and Online Payment safe.

Setting Up Online Financial Services

To use any of Quicken's online financial services, you must configure the appropriate Quicken accounts. This requires that you enter information about your financial institution and the account with which you want to use these online financial services features.

Applying for Online Financial Services

Before you can use Online Account Access or Online Payment (or Quicken Bill Pay), you must apply for it. I tell you how at the end of Chapter 3. Normally, all it takes is a phone call, although some banks and credit card companies do allow you to apply online. The process usually takes a week, but may take less. You'll know that you're ready to go online when you get a letter with setup information.

The setup information your financial institution sends usually consists of the following information:

- **A PIN (personal identification number)**   You'll have to enter this code into Quicken when you access your account online. This is a security feature, so don't write down your PIN on a sticky note and attach it to your computer screen. There is a chance that your bank may send this information separately for additional security.

- **A customer ID number**   This is often your Social Security number or taxpayer identification number.

- **The bank routing number**   This information tells Quicken which bank your account is with. You may not get this information for a credit card account.

- **Account number for each online-access-enabled account**   This tells your financial institution which account you want to work with.

For Web Connect, there may not be a formal application process. Visit your bank's Web site to see if your bank offers the ability to access account information online. If it does, you'll probably have to register with the Web site (or your bank) to receive a user or customer ID and password. This will enable you to access your account information while keeping it private. Next, check to see if the Web site allows you to download Web Connect (.QFX) files. If so, you have all the information you need to take advantage of this feature.

Caution   *Web Connect .QFX files are not the same as Quicken .QIF files. Although .QIF files can be imported into Quicken, as discussed in Appendix A, Web Connect .QFX files offer additional interactivity for reviewing and matching transactions, as discussed in this chapter.*

Enabling Online Account Access and Online Payment

With a PIN, routing number, and account numbers in hand, you're ready to set up your account(s) for online financial services features. There are a number of ways to set up. Rather than cover them all, I'll cover the most straightforward method.

Note   *Before you can set up online banking for an account, you must create the account. I explain how to create accounts in Chapter 2.*

Tip   *The Quicken Assistant can also step you through the process of setting up online financial services for bank, credit card, or investment accounts. You can give it a try by choosing Activities | Set Up Online Services.*

Begin by choosing Online | Enable Online Account. The Select Account to Enable dialog, which is illustrated next, appears. Select the account for which you want to enable online banking and click OK.

The Enable Online Banking window should appear. Use it to set online banking options.

Note   *You can also open the Enable Online Banking window for an account by clicking the Enable Online Banking button in the Edit Account window. I tell you about the Edit Account window in Chapter 2.*

Selecting Online Banking Features

Start by turning on the check box for each online banking feature you plan to use:

- **Enable Account Access** allows you to download transactions and balances and transfer funds between accounts.
- **Enable Online Payment** allows you to send payment instructions for paying bills and making other payments online. You can also turn on this check box if you plan to use Quicken Bill Pay.
- **Enable Web Connect Account Access** allows you to download transactions and balances from your bank's Web site in a Web Connect file. This option is only available when the other two options are not selected; likewise, if this option is selected, the other two options are not available.

Enabling an Account for Online Account Access, Online Payment, or Quicken Bill Pay

Next, you need to enter information about your financial institution and account. Here are the options that appear in the Enable Online Access dialog with one or both of the first two options enabled:

- **Financial Institution** is the name of your bank or credit card company. You can enter this information by typing it into the edit box. As you type, Quicken attempts to match the name with the names in its database. If you prefer, you can click the Financial Institutions button to display the Financial Institutions list window, shown next. Then select the name of your bank or credit card company and click Use to enter it into the Financial Institution edit box. This prevents you from entering an invalid financial institution name.

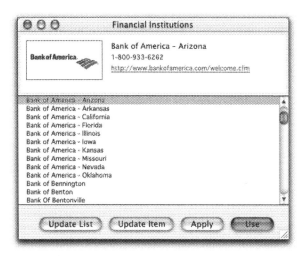

Note   *If you're using Quicken Bill Pay, enter Quicken Bill Pay in the Financial Institution edit box.*

- **Routing Number** is the routing number provided by your financial institution. This number may not be required when entering information for a credit card account.
- **Account Number** is your account number. Enter the entire number, without spaces or dashes.
- **Account Type** is the type of account. For a bank account, your options are None, Checking, Savings, Money Market, and Line of Credit. (If you're setting up a credit card account, Credit Card is also offered as an option.) Be sure to choose the correct account type from the pop-up menu.

Caution   *If you enter the incorrect account type, the online banking feature will not work. If your financial institution tells you what kind of account to enter, use that account type, even if it seems incorrect. For example, my bank instructed me to classify my money market account as a savings account. If I don't follow my bank's instructions, online banking for that account just won't work.*

- **Customer ID** is usually your Social Security number, but it may be another number provided by the bank. Be sure to enter the correct number.

Note   *When setting up a Quicken credit card account for online banking, you may also have to provide a PIN. Enter it in the appropriate edit box. The PIN is stored in your Quicken data file and is automatically used when you connect.*

When you've finished entering information in the Enable Online Banking window, click Save. A Service Agreement Information dialog may appear next. It tells you that online financial services are provided by your financial institution and not Intuit. (I think the lawyers at Intuit whipped this one up.) Read the contents of the dialog and click OK.

Enabling an Account for Web Connect

If you're going to use Web Connect to download data from your financial institution's Web site, the options that appear in the Enable Online Access dialog look like this:

Enter the name of your financial institution. As you type, Quicken attempts to match the name with the names in its database. If you prefer, you can click the Financial Institutions button to display the Financial Institutions list window, shown earlier. Then select the name of your bank or credit card company and click Use to enter it into the Financial Institution edit box. This prevents you from entering an invalid financial institution name.

Next, click Download Transactions. Quicken launches your Web browser and connects to your financial institution's Web site. If a Log In page appears, use it to enter the user or customer ID and password to access your account information on the Web site. Then follow links on the site to download the Web Connect (.QFX) file for your account statement. If a dialog appears telling you that your Web browser doesn't know how to handle the type of file you're downloading, use the dialog's options to save the file into your Documents folder. If Quicken does not automatically become the active application and import the file, switch back to

Quicken and choose File | Import Web Connect. Then use the Open dialog that appears (shown next) to locate, select, and open the file you downloaded.

The Select Account to Enable dialog, which is shown next, should appear. Select one of the radio buttons and set other options as necessary to identify the correct account. Then click OK. The Download Transactions window, which I discuss later in this chapter, should appear, with the downloaded transactions in the top half of the window (see Figure 5-2).

Note   *The exact steps you follow to enable an account for Web Connect may vary depending on your financial institution. If these instructions don't work for you, contact your financial institution. Chances are, they have a Web page with specific instructions for downloading Web Connect files from their Web site; print that page and use it as a guide.*

Verifying that an Account Has Been Enabled

You can verify that an account is enabled for online financial services by consulting the Account list window. Choose Lists | Accounts or press COMMAND-A. As shown next, a tiny lightning bolt appears beside the name of each account for which online banking has been enabled.

Downloading Transactions

When you enable Online Account Access or Web Connect, you can use the Download Transactions window to download transactions from your financial institution and compare them to transactions in your account register. You can check off the transactions that appear in your register and add the transactions that don't. This enables you to see which transactions have cleared and prevents you from failing to enter transactions.

In this section, I explain how to download, compare, and accept transactions in the Download Transactions window.

Opening the Download Transactions Window

Choose Online | Download Banking Transactions or choose Banking Transactions from the Dnld button near the top of the Banking tab. Figure 5-1 shows what this window looks like before transactions have been downloaded.

Figure 5-1 • The Download Transactions window enables you to download, compare, and enter transactions.

Downloading Online Account Access Data

To download transactions from your financial institution, begin by selecting the bank or credit card company name from the first pop-up menu in the Download Transactions window (see Figure 5-1). Then click Get Online Data. Your computer will connect to the Internet and display a Connection Status dialog. A PIN dialog like the one shown next should appear. Enter your PIN in the edit box and click OK.

Note   *The first time you download transactions from your bank or credit card company, you may be prompted to change your PIN. Follow the instructions that appear in the dialog to continue. From then on, be sure to use your new PIN.*

Tip   *You can change your PIN any time you like by clicking the Change PIN button in the PIN dialog. The dialog that appears prompts you to enter your current PIN once and your new PIN twice. When you click OK, your PIN is changed. Be sure to use the new PIN from then on.*

Quicken displays a Connection Status dialog as it downloads transactions. When the connection is finished, Quicken displays the Online Transmission Summary dialog, shown next. It summarizes the transactions that were downloaded. You can click Print to print the summary for reference if desired.

Note   *The first time you connect, your financial institution sends all transactions still stored on its server—normally 30 to 90 days' worth. After that, only new transactions will be downloaded.*

When you've finished reviewing the summary, click OK to return to the Download Transactions window, where downloaded transactions appear in the top half of the window (refer to Figure 5-2).

Downloading Web Connect Data

To download transactions from your financial institution with Web Connect, begin by selecting the bank or credit card company name from the first pop-up menu in the Download Transactions window (see Figure 5-1). Then click Get Online Data. Quicken launches your Web browser and connects to your financial institution's Web site on the Internet.

If a Log In screen appears, use it to enter your user ID and password so you can access your account information on the Web site. Then use links to navigate to the screen where you can download transaction information in Web Connect format and download the Web Connect file. If a dialog appears telling you that your Web browser doesn't know how to handle the type of file you're downloading, use the dialog's options to save the file into your Documents folder. If Quicken does not automatically become the active application and import the file, switch back to Quicken and choose File | Import Web Connect. Then use the Open dialog that appears (shown earlier in this chapter) to locate, select, and open the file you downloaded.

All this should sound familiar—it's almost the same procedure you followed to enable the account for Web Connect, as discussed earlier in this chapter. When the file has been imported into Quicken, the new transactions appear in the Downloaded Transactions window (refer to Figure 5-2).

Note *As mentioned earlier, procedures for using the Web Connect feature vary from one financial institution to another. For detailed instructions about using Web Connect, contact your financial institution.*

Comparing Downloaded Transactions to Register Transactions

Once the information has been downloaded (and, if necessary, imported into Quicken), you can compare the downloaded transactions to the transactions already entered in your account register. This enables you to identify transactions that you neglected to enter or that you entered incorrectly.

In the Download Transactions window, select the account for which you want to compare transactions. As shown in Figure 5-2, the downloaded transactions appear in the top half of the Download Transactions window.

Figure 5-2 • The Download Transactions window, with some transactions to compare and enter

The Status column in the top half of the window identifies two types of transactions:

- **Match** identifies downloaded transactions that match those in the register.
- **New** identifies transactions that do not appear to be in the register.

Checking Off a Matched Transaction   If a transaction matches one in the register, you can check it off by clicking in the ✔ column beside it to place a check mark there.

Tip   *You can view a matched transaction by clicking it in the top half of the window to select it in the bottom half of the window.*

Entering and Checking Off a New Transaction   To enter a new transaction into the register, select the new transaction in the top half of the window. Quicken begins preparing a register transaction entry for it in the bottom half of the window. Fill in the missing details, including the payee, category, and memo, as shown in Figure 5-2. Then click Record. Quicken records the transaction and changes its status in the top half of the window to "Match." You can then click in the ✔ column beside the transaction to place a check mark there.

Tip   *Because Quicken will automatically enter a date, transaction number, and amount—and, in the case of a debit card transaction or electronic payment, the payee and category (based on previous memorized transactions)—using this method to enter a transaction can be much faster than entering it manually in the account register window.*

Matching a New Transaction   If a downloaded transaction identified as New should match one in the register, you can modify the information in the register to match the information in the downloaded transaction. When you click Record for the register transaction, the word "Match" should appear beside the downloaded transaction. You can then click in the ✔ column beside the transaction to place a check mark there.

Unmatching a Matched Transaction   If a matched transaction really shouldn't be matched, select it in the top half of the window and click Unmatch. You can then treat it as a new transaction.

Deleting a New Transaction   To delete a new transaction, select the transaction in the top half of the window and click Delete. The transaction is removed from the downloaded Transaction List.

Tip   *This option is especially useful the first time you download transactions. You may download transactions that have already been reconciled. Use the Unmatch button to unmatch them as necessary, and then use the Delete button to delete them from the downloaded Transaction List.*

Accepting All Checked Transactions   To accept all transactions that you have checked off in the top half of the window, click the Accept ✔ Items button. This removes the items from the top half of the window and places a *C* beside them in the Clr column of the register window. (I explain how the Clr column works in Chapter 15.)

Finishing Up   When you've finished comparing downloaded transactions to register transactions and have accepted the checked transactions, you can close the Download Transactions window. If transactions still appear in the top half of the window, they'll remain there. You can work with them the next time you open the Download Transactions window.

Caution   *Transactions with a New status in the top half of the Download Transactions window may not be entered in your account register. Thus, your register balance may be misstated until you accept all downloaded transactions.*

Making Payments

You can make online payments from any account for which the Online Payment feature is enabled. Use the Set Up Payee window to enter information for each organization or individual you want to pay with online payments. Then, when you're ready to make a payment, use the Enter Online Payment window to enter payment information. Use the Out Box to send your payment instructions to the bank and you've finished.

In this section, I provide the details for all of these steps.

Entering Online Payee Information

To send payments from your account, your bank must know who and where each payee is. To ensure that your account with the payee is properly credited, you must also provide account information. You do this by setting up online payees.

Opening the Payees Window

Choose Online | Payments | Online Payees to display the Payees list window. This window, which is shown next, lists all the payees for which you have provided payment information.

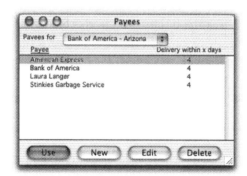

Buttons at the bottom of the window enable you to work with window contents:

- **Use** copies the selected payee's name into the Payee field of the Enter Online Payment window.
- **New** enables you to enter information about a new payee.
- **Edit** enables you to modify information about the selected payee.
- **Delete** removes the selected payee's information from the Payees list.

Note   *Deleting a payee simply deletes the payee's information from the Payees list. It does not change any transactions for a payee. You cannot delete a payee for which unsent payment instructions exist in the Out Box window.*

Creating a New Payee

To create a new online payee, click New. Then fill in the edit boxes in the Set Up Payee dialog, shown here, and click Create.

When you click Create, a dialog containing the information you just entered appears. Check the information in this box and click Yes. The payee is added to the list with the delivery lead time of 4. I explain what delivery lead time is all about later in this chapter.

Caution   *Check the payee information carefully! If there is an error, your payment might not reach the payee or it might not be properly credited to your account. Remember, your bank will not be sending a billing stub with the payment—just the check.*

Modifying a Payee

If necessary, you can change information for a payee. (I did this recently when one of my payees moved to a new location.) Select the payee name in the Payees window and click Edit. Then use the Edit Payee window, which looks and works just like the Set Up Payee window shown earlier, to change the payee's information. Click Change to complete the change.

Entering Payment Instructions

To send a payment to a payee, you must enter payment instructions. The easiest way to do this is with the Enter Online Payment window, shown next. To open this window, begin by opening the register for the account from which the payment will be made. Then choose Online | Payments | Enter Payment.

As you can see, this window looks and works a lot like the Write Checks window, which I cover in Chapter 4. Here are the details about the information you have to enter:

- **Delivery Date** is the date you want the payee to receive payment. This is the date the bank will either write on the check or make the electronic funds transfer. The check may be received before that date, depending on the mail. The date you enter, however, must be at least the same number of business days in advance as the delivery lead time for the payee—usually four days. That means if you want to pay a bill on Wednesday, August 29, you must enter and send its instructions to your bank on or before Friday, August 24. Quicken will adjust the date for you if necessary.

Tip   *Whenever possible, I give the bank an extra two days. So, in the previous example, if the bill is due on August 29, I'd instruct the bank to pay on August 27. This isn't because I don't have confidence in Quicken or my bank. It's because I have less confidence in the postal service.*

- **Pay to the Order of** is the online payee to receive payment. Quicken's QuickFill feature fills in the payee's name as you type it. If you enter a payee that is not in the Payees list, Quicken offers to set up a new payee for you. This enables you to create online payees as you enter payment instructions.

- **$** is the amount of the payment.
- **Category** is the category in which the payment should be recorded. You can enter a category, choose one from the pop-up menu, or click the Open Split triangle to enter multiple categories.

When you've finished entering information for the transaction, click Put In Out Box. The transaction is added to the Out Box window, which I discuss a little later. You can repeat this process for as many payments as you want to make.

Tip   *You can also enter online payment instructions in the account's register window. Be sure to select Send in the Number field. When you click Record, Quicken adds the instruction to its Out Box window.*

Scheduling Repeating Online Payments

Some payments, such as your rent or your monthly cable television bill, are exactly the same every month. You can set these payments up as repeating online payments.

Here's how it works. You use the Enter Transaction window, which I discuss in detail in Chapter 14, to enter payment information for an online payee. Be sure to click the Online Payment button (which looks like a lightning bolt) in the window. Enter the frequency, duration, and reminder information as desired in the bottom of the window. Here's an example of what a repeating online payment might look like:

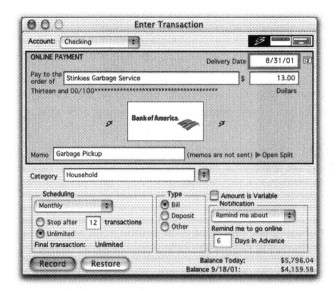

When you click Record, the payment is scheduled just like any other scheduled transaction. But each time the transaction needs to be recorded, Quicken either reminds you about it in its Upcoming Bills and Scheduled Transactions window or automatically puts the payment instruction in its Out Box for delivery to the bank with your other payment instructions.

Setting Up Online Loan Payments

You can also set up loan payments as repeating online payments. Just follow the instructions in Chapter 9 to set up a loan. In the Preview Payment window, which is shown next, select the Online Payment radio button. This enables you to schedule the payment as a repeating online payment.

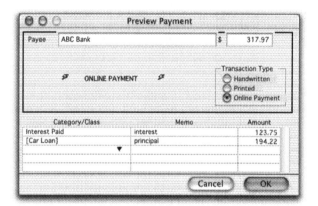

Sending Payment Instructions

Remember the bills I told you about? The ones waiting on a table by the door to be mailed? Payment instructions that have not yet been sent to the bank are just like those stamped envelopes. They're ready to go, but they won't get where they're going without your help.

Once your payment instructions have been completed, you must connect to your bank to send the instructions. Choose Online | Out Box. The Out Box window (see Figure 5-3) appears. It lists all of the transactions waiting to be sent, as well as other instructions to your bank.

Figure 5-3 • Use the Out Box window to send instructions and e-mail to your financial institution.

Tip   As you can see in Figure 5-3, Quicken's Out Box also includes instructions to update account statement data—in other words, download transactions. But although you can use this window to download transactions, you must switch to the Download Transactions window to review and accept them, as discussed earlier in this chapter.

Make sure check marks appear beside each instruction you want to send. Then click Send Now. In most cases, a PIN dialog like the one shown earlier in this chapter should appear. Enter your PIN in the edit box and click OK.

If you have a dial-up connection to the Internet, your computer connects and Quicken displays a connection status dialog while it exchanges information with your financial institution. When the connection is finished, Quicken displays the Online Transmission Summary window shown earlier in this chapter. It summarizes the online session and provides details about payment instructions that were sent. You can click Print to print the summary for reference if desired.

In the account register window, a check number is assigned to each payment instruction you sent and a lightning bolt icon appears in the Number field:

| 8/31/01 | 5038 | Stinkies Garbage Service | | 13.00 | | 5,365.07 |
| | | Household | | | | |

Canceling a Payment

Occasionally, you may change your mind about making a payment. Perhaps you found out that your spouse already sent a check. Or that you set up the payment for the wrong amount. For whatever reason, you can cancel an online payment that you have sent to your bank—as long as there's enough time to cancel it.

Here's how it works. When you send a payment instruction to your bank, it waits in the bank's computer. When the processing date (determined by the number of days in the payee's delivery lead time and the payment date) arrives, the bank makes the payment. Before the processing date, however, the payment instructions can be canceled. If you send a cancel payment instruction to the bank before the processing date, the bank removes the instruction from its computer without sending payment to the payee. Quicken won't let you cancel a payment if the processing date has already passed. If you wait too long, the only way to cancel the payment is to call the bank directly and stop the check.

Tip   *Canceling a payment instruction isn't the same as stopping a check. If you send the cancel payment instruction in time, the check will never be prepared. There should be no bank fee for canceling a payment instruction.*

Canceling an Online Payment

In the account register window, select the payment you want to cancel. Then choose Online | Payments | Cancel Payment. If it isn't too late to cancel the payment, a dialog like the one shown next will appear. Click the Put In Out Box button to add the cancellation instruction to the Out Box window or Send Now to send the cancellation instruction immediately.

● **Caution** *You must send the cancel payment instruction to your bank to cancel a payment. If you don't send the instruction immediately by clicking Send Now, be sure to use the Out Box to send the instruction before quitting Quicken. If you fail to do this, the cancel payment instruction may not reach your bank in time to cancel the payment.*

Stopping All Future Payments for a Repeating Online Payment

In the Scheduled Transactions tab of the Upcoming Bills and Scheduled Transactions window (which is discussed in detail in Chapter 14), select the payment you want to stop and click Delete. Click Yes in the confirmation dialog that appears. The transaction is removed from the list and no further payment instructions will be created or sent to your bank.

Exchanging E-mail with Your Financial Institution

You can use Quicken to exchange e-mail messages for any financial institution for which you have the Online Account Access feature enabled. This is an easy way to communicate with your bank or credit card company about issues that are not time-sensitive.

● **Caution** *If you need to communicate about a time-sensitive issue— such as a lost or stolen checkbook or credit card—do not use Quicken's e-mail feature. Instead, drop everything and call your bank or credit card company immediately.*

Opening the E-mail Window

Quicken's E-mail window enables you to create new e-mail messages, read incoming e-mail messages, and review e-mail messages waiting to be sent. To open this window, choose Online | E-mail. The window might look something like this with the Create New Mail view option selected:

Creating an E-mail Message

In the E-mail window, select the Create New Mail view option. Then fill out the e-mail form (consult the previous illustration) by entering a subject and message. When you have finished, click Put In Out Box to add the message to your Out Box, or Send Now to send the message immediately.

Tip *You can also send an e-mail message about a specific transaction. Open the account register in which the transaction appears, select the transaction, and choose Online | Payments | Payment Query. Quicken creates an e-mail message that already includes a subject and all information about the transaction. Just add your message text and click Put In Out Box or Send Now to save it.*

Exchanging E-mail Messages

Using e-mail is a lot like having a box at the post office. When you write a letter, you have to get it to the post office to send it to the recipient. When you receive a letter, you have to go to the post office and check your box to retrieve it. E-mail works the same way. Connecting is a lot like going to the post office to send and retrieve messages. If you don't use the Send Now button to send an e-mail message right after you compose it, you'll have to use the Out Box to send the message with your other instructions.

In the Out Box window (see Figure 5-3), select the financial institution for which outgoing messages are waiting to be sent and click Send Now. Quicken displays the PIN dialog; enter your PIN and click OK. Then wait while Quicken establishes an Internet connection with your financial institution and exchanges e-mail.

When Quicken is finished, it displays the Online Transmission Summary dialog. Review the information in this dialog and click OK.

Reading an E-mail Message

When your financial institution sends you an e-mail message, it appears in the E-mail window. To read the message, open the E-mail window and select the Incoming Mail view option. Then select the message you want to read. Its contents appear in the bottom half of the window. If desired, you can click Delete Mail to delete the message when you've finished with it or click Reply to compose a reply.

Transferring Money Between Accounts

If you have more than one account enabled for Online Account Access at the same financial institution, you can transfer money from one account to another.

Tip   *You can take advantage of this feature to maximize the interest earned on your money. Keep excess funds in an interest-bearing savings or money market account. Then, the day before a transaction will be made, transfer the funds to cover the transaction from the interest-bearing account to your checking account. Your money stays where it earns interest as long as possible, but is transferred just in time to make the payment.*

Preparing an online transfer is very much like preparing any other account transfer in Quicken. Choose Online | Transfer Money | Online to open the Transfer Money Online window, which is shown next. (This window looks and works very much like the Transfer Money window I discuss in Chapter 4.) Fill in the amount and account information and click Put In Out Box.

Note   *If all your accounts are enabled for online financial services, the Transfer Money submenu is replaced by a Transfer Money Online command. Use that command to open the Transfer Money Online window shown here.*

As with payment instructions, you must send transfer instructions to your bank in order for the transaction to take place. If you don't use the Send Now button to send the instruction immediately, make sure you use the Out Box to send the instruction with all of your other instructions.

In the Out Box window (see Figure 5-3), select the financial institution for which transfer instructions are waiting to be sent and click Send Now. Quicken displays the PIN dialog; enter your PIN and click OK. Then wait while Quicken establishes an Internet connection with your financial institution and sends the instructions.

When Quicken is finished, it displays the Online Transmission Summary dialog. Review the information in this window and click OK.

Tracking Your Investments

This part of the book explains how you can use Quicken to track your investments. It begins by explaining the basics of tracking investments in Quicken, then goes on to explain how you can use Quicken's online investment tracking features to download investment transactions from your brokerage firm and exchange investment information with Quicken.com. Finally, it provides a wealth of information you can use to invest wisely and maximize your investment returns.

This part has three chapters:

Chapter 6: Investment Tracking Basics

Chapter 7: Using Online Investment Tracking Tools

Chapter 8: Maximizing Investment Returns

Part Three

Investment Tracking Basics

In this Chapter:

- *Investment basics*

- *Working with investment accounts*

- *Adding and editing securities*

- *Recording investment transactions*

- *Viewing investment information*

- *Tracking the market value of investments*

Investments offer individuals a way to make their money grow. Although more risky than deposits made to an FDIC-insured bank, stocks, bonds, mutual funds, and other types of investments have the potential to earn more. That's why many people build investment portfolios as a way to save for future goals or retirement.

In this chapter, I tell you a little about investments and portfolio management, and then explain how you can use Quicken to keep track of the money you invest.

Investment Basics

Quicken enables you to record your investment transactions and track your portfolio value. With the information about your investments that you enter into Quicken, you can see how various investments perform, generate reports for tax time, and get a clear picture of what your investments are worth.

Before learning how to use Quicken to track your investments, here's a review of what investments and portfolios are.

Tip   *You may prefer to work with investment accounts and securities while in the Investing tab's work environment. By default, this tab has buttons and menus commonly used for investing-related transactions. I tell you how to switch tabs in Chapter 1 and how to customize tabs in Appendix B.*

Types of Investments

An *investment* is a security or asset that you expect to increase in value and/or generate income. There are many types of investments:

- **A certificate of deposit, or CD,** is an account with a bank or other financial institution. It earns a fixed rate of return and has a predetermined maturity date. Withdrawals before the maturity date normally result in penalty fees, which can exceed earned interest. CDs on deposit with a bank are normally FDIC-insured against loss.

- **A money market fund** is an account with a bank or other financial institution that earns interest based on short-term cash values. Money market funds are not FDIC-insured against loss.

- **Stocks** represent part ownership of an organization. Stock investments can earn you money by paying dividends or appreciating in value.

- **Bonds** represent loans to an organization. Bonds can earn you money by paying interest either during the bond's term or at its maturity date.
- **Treasury bills** represent loans to the U.S. government. They are issued at a discount and redeemed at face value; the difference between the two prices are the earnings.
- **Mutual funds** consist of multiple investments owned by many people. When you buy into a mutual fund, you pool your money with other investors to buy stocks, bonds, or other securities. Mutual funds can earn you money by paying dividends and interest and appreciating in value.
- **Annuities** are regularly funded accounts that earn interest or dividends paid in the future.
- **401(k) and 403(b) plans** are employer-funded retirement investments. They can consist of stocks, bonds, mutual funds, or any other type of investment.
- **IRAs, SEPs, and Keogh accounts** are employee-funded retirement investments. They have special tax implications and rules for funding. They can consist of stocks, bonds, mutual funds, or any other type of investment.
- **Real estate** is land or buildings. Real estate investments can earn money from rental or lease income and by appreciating in value.

Most investments can also earn you money if you sell them for more than you paid for them. I provide more specifics about investments and retirement planning in Chapters 8 and 13, respectively.

The Importance of Portfolio Management

The term *portfolio* refers to the total of all of your investments. For example, if you have shares of one company's stock, shares in two mutual funds, and a 401(k) plan account, these are the items that make up your portfolio.

At this point, you may be wondering why you should bother including investment information in your Quicken data file. After all, you may already get quarterly (or even monthly) statements from your broker or investment firm. What you may not realize, however, is how you can benefit from keeping a close eye on your investments. Take a look at what portfolio management with Quicken can do for you.

Centralizing Your Investment Records

Unless you have only one brokerage account for all your investments, you probably get multiple statements for the stocks, bonds, mutual funds, and other investments in your portfolio. No single statement can provide a complete picture of your portfolio's worth. Quicken can, however. By entering the transactions and values on each statement within Quicken, you can see the details of your entire portfolio in one place.

Knowing the Value of Your Portfolio on Any Day

Brokerage statements can tell you the value of your investments on the statement's ending date, but not what they're worth today. Or what they were worth on August 14, 2001. Quicken, however, can tell you what your portfolio is worth on any day for which you have entered security prices. And it can estimate values for dates without exact pricing information.

Tip *If you like to keep your portfolio's value up to date with the latest security prices, retrieve prices online. I show you how to take advantage of this feature in Chapter 7.*

Keeping Track of Performance History

Manually compiling a complete pricing and performance history for an investment is no small task, especially for periods spanning multiple statements. If you consistently enter investment information in your Quicken data file, however, preparing performance charts and reports is as easy as choosing a menu command or clicking a button.

Calculating Your Return on Investment

Return on investment varies from one investment to another. Quicken enables you to see the return on investment for each security you hold—all in one place!

Tip *Use this feature to make better financial decisions. When you're ready to invest more money in your portfolio, it's easy to see which holding is doing the best— and may deserve more funding.*

Calculating Capital Gains Quickly and Easily

Calculating the gain on the sale of an investment isn't always easy. Considerations include not only the purchase and selling prices, but commissions, fees, stock splits, and purchase lots. Quicken can take all the work out of calculating capital gains—even if you're just considering the sale and want to know what its impact will be. This is extremely helpful at tax time, as I discuss in Chapter 11.

Setting Up Accounts

In Quicken, you track investments in special investment accounts. These accounts store all information about investment transactions.

In this section, I tell you about the types of investment accounts Quicken offers and provide information about three methods for setting up account balances.

Investment Accounts

Quicken offers two types of investment accounts to track the balances and values of your investments: portfolio and mutual fund.

Portfolio accounts　A portfolio account is used to track a variety of investment types, including brokerage accounts, stocks, bonds, and multiple mutual funds.

Mutual fund accounts　A mutual fund account is used to track a single mutual fund.

Tip　*There are all kinds of investments. Sometimes it's not clear what kind of Quicken account is best for a specific investment. Table 6-1 offers some guidance.*

Type of Investment	Type of Account
CDs	Bank or Portfolio
Money market funds	Bank
Stocks in your possession	Portfolio
Brokerage account with one or more securities	Portfolio
Bonds	Portfolio
Savings bonds	Portfolio or Asset
Treasury bills	Portfolio or Asset
Mutual funds	Portfolio (for multiple mutual funds) or Mutual Fund (for a single mutual fund)
Variable or fixed annuities	Portfolio or Asset
Retirement plans, including 401(k), 403(b), IRA, SEP, or Keogh	Portfolio (for stocks, bonds, or multiple mutual funds) or Mutual Fund (for a single mutual fund)
Real estate and real estate investment trusts (REITs) or partnerships	Asset

Table 6-1 • Quicken Accounts for Various Investment Types

I explain how to set up accounts in Chapter 2. You can have as many investment accounts as you need to properly represent the investments that make up your portfolio.

Account Setup Options

When you set up your Quicken investment accounts, you have three options for setting up account balances: entering all historical information, entering data for this year, and entering data as of your Quicken start date.

Entering All Historical Information

Entering all historical information means entering all transactions for the securities you currently have on hand. This option can be time consuming, but I think it's worth the extra effort. It has several benefits:

- You will have exact cost information for all securities you purchased. This enables you to distinguish between purchase lots within Quicken, so you can create accurate reports of capital gains and losses. That'll come in handy when it's time to fill out Schedule D of your tax return.
- You will have complete dividend and interest income information for the current year. This means you can use Quicken's investment income and losses reports to get the information you'll need for Schedule B of your tax return.
- You can accurately track security performance for the full amount of time you've owned each security.
- All of your investment records are centralized in one place, making it easy to find data and compare investment performance.

To enter all historical information, gather together all of your investment records for the securities you currently own and enter each transaction into Quicken as discussed later in this chapter.

Entering Data for this Year

A quicker but less accurate way to set up investments in Quicken is to enter only data for the current year. Here are some of the pros and cons of this method:

- Since you don't have to go back as far for transaction and balance information, your records should be easier to find.

- Since there are less transactions to enter, you can enter them more quickly.
- You will have complete dividend and interest income information for the current year, so you can use Quicken's investment income and losses reports to get the information you'll need for Schedule B of your tax return.
- You will not be able to generate accurate capital gains and losses reports for securities purchased prior to the current year.
- You will not be able to track security performance for the entire time you've owned a security purchased prior to the current year.

To enter current year data, begin by entering share balances for all securities you owned as of January 1 using the Move Shares In investment action. Use security prices as of December 31 of the previous year. Then enter all new transactions since the beginning of the year as discussed later in this chapter.

Entering Data as of Your Quicken Start Date

The quickest but least accurate way to set up investments in Quicken is to enter share balances as of the date you set up your Quicken data file. Unless that date happens to be January 1, you won't be able to generate accurate reports of investment income or losses for the current year. You also won't be able to generate accurate reports of capital gains or losses for any security you owned as of your Quicken start date.

To enter current year data, begin by entering share balances for all securities you owned as of the current date using the Move Shares In investment action. Use security prices for the same date.

Setting Up Securities

Before you can start recording investment transactions and tracking your portfolio's worth, you need to set up the securities that you own or want to track. The easiest way to do this is with the Securities list window.

Note   *If you created a Mutual Fund account, that account is automatically listed as a security, too. You can edit its security information to provide additional details not entered when you created the account. I explain how later in this section.*

Working with the Securities List Window

The Securities list window, which is illustrated next, simply lists the securities in Quicken's data file. You can use this window to add, edit, or delete securities, including *WatchList securities*—securities you don't own but want to monitor. To open this window, choose Lists | Securities.

Buttons at the bottom of the window enable you to work with list items:

- **Use** enables you to use the currently selected security in a transaction. This option is only available when you are entering a transaction.
- **New** enables you to create a new security.
- **Edit** enables you to modify the currently selected security.
- **Delete** removes the currently selected security. Clicking this button displays a confirmation dialog. You must click Yes in that dialog to delete the security from your data file.

Caution *Do not delete a security for which you want to maintain historical information, even if you no longer own it. Deleting a security removes all record of the security from your Quicken data file. If you want to keep the information but don't want to see the security in lists, hide the security instead. I tell you how later in this chapter.*

Adding a New Security

To add a new security to your Quicken data file—either as a holding or a WatchList item—click New in the Securities window. The Set Up Security window, which is shown next, appears. Use it to enter information about the security and click Create.

Here's a quick rundown of the information you can provide about each security you enter:

- **Security** is the name of the security.
- **Symbol** is the security's ticker symbol. This information is not required unless you plan to use Quicken's Quotes feature to download security prices from the Internet. (I tell you more about downloading stock prices in Chapter 7.)
- **Type** is the type of security. You can use the pop-up menu to select one of four predefined types: Bond, CD, Mutual Fund, or Stock. You can also choose Edit from the pop-up menu to display the Types window, shown next, and add or remove security types.

- **Goal** is your intended investment goal for the security. You can use the pop-up menu to select one of five predefined types: College Fund, Growth, High Risk, Income, and Low Risk. You can also choose Edit from the pop-up menu to display the Goals window, shown next, and add or remove investment goals.

- **Notify If Price Is** options enable you to set a high and low price for the security. When the security price reaches either of the values you enter, Quicken notifies you. This feature is especially useful when you use the Quotes feature to download security prices from the Internet, as I discuss in Chapter 7.
- **Taxable** indicates whether the security is taxable. For example, although most investments are taxable, investments such as municipal bonds may not be. You click to toggle this check box on or off as necessary for the security.
- **Hide In Lists** indicates whether the security should appear in lists such as the Securities list. You can turn on this check box to hide a security you don't need to use in transactions but want to keep historical information for.

Tip   *You can display hidden securities in the Securities list window by turning on the Show Hidden Securities check box in the bottom of the window. Hidden securities will appear in italics.*

Editing a Security

You can edit a security to add or change information you previously entered for it. Select the security's name in the Securities window and click Edit. The Edit Security window, which looks and works just like the Set Up Security window shown earlier, appears. Enter or edit information in the window and click Change to save your changes.

Recording Investment Transactions

The most important part of properly tracking investments is recording all investment transactions. This includes purchases, sales, dividends, and other activity affecting your portfolio's value.

In this section, I provide instructions for entering most common investment transactions using Quicken's Investment Actions feature.

Before You Start

Before you enter a transaction, you must have all of its details. In most cases, you can find the information you need on a confirmation form or receipt you receive from your broker or investment firm. The information varies depending on the transaction, but it should include the security name, transaction date, number of shares, price per share, and commissions or fees.

Working with an Investment Register

You can enter security transactions into the account register window for the investment account (see Figure 6-1) that the transaction affects. To open an investment register, use one of the following techniques:

- Choose Lists | Accounts or press COMMAND-A to display the Accounts list window. Then double-click the name of the account for which you want to use the register.
- Choose the name of the register from the Rgstrs button menu at the top of the Investing tab.
- Click the button for the account near the top of the Investing tab.
- Double-click the name of the account in the Portfolio window (see Figure 6-3, later in this chapter).

As shown in Figure 6-1, an investment account register looks similar to the account register for a banking or credit account window. It enables you to view, enter, and edit transactions for an investment account.

You can use buttons at the bottom of the register window to enter investments and open other windows:

- **Record** saves the transaction you are currently entering.
- **Restore** reverts the current transaction back to the way it was before you began changing or entering it.

Date	Action	Security	Memo	Shares Out / Cash In	Shares In / Cash Out	Share Price / Commission	Clr	Cash Balance
		Transfer						
2/1/01	RD	AT&T			0.115	23.950		
		•Div Income			3.06	0.31		0.00
2/2/01	BUY	AT&T			3.991	23.8008		
		[Checking]			100.00	5.01		0.00
6/25/01	MS	Dow Chemical			307	32.820		
		[DRIPs]						0.00
8/14/01	SELL	AT&T		20		20.200		
		•Realized Gain		394.01		9.99		394.01
8/14/01	BUY	*Security*		*Shares In*	*Share Price*			
		Transfer	*Memo*	*Cash Out*	0.00			

Record Restore Actions Portfolio   Cash Balance $394.01
                                       Market Value $11,800.04

Figure 6-1 • Use an investment account register window, like this one for a portfolio account, to record investment transactions.

- **Actions** displays the Investment Actions window, shown in Figure 6-2, which lists common transactions for investment accounts. Double-clicking an option displays a form for entering the transaction.
- **Portfolio** opens the Portfolio window (see Figure 6-3), which I discuss later in this chapter.

Using Investment Actions

The easiest way to enter an investment transaction is with Investment Actions, a Quicken feature that displays a custom form for many kinds of investment transactions. To display a list of investment actions, click the Actions button at the bottom of the register window (see Figure 6-1) or choose Activities | Investment Actions. The Investment Actions window, which is shown in Figure 6-2, appears.

Tip *Experienced Quicken users may prefer to enter transactions directly into the account register for an investment account. A pop-up menu in the transaction's entry area offers appropriate transaction codes for all kinds of transactions. You can explore this feature on your own once you're accustomed to entering transactions with Investment Actions.*

Here's a quick overview of the transactions you can enter with Investment Actions:

- **Buy** adds shares to an investment account with an exchange of cash. Use this option for purchase transactions.

Figure 6-2 • The Investment Actions window lists common investment transactions.

- **Move Shares In** adds shares to an investment account without an exchange of cash. Use this option for securities obtained as a result of a gift or inheritance.

- **Sell Shares** removes shares from an investment account with an exchange of cash. Use this option for sale transactions.

- **Move Shares Out** removes shares from an investment account without an exchange of cash. Use this option for giving shares as gifts or writing off shares of a company that has gone out of business.

- **Stock Split** enables you to record additional shares received as a result of a stock split.

- **Dividend** enables you to record income from dividends paid on shares of a security.

- **Interest Income** enables you to record income from interest paid on cash balances.

- **Capital Gain Long** enables you to record income received from a long-term capital gains distribution.

- **Capital Gain Short** enables you to record income received from a short-term capital gains distribution.

Tip   *Capital Gain Long and Capital Gain Short transactions are relatively common with mutual funds that are not set up to reinvest income.*

- **Return Of Capital** enables you to record the return of part of your investment capital.
- **Reinvest Interest** enables you to account for interest income that is reinvested in the security.
- **Reinvest Dividend** enables you to account for dividend income that is reinvested in the security.
- **Reinvest Long** enables you to account for long-term capital gains that are reinvested in the security.
- **Reinvest Short** enables you to account for short-term capital gains that are reinvested in the security.

Tip *The Reinvest options are common with mutual funds that are set up to reinvest income. The Reinvest Dividend option is common with dividend reinvestment programs (DRIPs).*

- **Transfer Money** enables you to record a transfer of funds from one account to another.
- **Misc. Income** enables you to record investment income other than interest or dividends.
- **Misc. Expense** enables you to record investment expenses other than commissions.

You can open an Investment Action form window by double-clicking the transaction type in the Investment Actions window. These forms are generally self-explanatory and easy to use. Here are a few common transactions to illustrate how they work.

Purchases

A security purchase normally involves the exchange of cash for security shares. In some cases, you may already own shares of the security or have it listed on your WatchList. In other cases, the security may not already exist in your Quicken data file, so you'll need to set up the security when you make the purchase.

Start by double-clicking the Buy action in the Investment Actions window (see Figure 6-2). A Buy window like the one shown next appears. Enter information into each field and click Record.

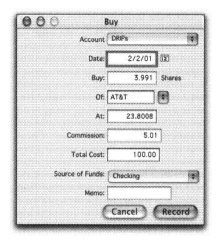

Here's the information you should enter:

- **Account** is the account to which you want to add shares. By default, the current account's name appears in this pop-up menu. Be sure to set the correct account in this field.

- **Date** is the date of the transaction. You can click the calendar icon to display a calendar of dates, if necessary. The date you enter should be the date of the transaction, not the date you entered it.

- **Buy** is the number of shares you purchased.

- **Of** is the name of the security you purchased. You can use the pop-up menu to pick a security in the Securities list. If you enter the name of a security that is not in the Securities list, Quicken displays a dialog like the one shown next, enabling you to select or set up a security.

- **At** is the price you paid per share. You can enter prices as decimal or fractional values. For example, 54.875 could also be entered as **54 7/8**. (Be sure to include a space between the whole number and the fraction.)
- **Commission** is the brokerage fee you paid to obtain the shares.
- **Total Cost** is calculated automatically by Quicken based on the number of shares, price per share, and commission. The only way to change this value is to change one of the other values.

Tip *You can use the Commission field to correct slight rounding differences that may occur when recording the purchase of fractional share amounts. This is relatively common when accounting for mutual fund and DRIP reinvestments. Just add a positive or negative number that makes the Total Cost field match the dollar amount of the transaction. Normally, this will only be 1¢ or 2¢, which shouldn't have much of an impact on your investment reports.*

- **Source Of Funds** is the account that was used to fund the transaction. If the purchase was paid for with cash in the investment account, you can leave this field blank; it will automatically use the same account. If the purchase was paid for with cash in another account—such as your checking account—be sure to choose the correct account.

Tip *To purchase stock on margin—credit offered by a brokerage firm—and later send a check to your brokerage firm to cover the purchase, leave the Source Of Funds field blank when entering the purchase transaction. Then, when you send a check to the brokerage firm, record the check in your checking account register, using the investment account as the transfer account in the Category field.*

- **Memo** is an optional memo you can include with the transaction.

When you click Record to save the transaction, Quicken adds it to the appropriate account register and updates cash and share balances as necessary.

Moving Shares into an Account

The Move Shares In action adds shares to an investment account without affecting the cash balance in any other account. You can use this action to record securities received as a gift or to record the beginning share balances for a security if you do not plan to enter all transactions for that security.

Double-click the Move Shares In action in the Investment Actions window (see Figure 6-2). A Move Shares In window like the one shown next appears. Enter transaction information and click Record.

This window has many of the same fields found in the Buy window shown earlier. Here are two tips for entering information:

- The date you enter should be the date you received the security (if you received it as a gift) or the date from which you want to begin tracking the security's value.
- The share price you enter should be the price as of the date you entered.

When you click Record to save the transaction, Quicken adds it to the appropriate account register and updates cash and share balances as necessary.

Sales

A security sale also involves the exchange of cash for security shares. Normally, you dispose of shares you already own, but in some instances, you may sell shares you don't own. This is called *selling short*, and it is a risky investment technique sometimes used by experienced investors.

Start by double-clicking the Sell action in the Investment Actions window (see Figure 6-2). A Sell window like the one shown next appears. Enter information into each field and click Record.

As you can see, this window is very similar to the Buy window shown earlier. The information you enter is basically the same; consult the section titled "Purchases," earlier in this chapter, for details. The only difference is the inclusion of a Net Proceeds field, which is the amount of money you will receive as a result of the sale. When you click Record to save the transaction, Quicken adds it to the appropriate account register and updates cash and share balances as necessary.

Quicken also enables you to select the shares you want to sell from individual purchase lots. You can use this feature for additional control over capital gains. For example, if you want to take advantage of long-term capital gains tax breaks, you could sell shares that have been in your possession for more than 12 months. If you want to record a loss, you could sell shares that cost more than the selling price. Obviously, your options will vary depending on the lots, their acquisition prices, and your selling price. To specify lots, select the sale transaction in the investment account register. As shown next, a Lots button will appear if the security you're selling has multiple lots.

When you click the Lots button, the Select Specific Shares (Lots) dialog, which is shown next, appears. Use it to select the lots you are selling and click OK.

Tip   *By controlling the term and amount of capital gains, you can minimize your tax bill.*

Dividend and Interest Payments

Many investments pay dividends, interest, or other income in cash. (That's why they're so attractive to an investor!) Recording this activity in the appropriate account register enables Quicken to accurately calculate performance, while keeping account balances up to date.

Caution   *Many mutual funds are set up to reinvest income, rather than pay it in cash. Do not use the forms in this section to record a reinvestment of income. Instead, use one of the Reinvest Earnings & Distributions options in the Investment Actions window (see Figure 6-2) to enter transaction information.*

Start by double-clicking the Dividend or Interest Income action in the Investment Actions window (see Figure 6-2). Then use the Dividend or Interest Income form that appears (both are illustrated next) to enter transaction information and click Record.

- If the income arrives as a check that you deposit to a bank account, the Destination Of Funds field should be the account to which you deposited the check. If the income is automatically deposited in your brokerage account, you can leave the Destination Of Funds field blank to increase the cash balance of that account.
- The Share Price field is optional; you don't have to enter information there unless you want to.

When you click Record to save the transaction, Quicken adds it to the appropriate account register and updates cash balances as necessary.

Other Transactions

Other transactions are just as easy to enter as purchases, sales, and dividends. Simply double-click the appropriate option in the Investment Actions window (see Figure 6-2), and then enter the transaction information in the window that appears. If you have the transaction confirmation or brokerage statement in front of you when you enter the transaction, you have all the information you need to enter it.

Entering Advanced Transactions

Some less common transactions are not included in the Investment Actions window (refer to Figure 6-2). Here are four that you might need to enter, along with instructions for entering them.

Stock Splits and Dividends

You can use the Stock Split action's form (shown next) to record stock received as a result of a stock split or a stock dividend:

Stock splits   The Stock Split form is designed for stock splits. Simply enter the split ratio in the fields provided. For example, if you got three shares of stock for every share you owned, enter 3 for 1 in the fields.

Stock dividends   A stock dividend is similar to a stock split in that you wind up with more shares than you originally had. In the first Split Ratio box, enter 1 plus the fractional number of shares you received per share of stock you own. In the second Split Ratio box, enter 1. So if you received 0.2 shares for every share you own, you'd enter 1.2 for 1 as the Split Ratio.

Exchange of Shares for IRA Custodial Fees

Some IRAs require annual custodial fees that are paid by deducting shares from your account. You can record this kind of transaction using the Sell action's form shown earlier in this chapter. Enter the number of shares paid and the per share price. Then enter the dollar amount of the fee in the Commission field to bring the Net Proceeds field to zero. You can leave the Destination Of Funds field empty. When you click Record, the share balance is changed, but the account's cash balance remains the same. The fee is recorded as a commission expense.

Accrued Interest for Bond Purchases

When you buy a bond after its original issue date, you normally pay accrued interest—the amount of interest earned but not yet paid—as part of the purchase price. There are two or three steps to properly recording this type of transaction.

1. Record the bond purchase as a Buy transaction.

Record the purchase of the bond, without the accrued interest, using the Buy action form.

2. Record the accrued interest as a Misc. Expense transaction.

Record the amount of the accrued interest, as a separate transaction, using the Misc. Expense form. Be sure to enter the correct Account and to select Accrued Int (at the bottom of the category list) as the Category. Here's an example of what it might look like:

> **Note** *If the bond is not taxable, use Accrued Int NT as the category.*

3. Record the accrued interest as a Transfer Money transaction.

If you paid for the accrued interest with cash from another Quicken account, use the Transfer Money form to transfer the funds from the account you used to pay to the accrued interest to the investment account you indicated in step 2. This will properly adjust the cash balance in the investment account. Here's what the form might look like:

> **Tip** *If you wrote a check to pay the accrued interest, you can simply use the investment account's name as the transfer account in the Category field for the check transaction. Then you can skip step 3.*

Stock Spin-Off

A stock spin-off occurs when a large company "spins off" one of its subsidiaries as a separate company with its own stock. As the investor, you keep the same number of shares of the parent company, which are now worth less because the company is smaller. But you also get shares in the new company. You need to record the change in value of the parent company while recording the receipt and value of the shares in the new company.

This is a two-step process, and you'll need all the divestiture statements you received from the parent company to complete it accurately.

1. Record the reduction of the parent company's value as a Return Of Capital transaction.

Record the value of the shares you received in the new company as a return of capital on the old company. The date of the transaction should be the date the spin-off occurred. Use the Return Of Capital action's form as shown here:

2. Record the acquisition of the new company's shares as a Buy transaction.

Use a Buy action form to record the purchase of the new company's shares on the spin-off date. To obtain a per-share price, divide the dollar amount entered in step 1 by the total number of shares acquired. When you complete the transaction and click Record, the cash added to the account in step 1 should be removed and the new shares properly recorded.

Editing Transactions and Adjusting Balances

Occasionally, you may need to edit transactions to correct errors or adjust the cash balance in an investment account. Here's how.

Editing Transactions

You can edit a transaction in the account register for the investment account (refer to Figure 6-1). Simply make changes to the appropriate fields and click Record.

Updating an Account's Cash Balance

You can adjust the cash balance in a brokerage account to account for rounding errors or other inconsistencies. Open the register for the account for which you want to change the balance. Then choose Activities | Adjust Balance to display the Adjust Balance dialog, shown next. Enter the correct balance and balance date in the top two edit boxes. In the Category box, choose a category to record the gain or loss of cash. Then click OK to record the transaction and change the account balance.

Viewing Your Investments

Quicken includes two different windows you can use to view information about your investments: the Portfolio window and the Security Detail window. Each window also offers options to add transactions or edit securities. Here's a closer look at them.

The Portfolio Window

The Portfolio window (see Figure 6-3) displays all of your investments in one place. Information can be viewed in a number of ways to show you what you need to see to understand the performance, value, or components of your portfolio.

To open the Portfolio window, use one of these methods:

- Choose Activities | Investment Portfolio or press COMMAND-I.
- Click the Portfolio button near the top of the Investing tab.
- Click the Portfolio button at the bottom of an investment account register window (see Figure 6-1).

Figure 6-3 • The Portfolio window shows all of your investments in one place.

The real strength of the Portfolio window is its flexibility. It includes many options for working with and viewing your portfolio.

Using Portfolio Window Options

You can customize the Portfolio window's appearance by using options at the top of the window. There are many view combinations—far too many to illustrate in this book. Here's a quick look at each option so you can explore them on your own.

Grouping by an Account or Field   The Group By options enable you to select the field by which securities are grouped. Choose from the following options on the pop-up menu:

- **Account**, which is the default selection shown in Figure 6-3, shows the securities grouped by account.
- **Security** shows the securities in alphabetical order by security name.
- **Type** shows the securities organized by security type. Security types are discussed earlier in this chapter.
- **Goal** shows the securities organized by investment goal. Investment goals are discussed earlier in this chapter.

Tip   *You can also change the sort order of securities in the Portfolio window by clicking a column heading to sort by that column. To toggle from ascending to descending order, click the button above the top of the vertical scroll bar in the window.*

Setting the Portfolio Date   You can use the Set Prices As Of edit box to set the date for which you want to view the portfolio. For example, suppose you want to see what your portfolio looked like a month ago, before a particularly volatile market period. Enter that date in the edit box. Or click the calendar button beside the edit box to display a calendar of dates, and then click the date you want to display. The window's view changes to show your portfolio as of the date you specified.

Customizing the Column Display   You can change the columns that are displayed in the Portfolio window. Click the Customize button to display the Portfolio Customization dialog, shown next. Click to toggle check marks for the columns you want to display, and then click OK to save your settings.

Here's a quick rundown of the available options:

- **Symbol** is the ticker symbol for the security.
- **Account** is the account the security is held in. This option is not available if the Portfolio window is grouped by Account, as shown in Figure 6-3.
- **Type** is the security type. This option is not available if the Portfolio window is grouped by Type.
- **Goal** is the investment goal. This option is not available if the Portfolio window is grouped by Goal.
- **Taxable Status** is the security's tax status.
- **Shares** is the number of shares owned.
- **Total Cost** is the cost basis for the security—what you paid to obtain it.

- **Average Cost Per Share** is the total cost of all the shares of a security divided by the number of shares. Quicken can calculate this value on the fly for individual securities and groups of securities.
- **Dollars Invested** is the total amount invested in a security. This includes dividend and capital gain reinvestments.
- **Income** is the amount of income received from the security.
- **Unrealized Gain Or Loss** is the dollar amount you would realize as a gain or loss if you sold the security at the most recently entered price for the Portfolio window date. I explain how to enter security prices near the end of this chapter.
- **Percent Gain Or Loss** is the percent change in the security's value.
- **Dollar Return** is the dollar amount of your return on investment for the security.
- **Percent Return** is the percent of your return on investment.
- **Percent Of Portfolio** is the percentage of your portfolio's value attributable to the security.
- **Market Value** is the total number of shares multiplied by the most recently entered price for the Portfolio window date.
- **Show Individual Acquisitions (Lots) For Each Security** instructs Quicken to show purchase lots under each security in the Portfolio window.

Tip   *You can change column width by dragging the right border of a column's heading to the right or left. When you release the mouse button, the column's width changes.*

Opening Registers and Security Detail Windows

You can open the register for an investment account or the Security Detail window for a security from within the Portfolio window (see Figure 6-3).

Opening an Investment Register   To open an investment register, use one of these techniques:

- Click the name of an account and then click the Register button at the bottom of the window.
- Double-click the name of an account.

Opening a Security Detail Window To open a Security Detail window, use one of these techniques:

- Click the name of a security and then click the Detail button at the bottom of the window. (The Register button shown in Figure 6-3 turns into a Detail button when a security is selected.)
- Double-click the name of a security.

Adding Securities to Your Portfolio or WatchList

The Portfolio window offers another way to add securities to your portfolio or to your WatchList, which appears at the bottom of the Portfolio window (see Figure 6-3). Click the Add Security button at the bottom of the window to get the process started. The tiny Security Name dialog appears. Use it to enter or select a security name.

Tip *If you enter a security name that is not in the Security list window, Quicken offers to let you set up or select the security, as discussed earlier in this chapter.*

When you click OK, the Add Security dialog, shown next, appears. It offers two options for adding the security:

- **Add Shares To Account** tells Quicken to add shares to one of your investment accounts. When you select this option and click OK, Quicken displays a dialog in which you can specify which investment action you want to use: Move

Shares In or Buy. Select an option there and click OK to display the appropriate action form for adding the shares.

- **Add Security To WatchList** tells Quicken to add the security to the WatchList in the Portfolio window so you can keep track of its prices. Figure 6-3 shows an example with two securities in the WatchList.

The Security Detail Window

The Security Detail window (see Figures 6-4 through 6-7) provides a wealth of information about a specific security, including value and performance information, transactions, and price or market value history. You can also use this window to edit security information and enter or edit prices.

To open the Security Detail window, use one of the following techniques:

- Choose Activities | Security Detail.
- Click the Detail button near the top of the Investing tab.
- Double-click a security name in the Portfolio window.

The Security Detail window has four tabs. Here's a quick overview of each tab and the features it offers.

Tip *When you open the Security Detail window, it automatically displays the last tab you viewed for the current security. You can switch to a different security by choosing a security from the pop-up menu at the top of the dialog or clicking the <<Prev Security or Next Security>> button.*

Setup Tab

The Setup tab (see Figure 6-4) provides setup information about the security. You can change any of the information in this tab by clicking the Edit button to display the Edit Security dialog. I explained how to edit a security earlier in this chapter.

Graph Tab

The Graph tab (see Figure 6-5) displays a graph of security prices that you have entered into your Quicken data file, either manually, as discussed later in this chapter, or automatically via Internet download, as discussed in Chapter 7. If sales volume amounts have been entered, they also appear in the graph.

Figure 6-4 • The Setup tab of the Security Detail window, which displays security setup information

Figure 6-5 • The Graph tab of the Security Detail window shows a chart of security prices.

Tip   *To get a better view of the graph, enlarge the Security Detail window. This window can be resized like any other Mac OS window.*

You can modify the graph by using options in the bottom of the Security Detail window:

Selecting a date range The Date Range menu enables you to select a period to display in the graph. Your options are One Week, One Month, One Quarter, One Year (shown in Figure 6-5), Three Years, Five Years, and All.

Charting multiple securities You can chart multiple securities in the same window by clicking Overlay Securities. A dialog like the one shown next appears. Click to place check marks beside each security you want to display on the graph. When you click OK, the graph is revised to show all securities you selected.

Customizing the graph display When you click Customize, the Customize Security Graph dialog appears. Click to place check marks beside each option you want enabled for the graph.

Prices Tab

The Prices tab (see Figure 6-6) displays all the price and volume information entered for the security. This is the same information used to create the graph in the Graph tab (refer to Figure 6-5). You can enter this information manually using the New and Edit buttons at the bottom of this window, as discussed later in this chapter. You can also enter it automatically via Internet download, as discussed in Chapter 7.

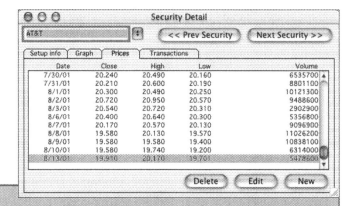

Figure 6-6 • The Prices tab of the Security Detail window lists all available security price and volume information.

Transactions Tab

The Transactions tab (see Figure 6-7) lists all of your transactions for a security. If you make the window wide enough, as shown in Figure 6-7, you can see columns for the Account, Date, Action (or transaction type), Shares, Price, Amount, Commission, and Total Shares (in the account after the transaction). Quicken automatically compiles this information from your account registers when you enter transactions.

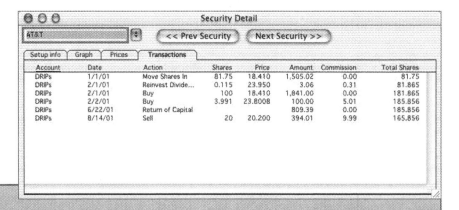

Figure 6-7 • The Transactions tab of the Security Detail window lists all of your transactions for a security.

Tip *You can quickly go to a specific transaction in an investment account register by double-clicking the transaction in the Transactions tab.*

Tracking Security Values

As you can see in the Portfolio window (refer to Figure 6-3), Quicken can automatically do all the math to tell you what your investments are worth—if you take the time to enter the per-share prices of each of your securities.

When you record transactions, Quicken automatically records the security price. It uses the most recently entered price as an estimate to calculate the current value of the investment. Of course, the Portfolio window is a lot more valuable with up-to-date security price information and a history of prices.

Note *If a security price is not for the current date, Quicken displays a gray diamond beside it to indicate that it is an estimate.*

You can enter price information two ways: manually (the hard way) and automatically (the easy way). I show you how to manually enter security prices in this chapter; to learn how to automatically enter prices via Internet download, skip ahead to Chapter 7.

Tip *If you track more than one or two securities and want to update price information more often than once a week, stop reading now. You don't want to enter security prices manually. Trust me. It's an extremely tedious task. Quicken's ability to download stock prices directly from the Internet—even five-year price histories—can save you tons of time and prevent data entry errors. And best of all, it's free. All you need is an Internet connection. Learn more about setting up an Internet connection in Chapter 3 and about downloading quotes in Chapter 7.*

Entering Security Prices

Manually entering security prices isn't really hard. It's just time-consuming. And the more securities you track, the more time-consuming it is. But without an Internet connection, this may be the only way you can enter prices into Quicken.

Start by opening the Security Detail window as instructed earlier in this chapter. Click the Prices tab to display its options (see Figure 6-6). Then click the New button at the bottom of the window. The New Price dialog, which is illustrated next, appears. Use it to enter price and volume information for a specific date. Then click Record to save the information in your Quicken data file.

Only two pieces of information are required in this dialog: Date and Close. Date is the date for which you want to enter the price. Close is the closing price on that date. If you're really ambitious, you can also enter the daily high, low, and volume for the date.

Modifying Security Prices

You can use two other buttons at the bottom of the Prices tab (see Figure 6-6) to work with prices:

- **Edit** displays the Edit Price dialog for the currently selected date. This dialog looks and works the same way as the New Price dialog.
- **Delete** removes the price information for the selected date.

Caution   *Removing a security price can affect the market value calculations and graph for the security for that date. Quicken will use the previous date's pricing information to estimate prices on the missing date. Quicken cannot plot graph points for dates for which no pricing information exists.*

Viewing Market Values and Performance

Once you've entered price information for your securities, you can view their market value and performance information in the Portfolio window (see Figure 6-3) and Graph tab of the Security Detail window (see Figure 6-5). You can use options within the windows to modify the display of information. I explained how earlier in this chapter.

Using Online Investment Tracking Tools

In this Chapter:

- *Downloading investment transactions*

- *Downloading current and historical security prices*

- *Exporting portfolio information to the Web*

- *Viewing your portfolio on the Web*

Quicken 2002 includes three powerful features that work with the Internet to help you keep track of the value of your portfolio.

The Online Account Access feature enables you to download investment transactions and account balances from financial institutions. This feature is brand new in Quicken 2002. Although only a few financial institutions supported this feature as this book went to press, new institutions are being added regularly.

The Quicken Quotes feature enables you to obtain current and historical quotes for individual stocks, mutual funds, and other investments. This automates the tracking of market values to keep your portfolio balance up to date. Quicken can also notify you, with a dialog, when a security you track reaches a high or low price you specify. This feature works for all stocks and mutual funds, no matter which brokerage firm you use for your investments.

The Portfolio Export feature enables you to export information from your portfolio accounts to your private Quicken.com account. You can then view your portfolio's current value from any computer with Internet access.

In this chapter, I tell you about these features and explain how they can help you save time and stay informed about your investments.

> **Tip**   *The instructions in this chapter assume that you have already configured your computer for an Internet connection. If you have not done so, do it now. Chapter 3 provides the instructions you need to set up and test an Internet connection. This chapter also assumes that you understand the topics and procedures discussed in Chapter 6, and builds on some of the basic concepts discussed in that chapter.*

Online Account Access

Online Account Access enables you to download transactions directly from the financial institutions with which you maintain investment accounts. Each transaction can then be entered into your Quicken investment account with the click of a mouse button. This feature is brand new in Quicken 2002.

> **Note**   *To use Online Account Access, your brokerage or investment firm must be a Quicken partner listed in the Financial Institutions window. Choose Online | Financial Institutions to view this list. You can learn more about Quicken partners in Chapter 3.*

Setting Up Online Account Access

To use Online Account Access, you must configure the appropriate Quicken accounts. This requires that you enter information about your financial institution and the account(s) you want to track.

Setting up Online Account Access for an investment account is similar to setting it up for a bank or credit card account. Choose Online | Enable Online Account. In the Select Account To Enable dialog, select the appropriate investment account and click OK. Then use the Enable Online Access dialog that appears to select the type of access you want to use, enter the financial institution's name, your account number, and your customer ID. Here's what it might look like:

When you click Save, Quicken saves the information you entered. You're all ready to go online.

Downloading Investment Transactions

To download investment transactions into Quicken, choose Online | Download Investment Transactions or click the Inv Dnld button near the top of the Investing tab. The Download Investment Transactions window, which is shown in Figure 7-1, appears. If necessary, choose the name of your financial institution from the Financial Institution pop-up menu. Then click the Get Online Data button. Quicken connects to the Internet and displays a dialog like the one shown next. Enter the PIN assigned by your financial institution and click OK.

Quicken communicates with your financial institution. It displays a Connection Status dialog as it works. When it's finished, it displays the Online Transmission Summary dialog, shown next, which summarizes the transactions that were downloaded.

If Quicken downloaded transactions, it then attempts to match the ticker symbols for the securities it downloaded to the ticker symbols for securities in your security list. It displays the Choose A Security dialog for any securities it doesn't recognize:

If the security corresponds to one in your security list, select the security it should match and click Match. Otherwise, click Add As New Security to add the downloaded security's information to your security list. You may have to repeat this process for several securities. When you're finished, you'll return to the Download Investment Transactions window (see Figure 7-1).

Comparing Downloaded Transactions to Register Transactions

Downloading transactions is half the job. The other half is to compare downloaded transactions to transactions already entered in your account register. You do that in the Download Investment Transactions window (see Figure 7-1).

Choose the account for which you want to compare transactions. As you can see in Figure 7-1, information about downloaded transactions appears in the top half of the window. The Status column identifies two types of transactions:

- **Matched** identifies transactions that match those in the register. You can select a matched transaction and click the Accept button to remove it from the list in the top half of the window.

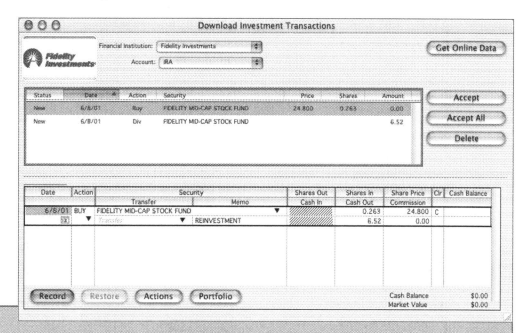

Figure 7-1 • The Download Investment Transactions window, with two downloaded transactions

- **New** identifies transactions that do not appear to be in the register. Otherwise, you can select a New transaction and click Accept to enter the transaction into your account register.

How you handle a transaction depends on its status and whether it already appears in the account register:

Accepting a Matched Transaction   To accept a matched transaction, select it in the top half of the window and click Accept.

Matching a Transaction   If the transaction is in the register but has different information—perhaps a different date or amount—you can modify the register transaction in the bottom half of the window and click Record to match it to the downloaded transaction. Then click Accept to accept it.

Entering a New Transaction   To enter a new transaction into the register, select it in the top half of the window and click Accept.

To Delete a Downloaded Transaction   To delete a downloaded transaction, select it in the top half of the window and click Delete.

Using Quicken Quotes

Consider the following scenario: you wake up one morning and realize that your future financial security is very important to you. (This happened to me about eight years ago.) You make a conscious effort to save and invest money. After a few years, you own shares of a few stocks and mutual funds, which you track in your Quicken data file. With your growing portfolio, you find that half the time you spend with Quicken is spent entering up-to-date stock quotes. You like keeping the market value information current, but you'd like to spend more of your time researching new investments and following news stories about the investments you already have.

With Quicken Quotes, you can download quotes throughout the day or at the day's end. If you miss a few days, don't worry. You can get up to five years of stock quotes for any company with the click of a mouse.

The cost? It's free to Quicken Deluxe users, courtesy of Intuit. All you need is an Internet connection.

Getting quotes online is easy—provided that you have properly set up your Quicken data file with required security information. In this section, I explain how to set up, download, and review online quotes. I also explain how you can download historical prices for securities you own or watch.

Setting Up Securities for Downloading Quotes

Before you can download a security's price, you must tell Quicken what the security's ticker symbol is. You do this by entering the ticker symbol for the security in the Set Up Security or Edit Security window. You may also want to set up the price notification feature to notify you of high or low prices. If you did all this when you first set up the security, you can skip this section. If not, read on.

Looking Up a Ticker Symbol

You can't download quotes for a security if its correct ticker symbol is not entered in Quicken. If you don't know a security's ticker symbol, you'll have to look it up.

Choose Online | Research Security Online to display the tiny Research Security dialog shown next. Enter the name of the security in the edit box and click Go Online.

Quicken launches your Web browser, connects to the Internet, and displays the Quicken.com home page. The Ticker Search page should also appear with a list of possible securities that match what you entered, as shown next.

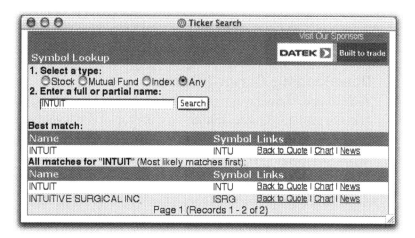

Note *If the Ticker Search page does not automatically appear, you can click the Don't Know the Symbol? link in the Quotes and Research area near the top of the Quicken.com home page to display it. Then use the form at the top of the Ticker Search page to select a security type and enter all or part of the security name. Click Search to display a list of possible matches, as shown previously.*

Entering the Ticker Symbol and Notification Prices

If necessary, switch back to Quicken. Then choose Lists | Securities to display the Securities window. Select the security for which you want to download quotes and click the Edit button. The Edit Security window, which is shown next, appears. Be sure the correct ticker symbol appears in the Security edit box. You can also set options to have Quicken notify you when the security reaches either a high or low price that you specify. When you've finished, click Change.

Repeat this process for each security for which you want to download quotes.

Downloading Current Quotes

You can update quotes any time you like. Choose Online | Update Security Prices or click the Quotes button near the top of the Investing tab. If you are not connected to the Internet, Quicken connects. A Quicken Quotes Progress dialog appears while Quicken requests and receives the security price information. When it's finished, a dialog appears, telling you how many quotes were downloaded.

When you click OK, a Download Summary window like the one shown next may appear. It displays any account value balance changes or price notifications.

		Download Summary			
Successfully downloaded quotes for 7 securities at 3:05:15 PM on 8/22/01.					

Investment account balance changes

Account	Previous Bala...	New Balance	Balance Chg	% Change
DRIPs	14,643.78	14,279.37	-364.41	-2.5%
Stock on Hand	27,410.40	28,831.68	1,421.28	5.2%

High/Low price notification

Security	Price	High Setting	Low Setting	Date
Intuit, Inc.	36.040	30		8/22/01

View Latest Prices

Tip You can fine-tune the account value balance changes by setting Quotes preferences. The value you enter determines the minimum percentage change in an investment account's balance for Quicken to notify you about the change. For example, with this option set to 2 percent (the default value), if an account's balance changes by 2.56 percent due to an increase (or decrease) in security market values, Quicken will notify you. If the account's balance changes by only 1.87 percent, Quicken will not notify you. I explain how to set preferences in Appendix B.

Note The prices downloaded by the Quicken Quotes feature during trading hours are delayed by 15 minutes or more. Mutual fund closing prices for the day are not updated until approximately 6:00 P.M. ET. Quicken does not download quotes for hidden securities.

In Quicken, market values of your securities are automatically updated when you download quotes. You can see recent prices for the securities you track by clicking the View Latest Prices button in the Download Summary window. Here's what it might look like:

Symbol	Volume	High	Low	Current	Change	Time/Date
AAPL	3107800	18.250	17.610	18.210	.290	8/22/01
T	6463600	19.440	19.210	19.270	-.090	8/22/01
T	6703200	19.790	19.250	19.360	-.130	8/21/01
T	6021700	19.580	19.280	19.490	.170	8/20/01
T	11312900	19.700	19.260	19.320	-.260	8/17/01
T	8005300	19.700	19.300	19.580	.030	8/16/01
AWE	7761200	16.460	15.740	15.800	-.580	8/22/01
AWE	5059500	16.590	16.200	16.380	-.160	8/21/01
AWE	4084100	16.560	16.250	16.540	-.050	8/20/01
AWE	5101900	16.600	16.260	16.590	-.080	8/17/01
AWE	6621300	16.800	15.980	16.670	.180	8/16/01
ADP	1029800	51.590	50.710	51.120	.240	8/22/01
ADP	1814300	51.990	50.100	50.880	.770	8/21/01
ADP	1337800	50.250	49.400	50.110	.510	8/20/01
ADP	1676700	49.990	49.390	49.600	-.450	8/17/01
ADP	1450900	50.200	49.300	50.050	.490	8/16/01
DOW	2014200	34.710	34.000	34.390	-.430	8/22/01
DOW	2022200	35.830	34.480	34.820	.380	8/21/01
DOW	2954000	34.440	33.770	34.440	-.120	8/20/01

All quotes are at least 15 minutes delayed

Viewing Portfolio Values

After downloading quotes, the Price and Market Value columns in the Portfolio window (see Figure 7-2) reflect the most recently downloaded prices for both the securities you own and WatchList items—even if you download quotes several times in the same day.

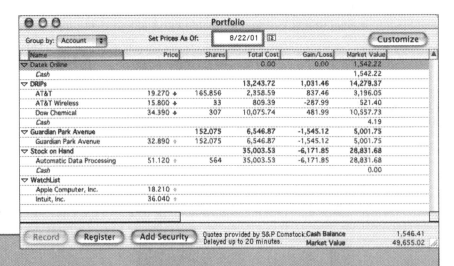

Figure 7-2 • The Portfolio window reflects the most recently downloaded prices for the day.

Symbols to the right of the security price indicate the price change:

- **Green up arrow** indicates that the security's price has risen since the last closing price.
- **Red down arrow** indicates that the security's price has fallen since the last closing price.
- **Black dash** (not shown) indicates that the security's price has not changed since the last closing price.
- **Gray diamond** (not shown) indicates that the security's price has not been downloaded since the start of the trading day.

 Note | *I tell you more about using the Portfolio window in Chapter 6.*

Getting Historical Prices

You can also download historical price information for the securities you track with the Quicken Quotes feature. Choose Online | Get Historical Prices or click the HistPrice button near the top of the Investing tab. Quicken displays the Download Historical Prices dialog, which is shown next. Choose a time period from the drop-down list at the top of the dialog. Make sure check marks appear beside all securities for which you want to get historical prices. Then click the Download button.

Quicken connects to the Internet and retrieves the information you requested. When it has finished, it updates the price information for each security.

You can review the quotes that were downloaded in the Security Detail window, as discussed in Chapter 6. Here's what the Graph tab looks like for one of my investments with historical information downloaded:

Web Portfolio Export

For years, Quicken.com has offered the My Portfolio feature, which you can use to track your portfolio's value online from any computer connected to the Internet. This makes it possible to see how your investments are doing while you're at work or away on business.

Quicken works directly with this feature by enabling you to export portfolio holdings to the Quicken.com Web site. This enables you to use the Quicken.com My Portfolio feature without a lot of tedious setup and updating. Every time you add or remove portfolio shares, simply export your portfolio to the Web. Then, when you view your portfolio online, it's in sync with your Quicken portfolio.

Note *To use the Portfolio Export feature, you must set up an account on Quicken.com. Setting up a Quicken.com account is part of the Quicken registration process discussed briefly in Chapter 1. If you did not set up a Quicken.com account when you registered Quicken, you can do so by choosing File | Register Quicken and following the instructions that appear onscreen.*

Exporting Your Portfolio to Quicken.com

To begin, choose Online | Portfolio Export. The Portfolio Export window, which is illustrated next, appears. Click to place check marks beside each portfolio account you wish to view on the Web. Then click Export.

Quicken connects to the Internet, checks your registration status with Quicken.com, and exports your portfolio. (During this process, it may prompt you to log in to Quicken.com; if so, just follow the prompts that appear onscreen.) When it is finished, it displays a dialog telling you that the accounts have been successfully exported.

Viewing Your Portfolio and Related Alerts Online

To view your portfolio on Quicken.com, visit the My Finances page on Quicken.com. From within Quicken, choose Online | To The Web | My Finances. If prompted, enter your user ID and password. Your portfolio's information should appear in the My Mini Portfolio area, as shown in Figure 7-3.

To get more information about your portfolio, click the Full Portfolio link in the Mini Portfolio area. This displays the Portfolio page, which might look something like the one in Figure 7-4.

Figure 7-3 • When you export your portfolio to Quicken.com, it appears in the Mini Portfolio area on the My Finances page.

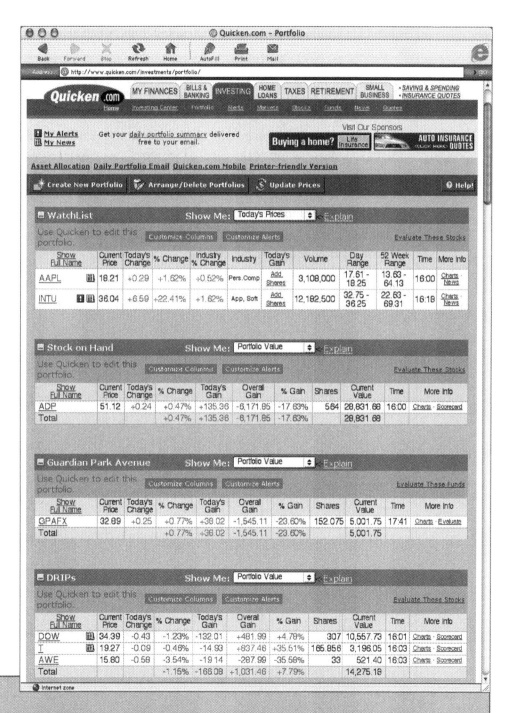

Figure 7-4 • You can see more information about your portfolio on the Portfolio page.

If basic quote information isn't enough about your portfolio, there's more information a mouse click away:

- Click the security's ticker symbol to go to the Quotes page for that security. From there, you can click on other links to get a wealth of information about the security.
- Click the red exclamation point icon beside a security's ticker symbol (or the Alerts link near the top of the page) to see alerts about your securities.
- Click the tiny newspaper icon beside a security's ticker symbol (or the News link near the top of the page) to see news headlines about your securities. Clicking the headline displays its news story.
- Click the Charts link for a security to view and customize charts of the security's prices and other information.

There's a lot more information than what's discussed here. When you have a few moments to spare, follow links to explore what's available.

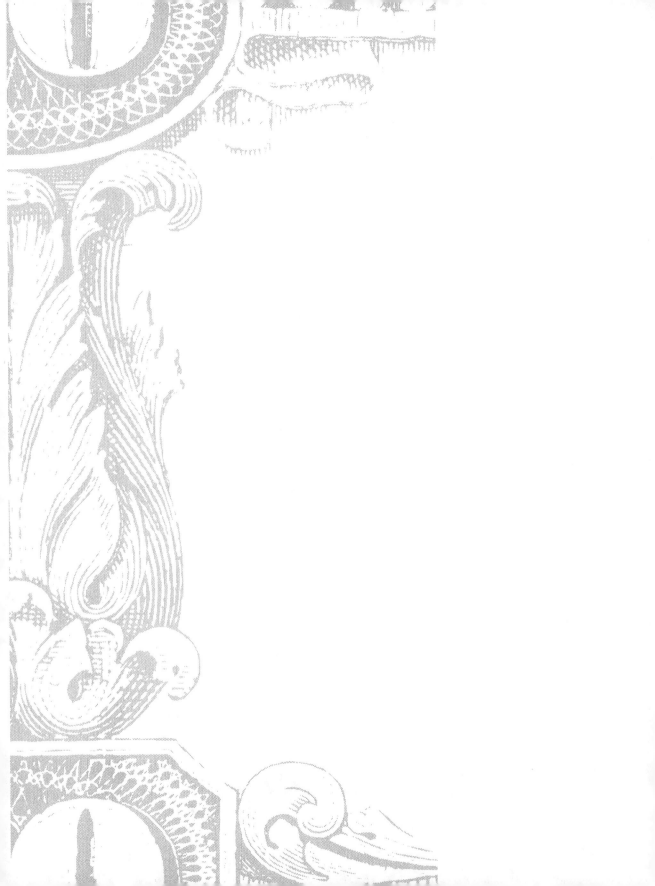

Maximizing Investment Returns

In this Chapter:

- *Types of investments*

- *Investment considerations*

- *Tips for getting started*

- *Researching investments online*

If you're good at managing your finances, you probably have a little left over every month. If you're concerned about risk and don't mind relatively low returns, the savings accounts and certificates of deposit offered by your local bank may be just the place for your money. But if you don't mind a little risk for the possibility of greater financial rewards, there's a good chance you've discovered Wall Street and investing.

In this chapter, I provide some basic information about investing, as well as what you can do to get started. I also tell you about the tools within Quicken and on Quicken.com that can help you research your investments to make smart financial decisions.

Tip　*If you think Wall Street and its risks are just for high rollers, skip this chapter for now and move ahead to Chapter 12. That's where I tell you about savings and the types of low-risk accounts you can open with your local bank.*

Investment Basics

An investment is a security that you purchase with the hope that it will rise in value and pay you interest or a dividend, or both. Investments differ from savings in several ways:

- An investment is somewhat more difficult to redeem for cash, thus making it less liquid.
- An investment's value varies depending on the market—what another investor is willing to pay for it—thus giving it the potential to be worth far more (or less) than you paid for it.
- An investment is not insured against loss, thus making it more risky.

In this section, I provide the information you need to understand what investments are available, what you need to know before deciding on a specific investment type, and the things you can do to get started as an investor.

Types of Investments

There are many types of investments, and each one has its pros and cons. Following is a summary of the most common types of investments.

Money Market Funds

A *money market fund or account* is an investment in short-term debt instruments such as certificates of deposit, commercial paper, banker's acceptances, Treasury bills, and discount notes. Although you can open a money market account with your local bank, it is not insured by the FDIC (Federal Deposit Insurance Corporation) as are most other bank accounts. The rate of return and value is not guaranteed. Money market funds earn income for investors by paying dividends.

Treasury Bills

A *Treasury bill* (or *T-bill*) is a short-term government security, sold through the Federal Reserve Bank by competitive bidding. T-bills are the most widely used of all government debt securities. They are backed by the full faith and credit of the U.S. government. T-bills earn money for investors by paying interest.

Stocks

A *stock* is part ownership of a corporation. Sold as shares through stock exchanges throughout the world (as well as privately, in the case of private corporations), their market values fluctuate daily. Thousands or millions of shares of any given stock can change hands each day. Stocks earn money for investors by paying dividends or rising in value.

Bonds

A *bond* is essentially a loan made by the investor to a company or government entity. Bonds earn money for investors by paying interest. The actual interest rate paid often depends on the stated interest rate and the purchase price of the bond.

Mutual Funds

A *mutual fund* is a group of securities held by a group of investors. When you invest in a mutual fund, your investment dollars are pooled with other investors. A fund manager buys and sells securities to maximize the fund's return. Mutual funds earn money for investors by paying dividends (which can often be automatically reinvested in the fund) or rising in value. In return for his or her services, the fund manager is paid a fee. Other fees may include *loads,* which can be applied when you invest or sell mutual fund shares.

There are thousands of mutual funds, each with its own "mix" of investment types. Investors—especially novice investors—find mutual funds attractive because an investment professional can make decisions for them.

Investment Considerations

When evaluating an investment, you should consider several important factors: return, risk, goal, and taxability.

Return

An investment's *return* is what it earns for the investor. Most investments earn money by paying interest, paying dividends, or rising in value.

Interest   *Interest* is a rate applied to the face or par value of a security that is then paid to the investor in cash. Treasury bills and bonds pay interest. Money market accounts pay dividends, although amounts are calculated like interest and often referred to as interest on bank statements.

Dividends   *Dividends* are per-share payments to shareholders. There are two types: cash and stock.

- **Cash dividends** pay a certain cash amount per share to each stockholder. For example, a $1-per-share cash dividend pays each stockholder $1 for each share held. Cash dividends are normally paid by large companies; smaller companies need cash to grow.

- **Stock dividends** pay a certain number of stock shares per share to each stockholder. A stock split is a type of stock dividend. For example, a 2-for-1 stock split doubles the number of shares each stockholder owns. Although this cuts the per-share value in half, the value is expected to rise again over time.

Capital Gains   A stock's price indicates what another investor is willing to pay for it. When the stock's price is higher than what you paid, you have a gain on your investment. When the stock's price is lower than what you paid, you have a loss on your investment. A capital gain (or loss) can be realized or unrealized:

- **Realized gains (or losses)** are the gains or losses you can record when you sell an investment. If an investment is taxable, the realized gain or loss must be reported on your tax return.

- **Unrealized gains (or losses)** are the gains or losses based on your purchase price and the current market value for investments you have not yet sold. Because the investment has not been sold, the gain is not realized and does not have to be reported on your tax return.

Risk

Risk is your chance of making or losing money on an investment. Although all investments have some element of risk involved, some investments are more conservative (less risky) than others.

There is a direct relationship between risk and return. The higher the potential return, the higher the risk. The lower the risk, the lower the potential return. For example, money market accounts and one-year T-bills are considered relatively conservative investments. On June 22, 2001, they earned an average of 4.46% and 3.35%, respectively. Stocks, on the other hand are considered more risky. On June 22, 2001, the rates of return for a one-year investment in Intuit, Amazon.com, and eBay were -4%, -63%, and 68%, respectively. As these examples show, you can make more money in the stock market, but you can also lose some.

Caution   *These examples are for illustrative purposes only. Exact accuracy is not guaranteed. I am neither recommending nor advising against an investment in any of these securities.*

Goal

Goal refers to your goal as an investor. You should choose an investment based on its ability to meet your goals. There are two main goals: income and growth.

- **Income investments** generate income for investors in the form of dividends and interest. Investors get regular cash payments. Income investments are popular with investors who are retired and living on fixed incomes. Income investments include money market accounts, T-bills, bonds, stocks of larger ("blue chip") companies, and some mutual funds.
- **Growth investments** grow in market value. Growth investments are popular with younger people who want to build a "nest egg" for their later years. Growth investments include stocks of smaller companies and some mutual funds.

Taxability

The *taxability* of an investment refers to how it is taxed. This matters most to individuals in high tax brackets. Generally speaking, investments fall into three categories: taxable, nontaxable, and tax-deferred:

- **Taxable investments** are fully taxed by the federal and local government. You must report and pay taxes on interest and dividend income, as well as capital gains. Capital losses can be deducted from income (within certain limitations) to reduce your tax bill. Visit the Taxes Department on Quicken.com or talk to your tax advisor for more information.

- **Nontaxable investments** are not taxed by the federal government. They may, however, be taxed by local governments such as your state government. Examples of nontaxable investments include municipal bonds.

- **Tax-deferred investments** are investments for which income is not taxed until it is withdrawn. An example is an investment set up as a tax-deferred annuity. In this case, you invest as much as you like. Income, when earned, is automatically reinvested into the account but is not taxed at that time. The value of the account continues to grow. When you're 59 1/2 years old, you can begin withdrawing money from the account. Income on the investment is taxed then, when you're likely to be in a lower tax bracket.

Getting Started

If you've never invested money before, the following sections outline some things you might want to consider doing to get started on the right track.

Doing Your Research

Would you go grocery shopping blindfolded? Groping around on the shelves for beef stew, only to wind up with dog food? Poking meat packages for porterhouse steak, only to wind up with bacon ends?

Investing without research is like shopping blindfolded. You spend money, but don't know what you've purchased until it's paid for. Even then, you may not know—until it's too late and you've lost money.

The Research Security feature and Investments Department on Quicken.com offer literally hundreds of resources you can tap into to get almost any information you can imagine about a company. Even if you don't know where to start, these features can help you search for stocks and mutual funds that meet criteria you specify. You can get news, price histories, and ratings. You can get financial results. You can even participate in message boards to see what other investors think is hot.

If you're not sure what you should be looking for, the Research Security feature and Investments Department can help, too. They offer links to basic information that goes far beyond the basics I provided at the beginning of this chapter. Spend a few hours learning about the types of investments that interest you. Then check out the individual investments themselves. Gather information before you make a decision.

Remember, it's your money. Put it where it'll work hardest for you.

Finding a Broker

If you decide to invest in stocks and bonds, you need a broker. (It's a lot cheaper than buying a seat on the stock exchange.) A stockbroker or brokerage firm can handle the purchases and sales of securities. Nowadays, there are three kinds of brokers:

- **Full-service brokers** can buy and sell securities for you, based on your instructions. But these people also research investments for you and tell you about the ones they think are hot. They also keep an eye on the securities you own and tell you when they think one of them may lose value. Based on their recommendations, you can buy or sell. Fees for full-service brokers are higher than any other—a typical stock purchase or sale could cost well over $100 in commissions. But you're getting more service for your money—you're paying someone to do investment research for you. If you decide to use a full-service broker, track his or her performance carefully. If your broker is not meeting your expectations, you might want to find another broker.

- **Discount brokers** can buy and sell securities for you, too. They usually don't offer any advice, though. They're much cheaper than full-service brokers—a typical stock purchase or sale could be $25 to $60.

- **Deep discount brokers** can also buy and sell securities for you. They don't offer advice either. They're dirt cheap—I've seen fees as low as $8 per trade.

You have two main ways to contact your broker to buy or sell stock:

- **Telephone trading** enables you to give buy or sell instructions by phone, either by speaking to someone at the brokerage firm or by entering information using your telephone keypad.

- **Online trading** enables you to enter buy or sell instructions using your computer and Internet connection. This is fast, convenient, and cheap. In fact, companies that offer both telephone and online trading usually offer online trading for less money.

Tip   *I've been using online trading for over three years now and I'm very happy with it. I can do more trades for less money. My brokerage firm can process orders within 60 seconds of receiving them. They even allow me to trade on margin—that's the brokerage term for "credit"—and pay interest on any cash balance in my account!*

If you're interested in telephone trading, you can find a broker the same way you'd find a bank: ask your friends or check your local phone book. Or ask your bank—some banks offer brokerage services or are connected with brokerage firms. You can also find broker information on Quicken.com.

If you're interested in online trading, your first stop should be Quicken.com. It provides information and links to a number of online brokerage firms. See what each one has to offer and select the one with the best deal for you.

Getting Advice from a Pro

If you don't want a full-service broker, but you do want investment advice, find a financial advisor. Many banks have financial advisors on staff and they can usually provide good, objective advice about investing. They often even handle investment transactions for you (which really makes them a full-service broker).

The trick (I think) is finding an advisor who is objective. Most of the ones I've spoken to deal only with certain types of investments or certain fund families. While these might be great investments, the fact that the advisor doesn't even deal with others makes me wonder how objective he or she can be.

Quicken.com also offers information and links for finding a financial advisor. If you can't get a good recommendation from a knowledgeable friend, be sure to tap into Quicken.com's online resources to see what's out there.

Remember to Diversify!

I'm not a financial planner and, in this lawsuit-crazy era we live in, I don't like to give advice. But here's a one-word piece of advice I must share, one that can help minimize your investment risks: *diversify*.

I can explain with my version of an old story. Farmer Joe has chickens. Every day, he takes a wicker basket to the hen house and collects the eggs. One day, on his way back from the hen house, the basket breaks, dropping the eggs all over the farmyard. As you can imagine, almost every egg breaks. That day, Farmer Joe learned the hard way that he should never put all of his eggs in one basket.

The eggs and basket story applies to your finances, too. If all your investment dollars are in one security and that security fails, you're liable to lose a lot of money. Now take that a step further. If all your investment dollars are in the stock market and the stock market takes a turn for the worse, you're also liable to lose money.

I'm not saying that you shouldn't have "favorite" investments or that you shouldn't invest in the stock market. I'm saying that you should spread your investment dollars among multiple securities and types of investments. If you don't put your eggs in one basket, you can't lose them all.

Quicken and Quicken.com Resources

Now that we've covered the basics, let's take an in-depth look at some specific
Quicken and Quicken.com features that can help you invest wisely and maximize
your investment returns.

Investment Reports and Graphs

Quicken offers a number of reports and graphs you can use to check on the
performance of your investments. Although I cover reports and graphs in Chapter 16,
here's a closer look at the reports and graphs that you can use to monitor your
investment performance and become a better investor.

Reports

To create an investment report, begin by opening the Reports window. Choose
Activities | Reports & Graphs | Reports, or click the Reports button near the top of
the Reporting tab. In the Reports window that appears, click the Investment tab to
display its options:

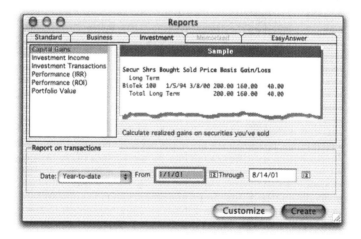

Here's a quick rundown of the reports you can access from this window:

- **Capital Gains** reports capital gains (and losses) from the sale of investment
  securities for a specific period. The report includes the security name, number
  of shares, purchase and sale dates, selling price, basis, and gain or loss.
- **Investment Income** displays the income and expenses from investments
  during a specific period.

- **Investment Transactions** provides a summary of all investment-related transactions for a specific period. The report includes the date, account, action, security name, category, price, number of shares, commission, cash amount, investment value, and net transaction value for each transaction.

- **Performance (IRR)** (see Figure 8-1) provides the internal rate of return of investments during a specific period. The report includes dates, actions, transaction descriptions, investments, returns, and average annual return on investment. This report offers a good way to compare the performance of one security to another.

- **Performance (ROI)** provides the return on investment during a specific period. The report includes dates, accounts, actions, transaction descriptions, investments, returns, and total return on investment.

- **Portfolio Value Report** provides the value of your investment portfolio on a specific date. The report includes the security name, number of shares, current price, cost basis, unrealized gain or loss, and balance for each security in your portfolio.

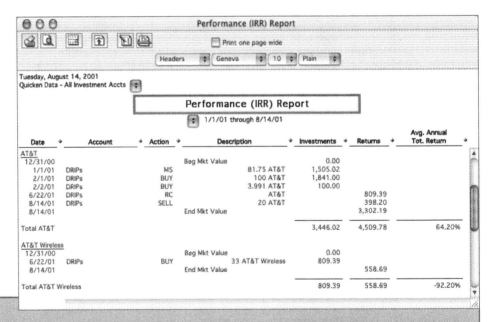

Figure 8-1 • A Performance (IRR) report shows investment performance with an annualized internal rate of return.

Graphs

You can create an investment graph from within the Graphs window. Choose Activities | Reports & Graphs | Graphs, or click the Graphs button near the top of the Reporting tab. The window looks like this:

There are three investment graphs to choose from:

- **Performance (IRR)** shows the annualized internal rate of return for each of the securities in your portfolio during a period you specify.
- **Performance (ROI)** shows the return on investment for each of the securities in your portfolio during the period you specify.
- **Portfolio Value** (see Figure 8-2) uses a stacked column chart to show the total value of your portfolio's investments for each month in the period you specify.

Capital Gains Estimator

Quicken's new Capital Gains Estimator feature enables you to estimate capital gains or losses and their related tax implications before you sell a security. The information it provides can help you make an informed decision about which security to sell.

Getting Started

Choose Activities | Planning Calculators | Capital Gains or click the CapGnEst button near the top of the Investing tab. The Capital Gains Estimator window, which is shown in Figure 8-3, appears. It lists all of the securities in your portfolio, along with the number available for sale and the current security price.

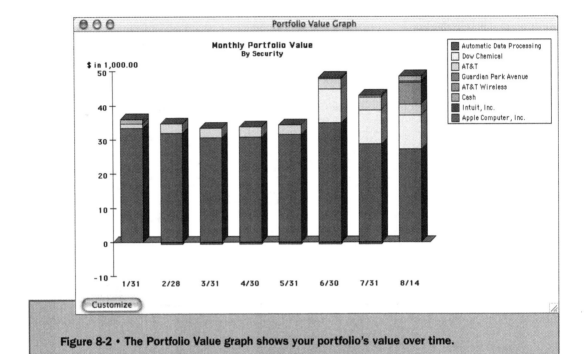

Figure 8-2 • The Portfolio Value graph shows your portfolio's value over time.

Figure 8-3 • The Capital Gains Estimator window, with security purchase lots displayed

Tip *You can click the triangle beside a security name to display all of the purchase lots for a security, as shown in Figure 8-3.*

If this is the first time you have used the Capital Gains Estimator, the Set Tax Rates dialog, which is shown next, appears on top of it. Use the Federal pop-up menu to select your Federal tax bracket or enter rates in the Short and Long edit boxes. You can also enter rates in the Short and Long edit boxes for your State tax rate. Then click OK to save the rates and work with the Capital Gains Estimator window.

Adding Proposed Sales

To select a security for sale, turn on the check box beside the security name or beside one or more of its lots. You can then change the values in the Sell Price and # To Sell columns for the selected security. The Proceeds, Cost/Basis, and Gain/Loss columns are automatically calculated, as shown in Figure 8-4.

Note *If you propose a sale that is less than all shares of a security or purchase lot, the check mark beside the security or lot turns into a dash as shown in Figure 8-4.*

Here are a few additional things you can do to set up proposed sales:

- To show only the securities that are included in proposed sales, choose Selected Securities from the Show pop-up menu. This is especially useful if you have many securities or lots and you want to see the proposed sales together without scrolling. You can choose All Securities from the Show pop-up menu to display all securities again.
- If you click Update Scenario, a dialog like the one shown next appears. Select the radio button for the type of update you want to perform and click OK. Update Prices updates the Sell Price to the most recently entered market price for a security. Reset Quantities resets the # To Sell column to the number of

securities owned. Update Holdings updates your holding information to match current balances.

Tip   *You should use the Update Prices and Update Holdings options in the Update Scenario dialog to update the contents of the Capital Gains Estimator window if your portfolio has changed since the last time you used it.*

- You can sort the proposed sales by any of the column headings. Just click on a column heading to change the order. Click again on the same heading to reverse the sort order for that column.

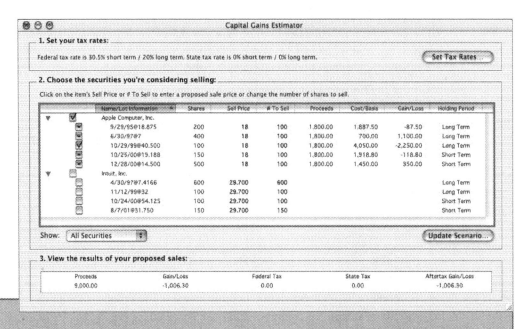

Figure 8-4 • The Capital Gains Estimator with several proposed sales to sell 100 shares from different purchase lots of the same security

Reading the Results

There are two ways you can use the results of Quicken's Capital Gains Estimator calculations. Either way can help you make an informed decision about your proposed sale.

Check the results of individual proposed sales in the middle of the window.   The pretax impact of each sale appears in the middle of the window. You can use this information to see which sale would best suit your needs. For example, suppose that on 8/15/01, you were interested in raising about $1,800 in cash by selling 100 shares of your Apple stock at $18 per share. You could set up proposed sales as shown in Figure 8-4 and use the Gain/Loss and Holding Period columns to determine which sale is best for you. If you've already recorded some long-term gains this year, you may want to sell the shares purchased on 10/25/99 to counter those gains with a big long-term loss. On the other hand, if you've recorded some short-term losses this year, selling the shares purchased on 12/28/00 to result in a short-term gain could help you at tax time.

Check the net post-tax results of all sales.   The bottom part of the Capital Gains Estimator window indicates the net effect of all of your proposed sales. For example, suppose that on 8/15/01 you decide to sell all of your holdings in Apple Computer, which is selling for $18 per share. The Capital Gains Estimator window might look like the one in Figure 8-5. The bottom of the window tells you how much cash you will receive from the sale, what your gain (or loss) would be, how much tax you'd expect to pay, and your post-tax gain (or loss).

Research Security

The Research Security feature offers quick access to information about stocks and mutual funds. Choose Online | Research Security Online, or click the Research button near the top of the Investing tab. The tiny Research Security window appears:

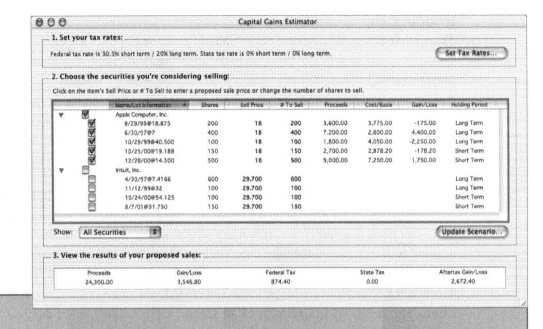

Figure 8-5 • This example shows how the sale of all shares of a security can affect your finances, including your tax return.

Enter a security name or ticker symbol in the edit box, or choose one of the securities in your Quicken data file from the drop-down list. Then click Go Online. Quicken connects to the Internet and displays the Quotes page for the security (see Figure 8-6).

You can click links along the left side of the page to view other information:

- **Quote** (shown in Figure 8-6) shows current price information (delayed approximately 20 minutes), trading volume, a number of ratios, and recent headline links.

- **Chart** displays a one-year chart of closing prices for the security. You can use menus in the chart window to modify the chart's display.

- **Intraday** displays a chart of security prices for the current day.

- **News** displays news headlines for the security. Click a headline to read the story.

- **One-Click Scorecard** prepares reports that help you evaluate a security before you invest, using a variety of well-known analysis techniques and strategies.

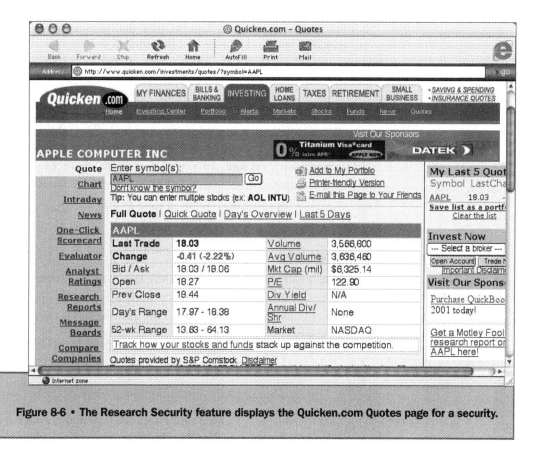

Figure 8-6 • The Research Security feature displays the Quicken.com Quotes page for a security.

- **Evaluator** displays a wide variety of performance and other evaluation information for the security.
- **Analyst Ratings** displays analyst ratings and estimates of earnings per share for the security. (This link was previously labeled Analyst Estimates on Quicken.com.)
- **Research Reports** displays links to free and for-purchase reports prepared by analysts about the security. (This link was previously labeled Analyst Research on Quicken.com.)
- **Message Boards** displays recent message board subjects for the security. These ratings and messages are submitted by Quicken.com Investing Channel message board participants. Click a message board subject to read the messages. (This link was previously labeled Rate & Discuss on Quicken.com.)
- **Compare Companies** displays a page you can use to compare the security to its competitors or other companies you specify.

- **Profile** displays a concise summary of the security, including contact information, exchange, sector, and business description.
- **Insider Trading** displays a list of the security trades conducted by company insiders.
- **Fundamentals** displays share information, valuation, growth rates, financial strength, and management effectiveness ratios. You may find this information helpful when evaluating the security or comparing it to a similar security.
- **Financial Statements** displays four years' worth of annual financial statement summaries for the security.
- **SEC Filings** displays a list of forms filed with the SEC by the company.

Portfolio Analysis

The Portfolio Analysis feature of Quicken.com is my favorite new investment feature, probably because it provides difficult-to-compile information about my portfolio, enabling me to look at it in new ways. This information is especially helpful for diversifying a portfolio.

Note   *To take advantage of this feature, you must export your portfolio to the Web as instructed in Chapter 7.*

Choose Online | To the Web | Portfolio Analysis or click the Analysis button near the top of the Investing tab. If necessary, Quicken launches your Web browser and connects to the Internet. It may prompt you for your Quicken.com user ID and password; if so, enter this information to continue. Finally, it displays a page with a simple form, allowing you to turn on check boxes for each of the accounts you want to include in the analysis. When you turn on the desired check boxes and click Go, the first page of the analysis, which shows asset allocation (see Figure 8-7), appears.

You can click links along the left side of the screen to get more analysis information:

- **Asset Allocation** (shown in Figure 8-7) indicates how your investments are allocated among various asset classes.
- **Model Allocation** shows a comparison of your portfolio's asset allocation compared to a model allocation with the same return. You can use this information to develop a more diversified portfolio.
- **Security Diversification** shows how your portfolio is divided among various securities.

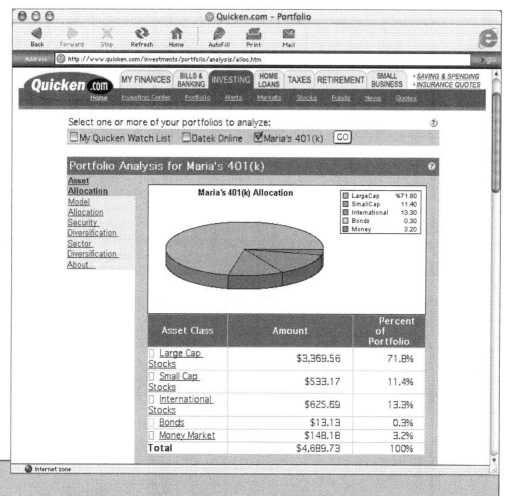

Figure 8-7 • The Asset Allocation screen of the Portfolio Analysis shows how your investments are allocated among various asset classes.

- **Sector Diversification** shows how your portfolio is divided among various industry sectors, such as technology, finance, and health.
- **About** explains what asset allocation is and why it's important. It's a good source of information if you've never considered diversification and need to learn more about it.

Each of these pages provides plenty of information about its contents, making the information useful to everyone—even complete novices.

Security Evaluator

Quicken.com's Security Evaluator feature offers another way to get in-depth information about a security. Choose Online | To the Web | Security Evaluator or click the Sec Eval button near the top of the Investing tab. If necessary, Quicken launches your Web browser, connects to the Internet, and displays the Security Evaluator's Getting Started page. Enter a ticker symbol in the edit box and click Go. The Evaluator screen for the security appears (see Figure 8-8).

Tip *You can also display this page by clicking the Evaluator link in the Quotes page shown in Figure 8-6.*

Figure 8-8 • Quicken.com's Security Evaluator screen provides growth, performance, and value information for a security.

You can click links on this page to learn more about the company, including its Growth Trends, Financial Health, Management Performance, Market Multiples, and Intrinsic Value. A Summary page provides concise information about the company. Each page of information is full of explanations and links to even more information.

The Investing Channel

The Security Evaluator, Research Security, and Portfolio Analysis features are a small part of Quicken.com's investment resources. There's a lot more where that came from in the Investing channel.

Choose Online | To The Web | Quicken.com. If necessary, Quicken launches your Web browser and connects to the Internet. Quicken.com's home page appears. Click the Investing tab near the top of the page. Figure 8-9 shows part of what this page had to offer on August 16, 2001. Explore this part of Quicken.com on your own to learn how it can help you maximize your investment returns.

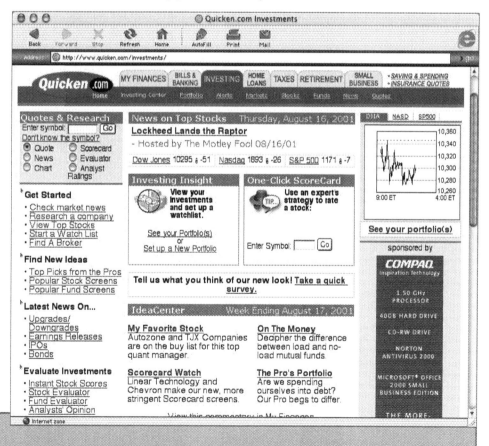

Figure 8-9 • Quicken.com's Investing channel offers a wealth of information about investing.

Note *Like everything else on the Internet, the contents of the Quicken.com Web pages can change daily. Don't be surprised if the features you find don't match the ones shown in Figure 8-9.*

Worksheets

Use the two worksheets on the following pages to help you compare and evaluate brokerage firms and mutual funds.

Broker Comparison Worksheet (page 1)			

Basic Information

Instructions: Enter information for each brokerage firm, one per column.

Company Name			
Agent Name			
Phone Number			
Type of Brokerage Firm (circle one)	Full/Discount	Full/Discount	Full/Discount
Comments			

Trading Fees

Instructions: Enter fees for each of the services listed. If fees vary based on the number of shares in the transaction, base the fee on 1,000 shares. If a service is not available, enter N/A. If a service is free, enter $0. Enter additional trading fees at the end of each section if necessary.

Broker-assisted telephone trading			
Market Orders			
Limit Orders			
Options (per trade)			
Options (per contract)			
Bonds			
Treasury Bills			
Mutual Funds			
Touch-tone telephone trading			
Market Orders			
Limit Orders			
Options (per trade)			
Options (per contract)			
Bonds			
Treasury Bills			
Mutual Funds			

Broker Comparison Worksheet (page 2)			
Online Trading			
Market Orders			
Limit Orders			
Options (per trade)			
Options (per contract)			
Bonds			
Treasury Bills			
Mutual Funds			

Other Fees

Instructions: Enter fees for each of the services listed. Enter additional fees at the end of this section if necessary.

Real-time Quotes			
Return Check Fee			
Wire Transfer Fee			
Stock Certificate Issuance Fee			
Check Writing Fee			
Stock Transfer Fee			
Cash Transfer Fee			

Interest Rates

Instructions: Enter the interest rate charged or paid for the following items.

Margin Rates (for <$50,000)			
Account Cash Balance Rates			

Mutual Funds Comparison Worksheet			

Basic Information

Instructions: Enter information for each fund, one per column.

Family Name			
Phone Number			
Fund Name			
Ticker Symbol			
Manager Name			
Manager Tenure			
Category			
Goal			
Minimum Initial Purchase			
Comments			

Ratings

Instructions: Enter ratings information from the fund's Morningstar profile.

Stars			
Return			
Risk			

Returns

Instructions: Enter the current average returns for each period listed. You can get this information from the fund's profile.

3 Months			
Year to Date			
1 Year			
3 Years			
5 Years			
10 Years			

Fees

Instructions: Enter values for the expense ratio and each of the fees charged by the fund.

Expense Ratio			
Front Load			
Deferred Sales Charge			
Redemption Fee			
12b-1 Fee			

Managing Your Assets and Debt

This part of the book explains how you can use Quicken to keep track of your general household finances. It starts with coverage of assets, such as a car and home, and the loans that you may have used to finance them. Then it moves on to some Quicken tools that can help you organize and keep track of important household information. Finally, it provides some useful information about how you can use Quicken and Quicken.com to save money on home, car, and insurance expenses.

This part of the book has two chapters:

Chapter 9: Monitoring Assets and Loans

Chapter 10: Minimizing Home, Car, and Insurance Expenses

Monitoring Assets and Loans

In this Chapter:

- *Setting up asset and liability accounts*

- *Tracking a loan*

- *Adjusting asset values*

Assets and liabilities are what make up your net worth. Bank and investment accounts, which I cover in Chapters 4 and 6, are examples of assets. Credit card accounts, which I cover in Chapter 4, are examples of liabilities. But there are other assets and liabilities you may want to track with Quicken, including a home, car, recreational vehicle, and related loans. By including these items in your Quicken data file, you can quickly and accurately calculate your net worth and financial fitness.

In this chapter, I explain how to set up asset and liability accounts to track your possessions and any outstanding loans you used to purchase them. I also tell you how you can adjust the balance of asset accounts to keep your Quicken data file up to date with the most current asset values.

The Basics

Before you begin, it's a good idea to have a clear understanding of what assets, liabilities, and loans are and how they work together in your Quicken data file.

Assets and Liabilities

An *asset* is something you own. Common examples might be your house, car, camper, computer, television set, and patio furniture. Most assets have value—you can sell them for cash or trade them for another asset.

Although you can use Quicken to track every single asset you own in its own asset account, doing so would be very cumbersome. Instead, you'll normally account for high-value assets in individual accounts and group lower-value assets together in one account. For example, you may create separate asset accounts for your home and your car, but group personal possessions such as your computer, television, and patio furniture in a single asset account. This makes it easy to track all your assets, so you have accurate records for insurance and other purposes.

A *liability* is something you owe—often to buy one of your assets! For example, if you buy a house, chances are you'll use a mortgage to fund it. The mortgage, which is a loan that is secured by your home, is a liability. You can use Quicken to track all of your liabilities, so you know exactly how much you owe at any given time.

Loans

A *loan* is a promise to pay money. Loans are commonly used to buy assets, although some folks often turn to debt consolidation loans to pay off other liabilities—I tell you more about that in Chapter 12.

Here's how it works: the lender gives the borrower money in exchange for the borrower's promise to pay it back. (The promise is usually in writing, with lots of signatures and initials.) The borrower normally pays back the loan with periodic payments to the lender that include interest on the loan balance or *principal*. In this way, the amount of the loan is reduced after each payment. The borrower also incurs interest expense while the lender earns interest income.

While most people think of a loan as something you owe (a liability), a loan can also be something you own (an asset). For example, say you borrow money from your brother to buy a car. In your Quicken data file, the loan is related to a liability— money that you owe your brother. In your brother's Quicken data file, the loan is related to an asset—money that is due to him from you.

Note *I tell you more about loans in Chapter 10, including how you can use Quicken.com to help you find the best loan deals.*

Setting Up Asset and Liability Accounts

To track an asset or liability with Quicken, you must set up an appropriate account. Quicken makes it simple by offering two kinds of accounts for tracking assets and liabilities: an asset account and a liability account. Chapter 2 explains how to use the Set Up Account window to create new Quicken accounts; refer to that chapter if you need instructions.

All transactions related to the asset or liability will be recorded in the account's register, which looks and works very much like the register for a bank, cash, or credit card account. The first transaction should be the account's opening balance:

- For an asset account, the opening balance should be the asset's fair market value on that date. You can estimate this amount or, if the asset is new, use the purchase price.
- For a liability account, the opening balance should be what you owe on that date. Do not include the amount of any interest you will pay.

Open the account's register by double-clicking its name in the Accounts list window or choosing its name from the Rgstrs button menu at the top of the Assets & Debt tab. Figure 9-1 shows an asset account register used to record the value of a house. If necessary, change the date to reflect the balance date. Then enter the opening balance in the Increase field and click Record.

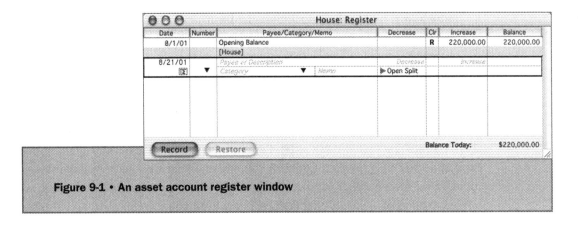

Figure 9-1 • An asset account register window

Tracking a Loan

Quicken makes it easy to track the principal, interest, and payments for a loan with regular recurring payments. Once you set up a loan and corresponding liability or asset accounts, you can make payments with Quicken using QuickFill, scheduled transactions, or online payments. The Loan feature keeps track of all the details so you don't have to.

The Loans Window

Quicken lists all of your loans in the Loans window. You can open this window by choosing Lists | Loans or by clicking the Loans button near the top of the Assets & Debt tab. Here's what the Loans window looks like with one loan already created:

Buttons at the bottom of the window enable you to create new loans or work with a selected loan in the list:

- **Use** enables you to use the selected loan in a transaction.
- **New** enables you to create a new loan.
- **Edit** enables you to modify the selected loan.
- **Delete** removes the selected loan from the list. This option does not delete transactions related to the loan—only the information Quicken uses to calculate loan interest and payments.
- **Payment Schedule** displays a list of payment details for each payment on the selected loan.

Setting Up a Loan

Setting up a loan is pretty straightforward. A pair of windows prompts you for all the information Quicken needs to make its loan calculation. To get started, click New in the Loans window.

Providing Basic Loan Information

The first window that appears is the Loan Interview window, shown next. Use it to answer basic questions about the loan:

Are you borrowing or lending this money?   This question establishes whether the loan should be treated as a liability (borrowing) or asset (lending).

Have any payments been made on this loan yet?   If you've had this loan for a while and are just entering it into Quicken now, chances are, the answer to this question will be Yes. Otherwise, if this is a brand new loan and you haven't made any payments yet, click No.

Have any prepayments been made on this loan?   This option is only available when you answer Yes to the previous question. It refers to additional payments made on the loan in excess of required payments. If you have made such payments, be sure to click Yes.

> **Tip** | *Many people—including me!—contribute additional funds each month to a loan to reduce the loan term and the total amount of interest paid. I tell you more about how you can take advantage of this to save money in Chapter 10.*

Is this a fixed-rate or variable-rate loan?   Fixed loan rates remain the same for the life of the loan. Variable loan rates change periodically over the life of the loan. Choose the appropriate option.

Does this loan have a balloon payment?   A balloon payment is a very large payment at the end of the loan term. This isn't very common, so if you're not sure whether your loan has a balloon payment, it probably doesn't.

Does this loan use U.S. or Canadian amortization?   *Amortization* refers to the way interest and payments are calculated for a loan. There are different methods in the United States and Canada. Choose the country of origin for your loan.

Do you want to start tracking from the first or the next payment?
This option appears in a dialog when you click Continue only if you have answered Yes to the question "Have any payments been made on this loan yet?" Select First if you want to start tracking from the first payment on the loan, even if it was made years ago. Select Next if you want to start tracking from the next loan payment forward.

Providing Loan Details

When you click Continue in the Loan Interview window, the Set Up Loan window appears. Use it to provide detailed information about your loan. Here's what it looks like when you borrow money:

Loan Info   The Loan Info area is for information about the loan itself. You must provide all requested information:

- **Name Of Lender** is the name of the individual or organization that loaned you the money.
- **Principal + Interest** is the amount of your monthly payment attributable to paying off the loan principal and interest.
- **PMI, Property Tax, Etc.** is the total amount of additional payments for private mortgage insurance (PMI), property taxes, homeowners insurance, and other fees you may have to pay with your mortgage. These fees are usually held in escrow to pay third parties, such as local governments and insurance companies.
- **Total Payment** is automatically calculated by Quicken. Check it to make sure it's right. Caution: If the Total Payment does not match the total periodic amount you pay on the loan, you probably made an error in one of the two edit boxes above it. Check the amounts you entered against statements or other documents provided by the lender.
- **Date Of Next Payment** is the date the next loan payment is due.

- **Frequency** is the frequency of loan payments. Your options are: Weekly, Every Two Weeks, Twice a Month, Every Four Weeks, Monthly, Every Two Months, Quarterly, Twice a Year, and Annually.
- **Payments Remaining** is the number of payments remaining on the loan.
- **Current Interest Rate** is the current interest rate on the loan. If you indicated that the loan has a fixed interest rate, this field will be labeled *Annual Interest Rate*.
- **Interest Category** is the Quicken category you want to use to record the amount of interest paid. This will normally be something like *Mortgage Int* or *Interest Paid*.
- **Principal Account** is the name of the account in which the loan balance is recorded. For a loan in which you borrow money, this will be the liability account you set up for the loan. For a loan in which you lend money, this will be the asset account you set up for the loan. Enter an account name; if the account does not exist, Quicken will offer to create it for you.
- **Balance Today** is the current balance of the loan. Normally, this will match the balance in the account you indicated as the principal account—in fact, Quicken may fill in the amount for you automatically. If it isn't the same, enter the correct amount and Quicken will update the balance in the loan account.

Note   *Other fields may appear in this window depending on options you selected in the Loan Interview window. Field names are self-explanatory, so you shouldn't have any trouble figuring out what to enter. Be sure to enter all requested information.*

Payment Options   Payment Options tell Quicken how you want to record your loan payments:

- **Confirm Payment Before Recording** tells Quicken to display a confirmation dialog when it's time to record the payment.
- **Schedule Payment On Calendar** tells Quicken to create entries on the calendar for the loan payments. This option ensures that you make payments on time by either automatically entering the payment or reminding you about it. I tell you more about this feature in the section titled "Scheduling Loan Payments," later in this chapter, and in Chapter 14.

Previewing Payments   You can view and edit the loan payment transaction by clicking Preview Payment. A window like the one shown next appears. Be sure to enter a category for the additional payments included with the loan (if applicable). If desired, you can split up this amount and allocate it to multiple categories by adding split lines. Make other changes as necessary and click OK to save the transaction.

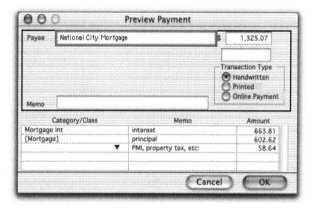

Note *The amount of the interest and principal paid will change automatically with each loan payment, so you should not change these amounts.*

Scheduling Loan Payments

If you turned on the Schedule Payment On Calendar check box in the Set Up Loan window, Quicken automatically displays the Schedule Future Transaction dialog (see below) as well as its calendar. Enter options in the dialog to set up the loan payment schedule and click Record.

Note *I tell you more about using the Schedule Future Transaction dialog in Chapter 14; be sure to consult that chapter if you need help setting scheduling options.*

When you click Record, a dialog like the one shown next may appear. It tells you about the transactions that will be scheduled. Select an option and click OK.

Viewing Loan Information

Quicken's Loans window offers two ways to get information about the loans in your Quicken data file.

Viewing and Editing Loan Details

You can review and, if necessary, edit the information for a loan at any time. This enables you to check values entered for a loan, change interest rate information, change payment amounts, and modify payment transactions.

In the Loans window, click to select the loan you want to view. Then click Edit to display the Edit Loan window. This window looks and works very much like the Set Up Loan window shown earlier in this chapter. Make changes as necessary and click Change to save them.

Viewing Payment Schedules

You can also view a loan's payment schedule to see what part of each payment is allocated to principal and interest.

In the Loans window, select the loan for which you want to view a payment schedule. Then click the Payment Schedule button. A window like the one shown next appears, providing details for each remaining loan payment. When you have finished reviewing the information in the table, you can click its Close box to dismiss it.

Date	Pmt	Principal	Interest	Balance
			6.875%	115,864.58
9/1/01	1	602.62	663.81	115,261.96
10/1/01	2	606.08	660.35	114,655.88
11/1/01	3	609.55	656.88	114,046.33
12/1/01	4	613.04	653.39	113,433.29
1/1/02	5	616.55	649.88	112,816.74
2/1/02	6	620.08	646.35	112,196.66
3/1/02	7	623.64	642.79	111,573.02
4/1/02	8	627.21	639.22	110,945.81
5/1/02	9	630.80	635.63	110,315.01
6/1/02	10	634.42	632.01	109,680.59
7/1/02	11	638.05	628.38	109,042.54

National City Mortgage Payment Schedule

Tip   *A payment schedule like the one Quicken maintains for each loan is also commonly known as a* loan amortization table.

Making a Loan Payment

If you do not take advantage of Quicken's scheduling feature to automatically record future loan payments, you must manually record loan payments. Quicken makes it surprisingly quick and easy to enter these transactions.

When you're ready to make a loan payment, open the account register or Write Checks window for the bank account you want to use to make the payment. When you enter the Lender name in the Payee field, Quicken automatically fills in the rest of the transaction, using amounts from the loan's setup and payment schedule. Quicken may display a Payment dialog like the one shown next, which you can use to confirm the loan information and, if desired, enter an additional prepayment amount. Click Record in the account register or Write Checks window and you're done.

National City Mortgage Payment

Current balance:	115,864.58
Annual interest rate:	6.875 %
Regular Payment:	1,266.43
Additional prepayment:	0.00
Other regular charges:	58.64

Cancel   OK

> **Tip**   *If you enter an amount in the Additional prepayment edit box of the Payment dialog, Quicken adds the amount to the total payment and deducts it from the loan principal account.*

What I think is great is that every time you make a payment, Quicken correctly enters the principal and interest paid and updates the information available through the Loans window. So the loan information is always up to date and the amount of the principal and interest paid should match statements from the lender.

Recording Other Asset Transactions

Part of tracking assets is keeping track of their current values and modifying account balances when necessary. Like a bank or investment account, which I discuss in Chapters 4 and 6, activity for an asset account appears in its account register.

In this section, I explain how you can record changes in asset values due to acquisitions and disposals, improvements, market values, and depreciation.

Adding and Disposing of Assets

The most obvious change in an asset's value occurs when you add or remove part of the asset. For example, I have a single asset account in which I record the value of my horses and related equipment. If I buy a new saddle, that increases the value of the account. Similarly, if I sell my horse trailer, that decreases the value of the account.

In many instances, when you add or dispose of an asset, there is an exchange of money. In that case, recording the transaction is easy: simply use the appropriate bank or credit card account register to record the purchase or sale and use the asset account as a transfer account in the category field. Here's what the purchase of a new saddle might look like in my credit card account:

8/21/01	Sports Saddle Company		975.90		1,784.13
	[Horses & Tack]	Saddle for Cherokee			

And here's the same transaction in my Horses and Tack asset account:

8/21/01	Sports Saddle Company			975.90	9,975.90
	[American Express]	Saddle for Cherokee			

If the asset was acquired without an exchange of money, you can enter the transaction directly into the asset account, using the Gift Received category (or a similar category of your choice) to categorize the income. Similarly, if the asset was disposed of without an exchange of cash, you can enter the transaction into the asset account register using the Gifts or Charity category (or other appropriate category) to categorize the write-off.

Updating Asset Values

A variety of situations can change the value of a single asset. The type of situation will determine how the value is adjusted. Here are three common examples.

Recording Improvements

Certain home-related expenditures can be considered improvements that increase the value of your home. It's important to keep track of improvements, because they raise the property's tax basis, thus reducing the amount of capital gains you have to record (and pay tax on) when you sell the house.

Tip *Your tax advisor can help you determine which expenditures can be capitalized as home improvements.*

Since most home improvements involve an expenditure, use a banking account register to record the transaction. Be sure to enter the appropriate asset account (House, Condo, Land, and so on) as a transfer account in the Category field. A home improvement expenditure might look something like this in a banking account register:

8/21/01	5039	Dan the Man Construction Co.		5,000.00		1,876.24
		[House]	New Deck			

And here's what the corresponding entry looks like in an asset account register:

8/21/01	5039	Dan the Man Construction Co.			5,000.00	225,000.00
		[Checking]	New Deck			

Adjusting for Market Value

Real estate, vehicles, and other large-ticket item assets are also affected by market values. Generally speaking, real estate values go up, vehicle values go down, and other item values can vary either way depending on what they are.

To adjust for market value, open the account register for the asset account you want to adjust. Then choose Activities | Adjust Balance. The Adjust Balance window, shown next, appears. Enter the new balance and balance date in the first two edit boxes. Then choose a category in which to record the difference between the current balance and the new balance.

When you click OK, Quicken makes the adjustment. The adjusting entry is added to the account register, as shown here:

> **Tip**   If you don't want the adjustment to affect any category or account other than the asset, choose the same asset account as a transfer account.

Recording Depreciation

Depreciation is a calculated reduction in the value of an asset. Depreciation expense can be calculated using a variety of acceptable methods, including straight line, sum of the year's digits, and declining balance—consult your accountant or tax advisor for details. Normally, it reduces the asset's value regularly, with monthly, quarterly, or annual adjustments. Depreciation is commonly applied to property used for business purposes since depreciation expense on those assets may be tax deductible.

> **Tip**   If you think depreciation on an asset you own may be tax deductible, use Quicken to track the depreciation expense. Otherwise, depreciation probably isn't worth the extra effort it requires to track.

To record depreciation, create an entry in the asset account that reduces the value by the amount of the depreciation. Use a Depreciation Expense category to record the expense. The transaction might look something like this:

8/1/01	Depreciation Expense	125.31		19,374.69
	Depreciation			

Tip   *You can set up monthly, quarterly, or annual depreciation transactions as scheduled transactions so Quicken will automatically record them when they are due. I tell you about scheduled transactions in Chapter 14.*

Minimizing Home, Car, and Insurance Expenses

In this Chapter:

- *Types of loans*

- *Loan considerations*

- *Preparing for a major purchase*

- *Insurance basics*

- *Quicken.com resources*

- *Loan and insurance worksheets*

Possibly the biggest purchase you'll ever make is the purchase of a new home or car. These aren't the kinds of things you buy on a whim. They require research and planning. It's not only important to find the right living space or vehicle, it's important to get the right financing. You want the best deal on a loan, with a low interest rate and monthly payments that won't stretch your budget.

As your assets, family, and responsibilities grow, so does your need for insurance. Insurance can protect you from financial loss in the event of loss, theft, or damage to your assets. It can help you cover medical costs and make ends meet if illness or injury requires extensive medical care or prevents you from working. It can provide for your family if something happens to you.

In this chapter, I tell you about the tools within Quicken and on Quicken.com that you can use to learn more about financing a home or car and obtaining the insurance you need to protect your possessions and family. Along the way, I provide useful information about loans and insurance to give you a good idea of what's available. As you'll see in this chapter, Quicken can help you get the information you need to make informed decisions that can save you money.

Note *Like everything else on the Internet, the contents of Web pages can change daily. Don't be surprised if the features you find don't match the ones shown throughout this chapter.*

Mortgage and Loan Basics

Before you start shopping for a loan—or for a home or car, for that matter—it's a good idea to have an understanding of loan basics. What kinds of loans are there? What are their benefits and drawbacks? Which is the right one for your purchase? What things are important when comparing one loan to another? In this section, I answer all of these questions and more.

Types of Loans

There are several types of loans, some of which are designed for specific purposes. Here's a quick summary of what's available, along with their pros and cons.

Mortgage

A mortgage is a long-term loan secured by real estate. Most mortgages require a 10 percent or higher down payment on the property. Monthly payments are based on the term of the loan and the interest rate applied to the principal. The interest you pay on a mortgage for a first or second home is tax-deductible. If you fail to make mortgage payments, your house could be sold to pay back the mortgage.

A balloon mortgage is a special type of short-term mortgage. Rather than make monthly payments over the full typical mortgage term, at the end of the fifth, seventh, or tenth year, you pay the balance of the mortgage in one big "balloon" payment. Some balloon mortgages offer the option of refinancing when the balloon payment is due.

Home Equity Loans or Lines of Credit

A home equity loan or second mortgage is a line of credit secured by the equity in your home—the difference between its market value and the amount of outstanding debt. Your equity rises when you make mortgage payments or property values increase. It declines when you borrow against your equity or property values decrease. A home equity loan lets you borrow against this equity.

There are two benefits to a home equity loan: interest rates are usually lower than other credit, and interest may be tax-deductible. For these reasons, many people use home equity loans to pay off credit card debt, renovate their homes, or buy cars, boats, or other recreational vehicles. But, as with a mortgage, if you fail to pay a home equity reserve, your house could be sold to satisfy the debt.

Reverse Equity Loans

A reverse equity loan provides homeowners who own their homes in full with a regular monthly income. Instead of you paying the lender, the lender pays you. This type of loan is attractive to retirees who live on a fixed income. The loan is paid back when the home is sold—often after the death of the homeowner. (You can imagine how the next of kin feel about that.)

Car Loans

A car loan is a loan secured by a vehicle such as a car, truck, or motor home. Normally, you make a down payment and use the loan to pay the balance of the car's purchase price. Monthly payments are based on the term of the loan and the interest rate applied to the principal. Interest on car loans is not tax-deductible.

Personal Loans

A personal loan is an unsecured loan—a loan that requires no collateral. Monthly payments are based on the term of the loan and the interest rate applied to the principal. You can use a personal loan for just about anything. Some people use them to pay off multiple smaller debts so they have only one monthly payment. Interest on personal loans is not tax-deductible.

Loan Considerations

When applying for a loan, a number of variables have a direct impact on what the loan costs you now and in the future. Be sure to ask about all these things before applying for any loan.

Tip *The Loan Comparison Worksheet and Mortgage Comparison Worksheet at the end of this chapter enable you to take notes about the loans and mortgages you research. Use them to compare options and costs before you make a decision.*

Interest Rate

The interest rate is the annual percentage applied to the loan principal. Several factors affect the interest rate you may be offered:

- **Your credit record** A borrower with a good credit record can usually get a better rate than one with a bad credit record. Of course, if your credit record is really bad, you might not be able to borrow money at any rate.
- **The type of loan** Generally speaking, personal loans have the highest interest rates, whereas mortgages have the lowest. From highest to lowest between these two types are a used car loan, a new car loan, and a home equity reserve or line of credit.
- **The loan term** The length of a loan can vary the interest within a specific loan type. For example, for car loans, the longer the term, the lower the rate.
- **The amount of the down payment** The more money you put down on the purchase, the lower the rate may be.
- **Your location** Rates vary from one area of the country to another.
- **The lender** Rates also vary from one lender to another. Certain types of lenders have lower rates than others.

Tip *When we purchased our current home, we used a mortgage company rather than a bank and got a considerably lower rate than what the local banks were offering. It's worth looking into!*

Two kinds of interest rates can apply to a loan: fixed and variable.

- **Fixed rate** applies the same rate to the principal throughout the loan term.
- **Variable rate** applies a different rate to the loan throughout the loan term. For example, the loan may start with one rate and, each year, switch to a different rate. The rate is usually established by adding a certain number of percentage

points to a national index, such as Treasury bill rates. A cap limits the amount the rate can change. Mortgages with this type of rate are referred to as adjustable rate mortgages (ARMs).

Tip   *When we purchased our first home, in the mid-1980s when interest rates were high, we selected an ARM. When interest rates dropped, so did the rate on our mortgage. If we'd selected a fixed-rate mortgage when we bought that home, we would have had to refinance to get the same savings. But because rates were much lower when we bought our current home, we selected a fixed rate to protect us from possible rate increases in the future. We're glad we did! Current interest rates are two points higher than they were when we bought that home three years ago.*

Term

A loan's term is the period of time between the loan date and the date payment is due in full. Loan terms vary depending on the type of loan.

- Mortgage loan and home equity reserve loan terms are typically 10, 15, 20, or 30 years.
- Balloon mortgage loan terms are typically 5, 7, or 10 years.
- Car loan terms are typically 3, 4, or 5 years.

Down Payment

A down payment is an up-front payment toward the purchase of a home or car. Most mortgages require at least 10 percent down; 20 percent down is preferred.

Tip   *If you make only a 10 percent down payment on a home, you may be required to pay for the cost of private mortgage insurance. This protects the lender from loss if you fail to pay your mortgage, but increases your monthly mortgage payments.*

Application Fees

Most lenders require you to pay an application fee to process your loan application. This usually includes the cost of obtaining a property appraisal and credit report. These fees are usually not refundable—even if you are turned down.

Mortgage Closing Costs

In addition to the application fee and down payment, many other costs are involved in securing a mortgage and purchasing a home. These are known as closing costs. Here's a brief list of the types of costs you may encounter. Because they vary from lender to lender, they could be a deciding factor when shopping for a mortgage. Note that most of these fees are not negotiable.

- **Origination fee** covers the administrative costs of processing a loan.
- **Discount** (or **"points"**) is a fee based on a percentage rate applied to the loan amount. For example, 1 point on a $150,000 mortgage is $1,500.
- **Appraisal fee** covers the cost of a market-value appraisal of the property by a licensed, certified appraiser.
- **Credit report fee** covers the cost of obtaining a credit history of the prospective borrower(s) to determine credit worthiness.
- **Underwriting fee** covers the cost of underwriting the loan. This is the process of determining loan risks and establishing terms and conditions.
- **Document preparation fee** covers the cost of preparing legal and other documents required to process the loan.
- **Title insurance fee** covers the cost of title insurance, which protects the lender and buyer against loss due to disputes over ownership and possession of the property.
- **Recording fee** covers the cost of entering the sale of a property into public records.
- **Prepaid items** are taxes, insurance, and assessments paid in advance of their due dates. These expenses are not paid to the lender, but are due at the closing date.

Tip   *The Real Estate Settlement Procedures Act of 1974 requires that your lender provide a Good Faith Estimate of closing costs. This document summarizes all of the costs of closing on a home based on the mortgage the lender is offering.*

Preparing for a Major Purchase

Whether you're buying a home, car, or recreational vehicle, you'll need to do some planning before you make your purchase. In this section, I tell you what information a lender wants to know about you, as well as how you can determine what a loan will cost you.

Gathering Financial Fitness Information

Before anyone lends you money (except maybe Big Louie, who works out of the back room of a bar on the bad side of town), you'll need to provide some assurance that you can pay it back, with interest, within the allotted time. Before a potential lender starts examining your financial fitness, you should. Then you'll know in advance what the lender will discover, and if there are problems, you can fix them.

Your Net Worth

Start by taking a look at your net worth. If you've been faithfully recording all of your financial information in Quicken, this is easy. Choose Activities | Reports & Graphs | Reports, or click the Reports button near the top of the Reporting tab to display the Reports window. Click the Standard tab to display its options. Then select the Net Worth report and click Create. Quicken creates a Net Worth Report, which shows all of your assets and liabilities. The difference between these two is your net worth. The bigger this number is, the better off you are.

Tip   *You can customize the Net Worth report to include only the accounts you specify. I tell you more about creating reports in Chapter 16.*

Not all of the numbers on your Net Worth report will interest a lender. They're interested primarily in cash, cars, real estate, investments, credit card balances, and other debt. If your home inventory values your T-shirt collection at $5,000, so what? T-shirts aren't easily exchanged for cash to make mortgage payments.

Debt Reduction

If all of your assets and liabilities have been recorded in Quicken and your net worth is a negative number, stop right here! No one (except maybe Big Louie) will loan you money, because too many others already have. Turn to Chapter 12. You'll need to follow the advice and instructions there before you can even think about applying for a loan. You might also find the budgeting information in Chapter 13 helpful to get your spending under control.

Credit Report

A lender is also going to be very interested in your credit history. Credit reports are created and maintained by third-party credit monitoring organizations such as Equifax, Experion, and Trans Union. They know everything about your finances— sometimes even things that aren't true. Before you apply for a loan, you may want to see what a credit report says about you. If there are errors, you can get them fixed before someone uses them to form a bad opinion of you.

Quicken Deluxe users who have access to the Internet can obtain a free credit report as part of a trial offer from ConsumerInfo.com. Choose Online | To The Web | Credit Report to connect to the Internet and display a Web page that provides basic information about credit reports available to you and how you can obtain them (see Figure 10-1). Follow links to sign up for the trial program and get your credit report.

Getting Current Interest Rates

Before you can estimate the monthly payments on a loan, you need a good idea of what the current interest rates are. You have three ways to research this information: check the newspaper, call banks, or look it up on Quicken.com.

Caution *Interest rates change often, sometimes on a daily basis. Although short-term variations are usually small, rates more than a few weeks or months old usually aren't very accurate.*

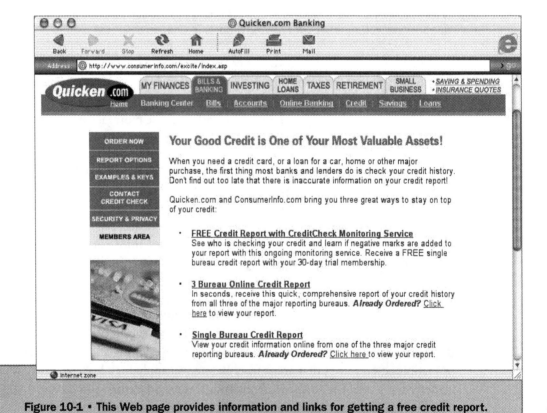

Figure 10-1 • This Web page provides information and links for getting a free credit report.

Checking a Recent Newspaper

Many banks and other lenders advertise their rates in the financial pages of the newspaper. Some newspapers summarize this information for you. For example, the big paper in my area, *The Arizona Republic*, has a weekly listing of organizations offering mortgages, complete with rates and phone numbers.

Checking with Local Banks

Get out the phone book and call a few banks in your area. Ask them what their rates are. Most banks will provide this information over the phone.

Looking Up Rates on Quicken.com

Quicken.com offers up-to-date rates on all kinds of loans. All you need is an Internet connection to check them for yourself.

Choose Online | To The Web | Bank Rates. Your computer connects to the Internet and displays the Banking & Credit channel's main page (see Figure 10-2). You can find average rates for home equity, car, and personal loans right on that page.

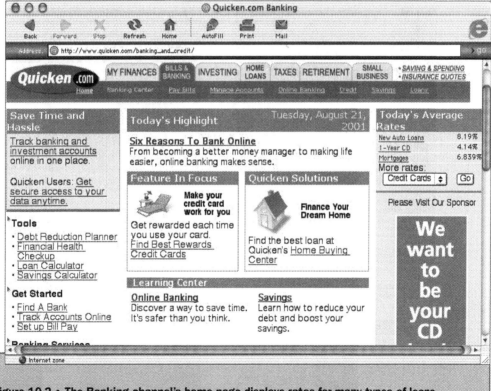

Figure 10-2 • The Banking channel's home page displays rates for many types of loans.

For mortgage rates and related information, choose Online | To The Web | Loan Rates. This displays the home page for the Quicken Loans Web site (see Figure 10-3). You can use this page to learn more about rates, get preapproved for a loan, or find loans to meet your special needs.

If all you're interested in is mortgage rates, choose Online | To The Web | Mortgage Rates. The Mortgage Tools Quick Rates page appears. Use the form on this page to enter information about the property and the type of mortgage you want. When you click Calculate, a list of loan terms appears, including the monthly mortgage payment amount (see Figure 10-4). You can use buttons and links on this page to learn more, have a mortgage company representative contact you, or even get preapproval for a mortgage.

Calculating the Cost of a Loan

Once you have an idea of what the interest rate for a loan will be, you can use one of two different tools within Quicken to determine how much the loan will cost you.

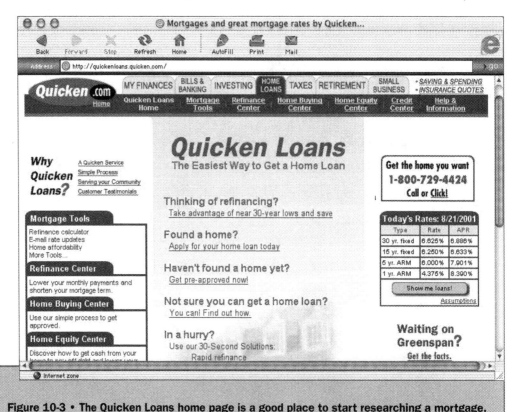

Figure 10-3 • The Quicken Loans home page is a good place to start researching a mortgage.

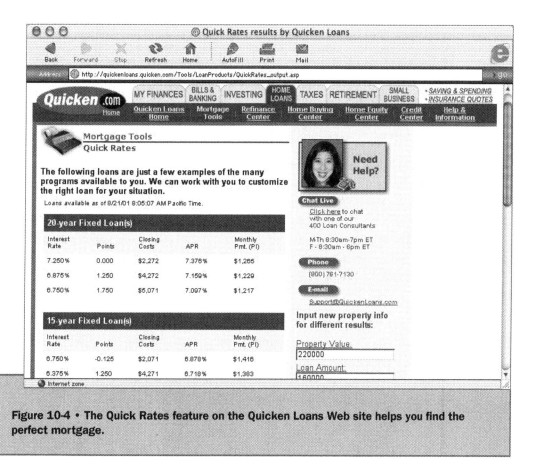

Figure 10-4 • The Quick Rates feature on the Quicken Loans Web site helps you find the perfect mortgage.

Loan Calculator

Quicken's Loan Calculator can quickly calculate the principal or periodic payment for a loan. Choose Activities | Planning Calculators | Loan. The Loan Calculator window appears:

Begin by selecting one of the two calculation options:

- To calculate the amount of loan you can afford, click the arrow beside Loan Amount. Then you can enter an affordable monthly payment in the Principal + Interest edit box.
- To calculate the periodic payment, click the arrow beside Principal + Interest. Then you can enter the amount of the loan in the Loan Amount edit box.

Enter values in the edit boxes. Be sure to choose the correct payment frequency from the Frequency pop-up menu. As you TAB from field to field, the loan is calculated and recalculated. You can try different values to play "what if" until you have a good idea of how the loan could work for you. With the information this provides, you should be able to tell whether you can afford the home or car you have your eye on. If you haven't started looking yet, it can tell you how much you can afford to spend.

You can use the two buttons at the bottom of the window to work with the loan entries:

- **Payment Schedule** displays an amortization table for the loan. It shows the amount of principal and interest paid for each payment, as well as the ending balance and accumulated interest paid. Here's an example:

	Principal	Interest	Prepayment	Balance	Total Interest
		10.500%		15,000.00	
1	191.15	131.25	0.00	14,808.85	131.25
2	192.82	129.58	0.00	14,616.03	260.83
3	194.51	127.89	0.00	14,421.52	388.72
4	196.21	126.19	0.00	14,225.31	514.91
5	197.93	124.47	0.00	14,027.38	639.38
6	199.66	122.74	0.00	13,827.72	762.12
7	201.41	120.99	0.00	13,626.31	883.11
8	203.17	119.23	0.00	13,423.14	1,002.34
9	204.95	117.45	0.00	13,218.19	1,119.79
10	206.74	115.66	0.00	13,011.45	1,235.45
11	208.55	113.85	0.00	12,802.90	1,349.30

- **Set Up Loan** displays the Set Up Loan window, which you can use to add the loan to your Quicken data file. I tell you how to use this window in Chapter 9.

Tip *You can use the Additional Prepayment edit box and Payment Schedule button in the Loan Calculator window to see how the loan's payment schedule would change if you made additional principal payments as part of each loan payment. To use this feature, enter a value in the Additional Prepayment edit box and then click the Payment Schedule button. Scroll to the end of the payment schedule that appears to see the new last payment number and total interest paid. With the example used here, an additional $50 per month prepayment would reduce the loan's term by ten months and reduce total interest paid by almost $800.*

Refinance Calculator

If you already own a home and are thinking about refinancing, you can try the
Refinance Calculator. Choose Activities | Planning Calculators | Refinance.
The Refinance Calculator window appears:

Enter values for your current mortgage and proposed mortgage in the edit boxes
to calculate your monthly savings with the new mortgage. As you TAB from field to
field, Quicken calculates the results. If you enter closing costs and points for the
proposed mortgage, you can even calculate how many months it will take to break
even after paying these fees.

For example, in the previous illustration, refinancing the mortgage would save
about $230 a month. It would take less than a year to save enough to cover the
refinancing costs. Based on this information, refinancing looks like a good idea.

There's also a refinance calculator on the Quicken Loans Web site. Choose
Online | To The Web | Home Refinance Calculator. This displays the Refinance
Calculator page of Quicken Loan's Mortgage Tools (see Figure 10-5). Fill out the
form that appears onscreen and click Calculate to see how your current mortgage
stacks up against a proposed mortgage. The benefit of this calculator over the one
built into Quicken is that it can automatically use national averages and current
estimates to perform calculations.

Figure 10-5 • The Refinance Calculator on the Quicken Loans Web site enables you to use national averages and estimates for its calculations.

Learning What You Can Afford

Of course, part of the home purchase planning process is learning what you can afford. The Quicken Loans Web site has tools to help you with this, too. Choose Online | To The Web | Home Affordability. This displays the Home Affordability page of Quicken Loan's Mortgage Tools (see Figure 10-6). Fill out the form online and click Calculate. The results page gives you low and high estimates of the purchase price of homes within your budget, along with details about monthly payments, down payments, and limiting factors.

Figure 10-6 • The Home Affordability page helps you learn what kind of home is within your budget.

Insurance Basics

Buying insurance can be baffling. Not only do you need to know what kinds of insurance are available, but you need to know which type you need, how much coverage you should have, and where you can get it.

In this section, I provide some basic information about insurance types and some of the terminology you need to know to understand what a policy covers.

Tip *Before you start shopping for insurance—whether you shop online via Quicken.com or by phone with a phone book—be sure you know the basic information about the type of insurance you want to buy. Understanding insurance options is the only way to be sure you are purchasing all the insurance coverage you need, without being sold extra coverage for the benefit of an insurance company or commissioned salesperson.*

Types of Insurance

If you think insurance is limited to home, life, and auto, think again. Here's a quick rundown of the different types of insurance available today.

Auto Insurance

Auto insurance covers specific auto-related losses you may incur during the term of the insurance policy. Auto insurance can be broken down into several parts:

- **Liability insurance**, which is required by law in most states, covers injuries or damage to others or their property. Many insurance advisors recommend that you carry enough liability insurance to protect all of your assets in the event of a lawsuit. This is usually much more than the minimum required by law.

- **Collision insurance** covers damage to your car when the damage results from colliding with another car or object or overturning your car. Although this coverage is not required by law, it is usually required by a lender if the car is purchased with an auto loan.

- **Comprehensive insurance** covers damage to your car when the damage results from causes other than a collision—for example, theft, hail, fire, flood, or vandalism. Although this coverage is not required by law, it is usually required by a lender if the car is purchased with an auto loan.

- **Uninsured and underinsured motorist insurance** covers injury or damage to you, your passengers, and your car in the event that your car is hit by someone who either doesn't have any insurance or doesn't have enough insurance to cover the cost of the accident.

- **Medical payments insurance** covers you and your passengers for reasonable medical (and funeral) expenses incurred as a result of an accident.

Auto insurance rates are affected by where you live, drive, and park your car; the make and model of your car; your age; and your driving record. Many insurance companies offer discounts for good drivers and multiple policies within the same household.

Home Insurance

Home insurance covers financial losses caused by theft, storms, fires, and other similar occurrences that could cause loss or damage to your home and property. It also covers damages resulting from injuries to other people for which you are held legally responsible.

There are different types of home insurance:

- **Homeowner's insurance** covers a house and the homeowner's property, including the house itself, other structures on the property, personal property within the house or on the property, and liability lawsuits brought against the homeowner for injuries sustained on the property.
- **Renter's insurance** covers the personal property of someone renting a home or apartment.
- **Condo or co-op insurance** covers the homeowner's personal property and liability lawsuits brought against the homeowner for injuries sustained within the condo or co-op.

Home insurance rates are affected by the value of your home, the location of your home, the year your home was built, and the proximity of your home to a fire hydrant or fire station.

Life Insurance

Life insurance is money that an insurance company pays to your named beneficiary when you die. There are several types of life insurance:

- **Term life** pays a specific lump-sum amount to your beneficiary when you die. A term life policy is designed specifically to protect your family by providing money to replace your salary and cover the cost of your funeral.
- Cash value policies, such as **whole life**, **variable life**, **universal life**, and **universal variable life** pay a specific lump-sum amount to your beneficiary when you die. But they also build a cash value account that you can use for non-insurance purposes while you're alive.

Annuities

An annuity is a contract between you and an insurance company in which you pay a premium and, in return, the insurance company promises to make benefit payments to you or to another named beneficiary. This is usually done through the use of investments managed by the insurance company.

Annuities can be classified by the timing of the benefit payments and how the annuity earnings accumulate:

Immediate vs. Deferred Annuities   An immediate annuity begins paying you benefits within one month to one year of its purchase. A deferred annuity accumulates earnings over a period of time, then begins paying you benefits after a specific date—typically a retirement date.

Fixed vs. Variable Annuities A fixed annuity guarantees a fixed rate of return for a specific time period. A variable annuity pays a return that varies based on the performance of the investments you select.

Business Continuation Insurance

Business continuation insurance protects your company from financial loss caused by the death or the long-term disability of a key employee. There are three types:

- **Business overhead expense (BOE) insurance** pays business overhead expenses, such as rent, salaries, and utilities, while a business owner is disabled.
- **Key person disability insurance** protects your company while a key employee is disabled.
- **Key person life insurance** covers the cost of losses due to the death of a key employee.

Disability Income Insurance

Disability income insurance covers a percentage of your lost income if you cannot work or perform the duties required by your occupation because you are disabled. The coverage and rates for disability income insurance vary depending on the broadness of the coverage and the amount of benefits to be paid.

Long-Term Care Insurance

Long-term care insurance covers the cost of long-term care, which includes custodial care, to help with the activities of daily life, whether at home or in a nursing home.

Medical Insurance

Medical or health insurance covers the cost of medical care. There are three different types:

- **Employer-provided medical insurance** is usually subsidized by your employer, making it more cost-effective than individual medical insurance. Medical plans vary from one provider and company to another.
- **Individual medical insurance** is available directly from insurance companies for individuals. This is often the only option for non-working or self-employed individuals and their families.

- **Medicare** Part A coverage provides mandatory basic hospitalization for all U.S. citizens over the age of 65. An additional voluntary program (Part B) provides coverage for doctor bills at a monthly cost. Medicare usually covers only 50 percent of the average senior citizen's health care bills and can be supplemented with Medigap insurance.

Umbrella Liability Insurance

Umbrella liability insurance may indeed cover you for injuring someone with your umbrella. But that's not its only purpose. It covers injuries to other people or damage to their property for which you are legally responsible. It's an expansion of the basic liability coverage of your auto and home insurance.

Insurance Terminology

Part of what makes buying insurance so tough sometimes is the terminology used to describe policy terms. Here are a few of the terms you should know when researching insurance policies.

Premium   A *premium* is the amount paid for an insurance policy. Premiums may be paid annually, semi-annually, quarterly, or on some other payment plan.

Binder   A *binder* is a temporary insurance policy issued while the paperwork on the permanent policy is being processed.

Renewal   A *renewal* is either a new policy or a document from the insurance company stating that the terms and conditions of your old policy remain in effect for a specific period of time.

Claim   A *claim* is your request for reimbursement at the loss of insured property. You file a claim with your insurance company after a loss has occurred.

Floater   A *floater* is a type of insurance policy that covers moveable property, such as jewelry.

Endorsement   An *endorsement* is an amendment to an insurance policy that changes its terms.

Named Perils   *Named perils* are specific dangers that a policy insures you against. These dangers are named in the insurance policy. For example, a homeowner's policy might include the following named perils: fire, hail, and wind.

Exclusion   An *exclusion* is an insurance policy provision that denies coverage for a certain type of loss. For example, flood damage is often excluded from homeowner's insurance policies. (If you live in an area prone to flooding, you can get flood insurance through the U.S. government.)

Limit A *limit* is the maximum amount a policy will pay on a covered loss. For example, if you have a $3,000 limit and the loss is $5,000, your insurance company will pay only $3,000.

Deductible A *deductible* is the amount of out-of-pocket expenses you have to pay before an insurance company begins paying on a covered loss. For example, if your car has $1,500 worth of covered damages and your deductible is $500, you pay $500 and the insurance company pays $1,000. If you have only $300 worth of covered damages, you pay the whole thing. In most cases, raising your deductible will lower your insurance premium.

Appraisal An *appraisal* is an evaluation of the value of the property you want to insure when you buy insurance or, of the amount of loss when you file a claim for covered property.

Depreciation *Depreciation* is the amount of money deducted from the value of an item to account for age and use. For example, if you paid $15,000 for your car four years ago, it may be worth only $9,000 today. The $6,000 difference is depreciation.

Replacement Value *Replacement value* is the amount it would cost to replace or rebuild a covered item based on current market prices. For example, the replacement cost of a three-year-old stereo system would be the amount it would cost to buy a comparable stereo system today.

Actual Cash Value *Actual cash value* is the amount you originally paid for an item minus the item's depreciation.

No-Fault Insurance *No-fault insurance* covers the cost of repairs and medical expenses for minor accidents, regardless of who caused the accident. No-fault insurance helps speed up the insurance process and lowers insurance costs, but may limit the right to sue for damages.

Researching Insurance Online

Quicken.com's Insurance Quotes channel (see Figure 10-7) offers a wide variety of resources you can consult to learn more about insurance and to shop for insurance online. Choose Online | To The Web | Quicken.com, then click the Insurance Quotes link near the top of the Quicken.com home page that appears.

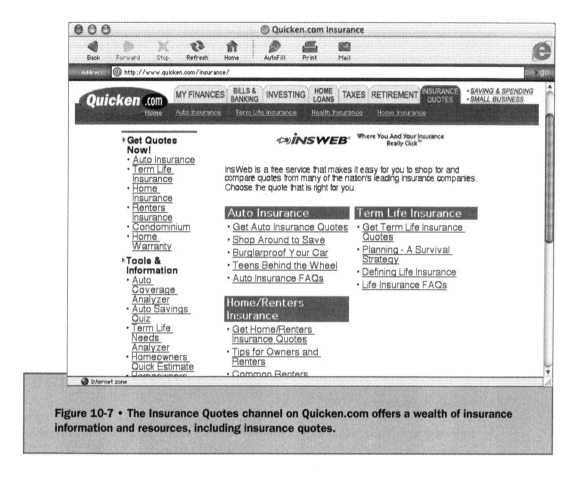

Figure 10-7 • The Insurance Quotes channel on Quicken.com offers a wealth of insurance information and resources, including insurance quotes.

Worksheets

Use the worksheets on the following pages to help you compare and evaluate different loans, mortgages, and insurance policies.

Loan Comparison Worksheet			

Basic Information

Instructions: Enter information for each loan, one per column.

Lender Name			
Contact Name			
Phone Number			
Comments			
Amount of Loan			

Rates and Fees

Instructions: Enter rate and fee values for each loan.

Application Fee			
Other Fees			
Term (in months)			
Annual Interest Rate			

Payment Calculations

Instructions: Calculate the monthly payments. Use the Loan Calculator within Quicken for accuracy (choose Planning | Financial Calculators | Loan). Then calculate the total of all payments and fees.

Monthly Payment			
Total Payments (Monthly Payment × Number of Months)			
Total Payments Plus Fees			

Mortgage Comparison Worksheet (page 1)						

Basic Information

Instructions: Enter information for each mortgage, one per column. Note: You can get most of this information from the Good Faith Estimate the lender should provide.

Lender Name			
Contact Name			
Phone Number			
Comments			

Purchase Price and Down Payment Information

Instructions: Enter the purchase price, down payment, and loan amount for each mortgage. For the best comparison, these should be the same.

Purchase Price						
Down Payment	%	$	%	$	%	$

Basic Loan Information

Instructions: Enter values for each mortgage. Then calculate monthly payments. Use the Loan Calculator within Quicken for accuracy (choose Planning | Financial Calculators | Loan). Total the monthly payments for the life of the mortgage.

Annual Interest Rate						
Term (in years)						
Fixed or Variable						
If Variable, Adjustment Period and Cap	Period	Cap	Period	Cap	Period	Cap
Monthly Payments						
Total Monthly Payments (Term × 12 × Monthly Payments)						

Mortgage Comparison Worksheet (page 2)							

Closing Costs

Instructions: Enter expected closing costs for each loan. Do not include prepaid amounts that are due at closing. Not all of these fees may apply; use space at the bottom of this section to enter other fees not listed here.

Origination Fee	%	$		%	$		%	$
Discount Fee (Points)	%	$		%	$		%	$
Credit Report Fee							
Lenders Inspection Fee							
Tax Service Fee							
Application Fee							
Underwriting Fee							
Courier Fee							
Settlement Fee							
Document Preparation Fee							
Notary Fee							
Administration Fee							
Title Insurance Fee							
Recording Fee							
City/County Tax Stamps							
State Tax Stamps							
Recordation Tax							

Mortgage Comparison Worksheet (page 3)		
Loan Program Fee			
Pest Inspection Fee			
Final Inspection Fee			
Total Closing Costs	$	$	$

Total Mortgage Costs

Instructions: Add the Total Monthly Payments to the Total Closing Costs to arrive at the total cost of each mortgage.

Total Mortgage Costs	$	$	$

Term Life Insurance Worksheet			
Basic Information			
Instructions: Enter information and values for each policy, one per column.			
Company Name			
Agent Name			
Phone Number			
Policy Name			
Coverage Amount			
Annual Premium			
Comments			
Features and Options			
Instructions: Check off the features and options included with each policy. If a feature or option is not included, leave the space blank. If it is available as an option for which you must pay more, enter an O (for option) or the additional amount you must pay. You can enter additional features and options at the bottom of the form.			
Guaranteed Level Premium			
Guaranteed Renewable			
Guaranteed Convertible			
Accelerated Death Benefit			
Disability Waiver Option			
Accidental Death Option			
Child Rider			
Other Insured Option			

Auto Insurance Worksheet (page 1)						

Basic Information

Instructions: Enter information for each policy, one per column.

Company Name			
Agent Name			
Phone Number			
Comments			

Coverage and Cost

Instructions: Enter the limits and/or deductibles for each category of coverage in one column and the corresponding premium cost in the other. You can enter additional coverage options at the bottom of the section. Be sure to subtotal the Premiums column.

Standard Coverage	Limits or Deductibles	Premiums	Limits or Deductibles	Premiums	Limits or Deductibles	Premiums
Bodily Injury Liability		$		$		$
Property Damage Liability						
Medical Payments						
Personal Injury Protection						
Uninsured/ Underinsured Motorist: • Bodily Injury • Property Damage						
Comprehensive						
Collision						

Auto Insurance Worksheet (page 2)						
Additional Coverage Options	Limits or Deductibles	Premiums	Limits or Deductibles	Premiums	Limits or Deductibles	Premiums
Rental Reimburse-ment		$		$		$
Towing/ Labor						
Emergency Road Service						
Electronic Equipment Protection						
Sound Reproducing/ Tapes and Compact Disks						
Auto Loan/ Lease Gap						
Premium Total	$		$		$	

Auto Insurance Worksheet (page 3)			
Discounts			
Instructions: Enter discounts offered by each insurance company. You can enter additional discounts at the bottom of the section. Be sure to total the discounts.			
Multipolicy	$	$	$
Multicar Coverage			
Safety Equipment			
Good Driver			
Antilock Brakes			
Antitheft System			
Driver Training			
Discount Total	$	$	$
Policy Cost			
Instructions: Subtract the discount total from the premium total to arrive at the total cost of the policy with the options you selected.			
Policy Cost	$	$	$

Saving Money and Achieving Your Goals

Part Five

This part of the book tells you about the Quicken and Quicken.com features you can use to save money on big-ticket items such as income tax, insurance, a home, or a vehicle. It shows you how using Quicken to help you make big financial decisions can save you money. It also highlights how you can use Quicken to help make your dreams come true. Its three chapters are:

Chapter 11: Saving Money at Tax Time

Chapter 12: Saving Money and Reducing Debt

Chapter 13: Planning for the Future

Saving Money at Tax Time

In this Chapter:

- *Tax planning basics*

- *Including tax information in accounts and categories*

- *Quicken Tax Planner*

- *Tax Deduction Finder*

- *Tax reports*

Chapter 11

Tax time is no fun. It can force you to spend hours sifting through financial records and filling out complex forms. When you're done with the hard part, you may be rewarded with the knowledge that you can expect a refund. But it is more likely that your reward will be the privilege of writing a check to the federal, state, or local government—or worse yet, all three.

Fortunately, Quicken can help. Its reporting features can save you time. Its planning features can save you money and help you make smarter financial decisions. By using the tax tools that are part of Quicken or available on Quicken.com, the next tax season may be a little less … well, *taxing*. In this chapter, I show you how.

The Importance of Tax Planning

Don't underestimate the importance of tax planning. Doing so can cost you time and money. In this section, I explain why tax planning is important and give you some tips on what you can do to plan for tax time.

Why Plan for Tax Time?

The following scenarios illustrate how a little planning now can save you time and money later.

Mary's Interest Expense Lesson

Mary is a homeowner who has been using her credit cards a little more than she should. She decides to cut up most of the cards and is now reducing her debt by paying a little more than the minimum monthly payment on each credit card account. Mary never considered the tax benefit of using a home equity loan, with tax-deductible interest, to pay off her credit card debt. Silly Mary doesn't even realize that the home equity reserve's interest rate might be half the rate she pays the credit card companies.

John's Capital Gains Lesson

John invests in the stock market. He's been holding shares in Company A for five years, in Company B for a year and a half, and in Company C for a few months. All three investments have been doing well. Now John wants to buy a new car. He needs to liquidate some of his investments for the down payment. Because selling all shares of Company C would give him just the right amount of money, he sells them. What John didn't consider is that the gain on the sale of Company C is recognized as a short-term capital gain. If he'd sold some shares of Company A or B, he could have recorded a long-term capital gain, which is taxed at a lower rate.

Jean's Record-Keeping Lesson

Jean's young daughter has a serious medical problem that requires frequent trips to a big city hospital 50 miles away and other trips to doctors all over the state. Jean drives her there in the family car or, if her teenage son needs the car for work, she takes a cab. Her daughter's condition has improved greatly and the prognosis is good. But Jean's family health insurance doesn't cover all the transportation costs for the hospital and doctor visits. She was just told by a friend that she can deduct the cost of medical transportation from her income taxes. She's spent hours trying to compile a list of the dates of all those long drives and she wishes she'd asked for cab ride receipts.

Pete's Estimated Tax Lesson

Pete is a freelance writer who is having a very good year. By the end of June, he estimated that he'd already earned twice as much as he did the previous year. To celebrate, he bought a new car and took a two-week vacation in Peru. He also invested heavily in a mutual fund with good returns and a high front-end load. He feels great to have finally made the big time. But the estimated tax payments Pete has been making this year aren't nearly enough to cover his April 15 tax bill. He never considered increasing the payments to reduce his year-end tax bill, investing in a tax-deferred annuity or tax-free municipal bond to reduce his taxable income, or even saving some of his cash for April 15.

Learn from Their Mistakes, Not Yours

Mary, John, Jean, and Pete may as well be real people—I'm sure plenty of people find themselves in their situations every year. These examples illustrate the point: understanding the tax rules and planning ahead for tax time can save you time and money.

What You Can Do

Unless you're a tax accountant, you probably don't know all the tax laws. Fortunately, you don't need to know all the laws, just the ones that can affect you. Then, with the knowledge of what you can include on your tax returns, you can take steps to make smart decisions and keep track of items you can deduct.

Learning About Tax Rules

At tax time, people fall into two categories: those who do their own taxes and those who find (and probably pay) someone else to do their taxes for them.

If you do your own taxes, you can learn a lot about tax laws by reading the tax forms and publications for your return. If you pay a tax preparer, you can really get your money's worth by asking him or her about how you could save money. Any good tax preparer should be able to tell you.

Either way, you can also learn tax rules and get tips and advice by consulting the Taxes channel at Quicken.com. Choose Online | To The Web | Tax Center. If necessary, your Web browser launches and connects to the Internet. The Taxes home page appears (see Figure 11-1). Follow links on this page to access all kinds of tax forms and publications, as well as tax calculation tools.

Figure 11-1 • The Taxes channel home page on Quicken.com is a great place to research tax questions and learn more about taxes.

Note   *Like all Web pages, the contents of the Quicken.com Taxes channel home page can change daily. So don't be surprised if the features you find don't match the ones shown in Figure 11-1.*

Saving Receipts and Recording Transactions

When you know what items are deductible, make a special effort to save receipts and record them in the proper Quicken categories. The receipts provide documentation for the expenditures, especially the date and amount. Recording them in the right account makes it possible to quickly generate reports of tax-deductible expenditures when it's time to fill out your tax returns.

Analyzing All Options Before Making a Decision

Many people make decisions based on limited information—or worse yet, no information at all. As a Quicken user, you have access to all kinds of information and decision-making tools. Use Quicken.com to learn about finance-related opportunities. Go the extra step to research how an opportunity could affect your tax bill. Finally, use tools within Quicken and on Quicken.com (many of which are discussed in this chapter) to help you make an informed decision.

Specifying Tax Information in Accounts and Categories

As discussed briefly in Chapter 2, Quicken enables you to specify tax-related information for accounts and categories. Including such information will help you at tax time. In this section, I tell you more about this feature, including why you should use it and how you can set it up.

Why Enter Tax Information?

By including tax information in Quicken accounts and categories, Quicken enables you to do several things:

Prepare tax reports   These reports summarize information by tax category or schedule.

Save time using the Tax Planner   This feature of Quicken Deluxe can import information from your Quicken data file based on tax information you enter.

Distinguish between taxable and non-taxable investments   This enables you to create accurate reports on capital gains, interest, and dividends.

Tip *By spending a few minutes setting up tax information for your accounts and categories, you can save hours compiling information for your returns.*

Setting Portfolio Accounts as Taxable

Investments can be taxable or nontaxable. It's important to distinguish between these two types of investments if you want Quicken to generate accurate reports of taxable income and expenses.

To check or change the tax status of a portfolio account, open the Accounts window, select the account you want to work with, and click the Edit button at the bottom of the Accounts window. The Edit Account dialog, which is shown next, appears. If the investment account is taxable, turn on the Taxable check box. Otherwise, turn it off. When you've finished, click Change.

Setting Categories as Tax-Related

Quicken can automatically generate tax reports that include tax-related income and expenses. How does it know what categories are tax-related? You tell it.

Choose Lists | Categories & Transfers or press COMMAND-L to open the Categories & Transfers window. As you can see in the next illustration, some categories may have a diamond in the Tax column. These are categories that have been set as tax-related.

Tip *Quicken sets tax information for many of the categories it creates automatically. Concentrate on the categories without the diamond in the Tax column; some of these may require tax information, depending on your situation.*

Select the category for which you want to change tax-related options. Then click the Edit button at the bottom of the window to display the Edit Category window, shown next. If the category's transactions should be included on your tax return as either income or a deductible expense, turn on the Tax-Related check box. Otherwise, turn it off.

As shown in the previous illustration, you can also assign tax link line items to categories within the Edit Category dialog. This is a new feature in Quicken 2002 that makes it easier to set tax information when you create or edit individual categories. To use this feature, turn on the Assign Tax Link check box, then select one of the tax return line items in the scrolling list. When you're finished setting tax information for the category, click Change to save your changes.

Repeat this process for all categories for which you want to change the tax-related status.

Quicken and Quicken.com Tax Tools

You don't have to wait until tax time to get tax help from Quicken and Quicken.com. It's there all year long, helping you minimize your taxes and plan for tax day by offering several excellent tax planning tools. Here's a look at two of them.

Quicken Tax Planner

One of the best reasons to think about taxes *before* tax time is to avoid surprises on April 15. Knowing what you'll owe before you owe it can help ensure that you pay just the right amount of taxes up front—through proper payroll deductions or estimated tax payments—so you don't get hit with a big tax bill or tax refund.

Quicken Tax Planner helps you estimate your federal income tax bill for 2001 and 2002. While this can help you avoid surprises, it can also help you see how various changes to income and expenses can affect your estimated tax bill.

Tip *You may think of a big tax refund as a gift from Uncle Sam. Well, it isn't. It's your money that Uncle Sam has been using, interest free, for months. When you overpay your taxes, you're giving up money that you could be using to reduce interest-bearing debt or earn interest on investment income. Make sure you don't overpay taxes throughout the year so you can keep your money where it'll do you the most good.*

Getting Started

To open Quicken Tax Planner, choose Activities | Planning Calculators | Tax. Figure 11-2 shows what the Quicken Tax Planner window might look like with the Base scenario displayed.

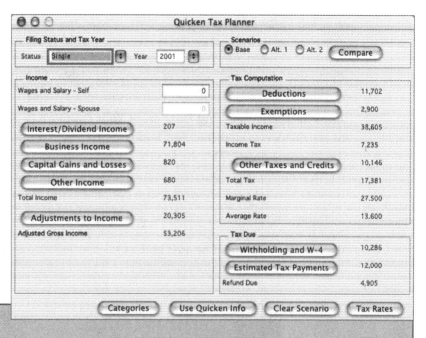

Figure 11-2 • Use the Quicken Tax Planner to estimate your year-end tax bill.

You can use the buttons at the bottom of the window to work with window contents:

- **Categories** displays the Categories & Transfers dialog, which you can use to check or change tax return line item assignments as discussed earlier.
- **Use Quicken Info** imports information from your Quicken data file into Quicken Tax Planner. This is a quick way to enter data based on actual amounts.
- **Clear Scenario** clears the entries in the current Quicken Tax Planner scenario.
- **Tax Rates** provides information about current tax rates. You can edit this information, if necessary, to account for changes in tax laws.

Entering Tax Planner Data

There are two ways to enter data into the Quicken Tax Planner: manually or automatically.

Manually Entering Income and Deductible Expenses   Manually entering data into the Quicken Tax Planner is pretty straightforward and easy to do. You can click buttons for various tax return categories and enter values into edit boxes. You might want to have some tax records on hand when you do this to help ensure accuracy. You can always reopen the Quicken Tax Planner window and make changes later if new information becomes available. All calculations are performed automatically for you based on your entries.

Automatically Entering Data from Your Quicken Data File   A quicker way to enter data is to click the Use Quicken Info button at the bottom of the Quicken Tax Planner window. This displays the Preview Information from the Quicken dialog, which is shown next. Quicken automatically annualizes the amounts entered into the data file, but you can override this option and use an actual amount by double-clicking a line item. For example, suppose it's October and you've already paid all your real estate taxes for the year. The actual amount in your Quicken data file is the amount that should be used in the Quicken Tax Planner, so you would set the annualize option to No for the Real Estate Taxes line item.

Note   To make the most of this feature, you must properly set up all tax links before importing Quicken data into the Quicken Tax Planner.

Using Scenarios

The Scenarios feature of Quicken Tax Planner enables you to enter data for multiple scenarios—a "what-if" capability that you can use to see tax impacts based on various changes in entry data. For example, suppose you're planning to get married and want to see the impact of the additional income and deductions related to your new spouse. You can use a scenario to see the tax impact without changing your Base scenario.

To use this feature, select the Alt. 1 or Alt. 2 scenario radio button in the Scenarios area at the top of the Quicken Tax Planner window. Then change or enter values in the Quicken Tax Planner window for the scenario. You'll see the results immediately.

If you have created multiple scenarios, you can compare them by clicking the Compare button in the Scenarios area. Here's what it might look like with three scenarios set up:

Tax Scenario Comparisons			
	Base Case	Alt. 1	Alt. 2
Filing Status	Single	Married-Separate	Married-Joint
Tax Year	2001	2001	2001
Adjusted Gross Income	31,016	31,016	82,470
Deductions and Exemptions	13,420	13,420	16,439
Taxable Income	17,596	17,596	66,031
Total Tax	9,370	9,370	19,240
Marginal Rate	15.000	15.000	27.500
Average Rate	8.510	8.510	15.170

Print Comparison   OK

Acting on Quicken Tax Planner Results

The Tax Due area in the Quicken Tax Planner window estimates the amount of refund or tax due based on the information you entered. If the Refund or Amount Due amount is large, you may want to adjust the amount of money you pay in taxes before the end of the year. There are two ways to do this:

- If you pay withholding taxes from your regular salary, submit a new W-4 form to adjust the amount of withholding you pay. You can usually get this form from your company's Payroll or Human Resources department.
- If you pay estimated taxes, adjust the amount of quarterly estimated payments.

Tip *In a few months, use the Quicken Tax Planner again to reassess the situation. You may find that another adjustment is necessary to make sure you minimize the amount of underpayment or overpayment.*

Finishing Up

When you've finished using the Quicken Tax Planner, click its Close button. This saves the information you entered so you can review or revise it in the future.

Tax Deduction Finder

One way to minimize taxes is to maximize your deductions. While Quicken can't help you spend money on tax-deductible items (that's up to you), it can help you identify expenses that may be tax-deductible—so you don't forget to include them on your tax returns.

The Tax Deduction Finder is a Quicken.com-based tax tool that can help you learn which expenses are deductible. You can use its question-and-answer interface to compile information and then provide a list of possible deductions based on your answers.

To open the Tax Deduction Finder, choose Online | To The Web | Tax Deduction Finder. Quicken launches your Web browser, connects to the Internet (if necessary) and displays a brief introduction page for the Tax Deduction Finder. Click the Start the Deduction Finder Now! link to get started.

Follow instructions that appear onscreen to explore various deduction possibilities. You'll be prompted to select check boxes and click buttons and links. Figure 11-3 shows an example. Work your way through the Deduction Finder to see results: a list of the deductions that may apply to you.

Figure 11-3 • The Tax Deduction Finder gathers information about your expenses to determine whether they are deductible.

Tax Reports

Quicken offers several different tax reports that can make tax time easier by providing the information you need to prepare your taxes. All of these reports are based on the tax information settings for the accounts and categories in your Quicken file.

Note *You can learn more about Quicken's reporting feature in Chapter 16.*

To create a report, begin by selecting Activities | Reports & Graphs | Reports or click the Reports button near the top of the Reporting tab. The Reports window, which is shown next, appears. It offers a number of reports you might find useful at tax time.

Tip *If you pay a tax preparation specialist, be sure to furnish him or her with an accurate Tax Schedule report from Quicken. Doing so may save the preparer time and reduce your tax preparation bill.*

Standard Reports   Two reports on the Standard tab of the Reports window are specifically for taxes:

- **Tax Schedule** summarizes tax-related transactions, organized by tax form or schedule and line item.
- **Tax Summary** summarizes tax-related transactions, organized by category and date.

Investment Reports The Investment tab also offers two handy reports for tax time:

- **Capital Gains** summarizes gains and losses on the sales of investments, organized by the term of the investment (short or long) and the investment account.
- **Investment Income** summarizes investment cash inflows and outflows, usually due to dividends, interest earned, and investment expenses.

Saving Money and Reducing Debt

In this Chapter:

- *Saving basics*

- *Investment savings calculator*

- *Reducing debt*

- *Budgeting*

- *Forecasting*

The best way to prepare for life events is to build up your savings. Saving money is an important part of financial management. Savings enable you to take vacations and make major purchases without increasing debt, help your kids through college, handle emergencies, and have a comfortable retirement.

In this chapter, I tell you about saving money and how tools within Quicken can help. I provide plenty of information about various savings accounts so you can learn about your savings options. If you're in debt and can't even think about saving until you dig your way out, this chapter can help you, too. It also covers Quicken tools for reducing your debt.

> **Tip**   *If you don't mind risk and want to earn higher income on your savings, consult Chapter 8. It discusses investments, including stocks, bonds, and mutual funds.*

Saving Basics

Remember when you got your first "piggy bank"? It may not have looked like a pig, but it had a slot for slipping in coins and, if you were lucky, a removable rubber plug on the bottom that made it easy to get the coins out when you needed them. Whoever gave you the bank was trying to teach you your first financial management lesson: save money.

As an adult, things are a little more complex. In this section, I explain why you should save, provide some saving strategies, and tell you about the types of savings accounts that make your old piggy bank obsolete.

Why Save?

Most people save money so there's money to spend when they need it. Others save for a particular purpose. Still others save because they have so much they can't spend it all. Here's a closer look at why saving makes sense.

Saving for "Rainy Days"

When people say they are saving for a rainy day, they probably aren't talking about the weather. They're talking about bad times or emergencies—situations when they need extra cash.

For example, suppose the family car needs a new transmission. Or your beloved dog needs eye surgery. Or your daughter manages to break her violin three days before the big recital. In the "rainy day" scheme of things, these might be light drizzles. But your savings can help keep you dry.

Here are a few other examples. Suppose your employer goes bankrupt and closes up shop. Or after a three-martini lunch with a customer, you get back to the office, tell your boss what you really think of him, and quit on the spot. Or after being poked one too many times in the butt by a bull, you find it impossible to continue your career as a rodeo clown. If your paychecks stop coming, do you have enough savings to support yourself or your family until you can get another source of income? On the "rainy day" scale, this could be a torrential downpour. Your savings can be a good umbrella.

Saving for a Goal

Planning for your future often includes planning for events that affect your life—and your wallet. Saving money for specific events can help make these events memorable for what they are, rather than what they cost.

For example, take a recently engaged couple, Norbert (my kid brother) and Missy. They plan to marry within a year and buy a house right away. Within five years, they plan to have their first child. That's when Missy may leave her job to start the more demanding job of mother and homemaker. Someday, they hope their children will go to college and they want to help cover the expenses. They also want to be able to help pay for their children's weddings. Eventually, they'll retire. And throughout their lives, they want to be able to take annual family vacations, buy a new car every six years or so, and get season tickets for the New York Knicks.

All of these things are major events in Norbert and Missy's lives. Saving in advance for each of these events will make them possible—without going into debt.

Saving for Peace of Mind

Some people save money because events in their lives showed them the importance of having savings. Children who lived through the Depression or bad financial times for their families grew up to be adults who understand the value of money and try hard to keep some available. They don't want to repeat the hard times they went through. Having healthy savings accounts gives them peace of mind.

Saving Strategies

There are two main ways to save: when you can or regularly.

Saving When You Can   When money is tight, saving can be difficult. People who are serious about saving, however, will force themselves to save as much as possible when they can. Saving when you can is better than not saving at all.

Saving Regularly   A better way to save money is to save a set amount periodically. For example, save $25 every week or $200 every month. Timing this with your paycheck makes sense; you can make a split deposit for the check. A savings like this is called an *annuity*, and you'd be surprised at how quickly the money can accumulate. Table 12-1 shows some examples based on a 4.5 percent annual interest rate.

Types of Savings Accounts

There are different types of savings accounts, each with its own benefits and drawbacks.

Month	Weekly Contributions				Monthly Contributions				
	$25	$50	$75	$100	$50	$100	$200	$300	$400
1	$100	$200	$300	$401	$50	$100	$200	$300	$400
2	$226	$452	$677	$903	$100	$200	$401	$601	$801
3	$327	$653	$980	$1,307	$151	$301	$602	$903	$1,205
4	$428	$856	$1,284	$1,712	$201	$402	$805	$1,207	$1,609
5	$555	$1,110	$1,665	$2,220	$252	$504	$1,008	$1,511	$2,015
6	$657	$1,314	$1,971	$2,628	$303	$606	$1,211	$1,817	$2,423
7	$759	$1,519	$2,278	$3,038	$354	$708	$1,416	$2,124	$2,832
8	$888	$1,776	$2,664	$3,552	$405	$811	$1,621	$2,432	$3,242
9	$991	$1,982	$2,974	$3,965	$457	$914	$1,827	$2,741	$3,654
10	$1,095	$2,190	$3,284	$4,379	$509	$1,017	$2,034	$3,051	$4,068
11	$1,225	$2,449	$3,674	$4,899	$560	$1,121	$2,242	$3,363	$4,483
12	$1,329	$2,658	$3,987	$5,316	$613	$1,225	$2,450	$3,675	$4,900

Table 12-1 • Your Savings Can Grow Over Time

Tip *All the accounts discussed in this chapter (except where noted) should be insured by the FDIC (Federal Deposit Insurance Corporation). This organization covers savings deposits up to $100,000 per entity (person or company) per bank, thus protecting you from loss in the event of a bank failure.*

Standard Savings Accounts   All banks offer savings accounts and most accommodate any balance. Savings accounts pay interest on your balance and allow you to deposit or withdraw funds at any time.

Holiday Clubs   A "holiday club" account is a savings account into which you make regular, equal deposits, usually on a weekly basis. Many banks offer these accounts, along with an option to automatically withdraw the deposit funds from your regular savings or checking account. The money stays in the account, earning interest until the club ends in October or November. The idea behind these accounts is to provide you with cash for the holidays, but there are variations on this theme, such as vacation club accounts that end in May or June.

Credit Union Payroll Savings   A bank isn't the only place where you can open a savings account. If your company has a credit union, it also offers a number of accounts. These accounts often offer the option of payroll savings deductions. This is a great feature for people who have trouble saving money, because the money comes out of their paychecks before they see (and can spend) it. It's as if the money never existed, when in reality it's accumulating in an interest-bearing account. In case you're wondering, the withdrawn funds are included in your taxable income.

Tip *I had a payroll savings account with the credit union of my last employer. Every time I got a raise, I increased the amount of the savings withdrawal so my take-home pay was almost the same. Before I left that job, I was saving $100 a week and I didn't miss a penny of it. Not bad!*

Certificates of Deposit   A certificate of deposit (CD) is an account, normally with a bank, that requires you to keep the money on deposit for a specific length of time. As a reward for your patience, your earnings are based on a fixed interest rate higher than what is available for a regular savings account. The longer the term of the deposit and the more money deposited, the higher the rate. At the CD's maturity date, you can "roll over" the deposit to a new account that may have a different interest rate, or you can take back the cash. If you withdraw the money before the CD's maturity date, you pay a penalty, which can sometimes exceed the amount of the interest earned.

Money Market Accounts   A money market account is actually a form of investment, but it should be included here because it is offered by many banks. It has a higher rate of return than a regular savings account, but is not insured by the FDIC. It is considered a conservative investment and can be treated just like a savings account for depositing and withdrawing money.

Interest-Bearing Checking Accounts   Many banks offer interest-bearing checking accounts. They usually have minimum balance requirements, however, forcing you to keep a certain amount of money in the account at all times. Although it's nice to earn money on checking account funds, the interest rate is usually so low that it's better to have a regular checking account and keep your savings in a savings account or money market account.

Quicken and Quicken.com Savings Tools

Quicken and Quicken.com offer a number of features to help you save money. Here are two of the most useful ones.

Investment Calculator

The Investment Calculator enables you to calculate savings annuities. Choose Activities | Planning Calculators | Investment & Savings. The Investment Calculator appears:

Begin by clicking one of the arrows to determine what should be calculated by Quicken:

- **Current Value** calculates the amount of money you should currently have saved based on the values you enter.

- **Contribution** calculates the minimum amount you should regularly contribute to savings based on the values you enter.
- **Future Value** calculates the total amount saved at the end of the savings period based on the values you enter.

Enter values throughout the window. Be sure to choose the appropriate contribution frequency from the pop-up menu. Most options are pretty straightforward and easy to understand. The Inflation options enable you to enter a predicted inflation rate, and then apply that rate to the calculation of the result. As you TAB from field to field, Quicken calculates a result. In the previous illustration, for example, Quicken has calculated that a monthly investment of $100 for ten years at 4.5 percent interest will yield $15,119.81. In this example, inflation is not taken into consideration.

Quicken.com Saving & Spending Channel

Quicken.com also offers information you may find helpful for saving money. The best place to start is within the Saving & Spending channel.

Choose Online | To The Web | Quicken.com to connect to the Internet and open the Quicken.com home page. Click the Saving & Spending link near the top of the page. The Saving & Spending channel's home page, which is illustrated in Figure 12-1, should appear.

As you can see, this page includes current savings rates as well as links to planners, calculators, and articles to provide information about saving money—and reducing debt, which I discuss next. Explore these features on your own to see how they can help you put aside more money for rainy days or achieving your dreams.

Reducing Your Debt

It's not easy to save money if most of your income is spent paying credit card bills and loan payments. If you're heavily in debt, you might even be having trouble keeping up with all your payments. If that's the case, stop thinking about saving for a moment and start thinking about reducing your debt.

Consumer credit is a huge industry. It's easy to get credit cards—sometimes too easy. And it's a lot easier to pay for something with a piece of plastic than with cold, hard cash. The "buy now, pay later" attitude has become an acceptable way of life. It's no wonder that many Americans are deeply in debt.

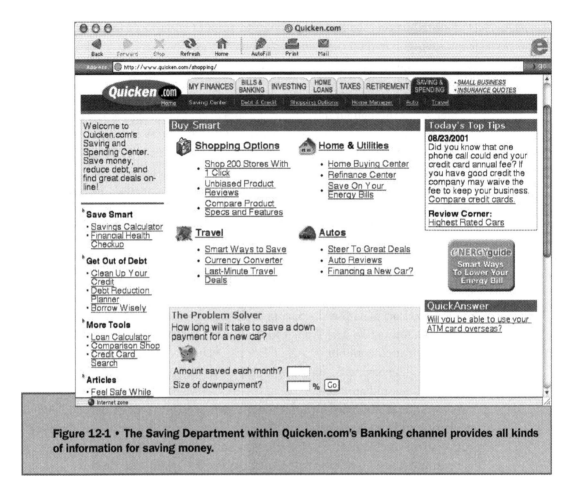

Figure 12-1 • The Saving Department within Quicken.com's Banking channel provides all kinds of information for saving money.

Those credit card bills can add up, however. And paying just the minimum payment on each one only helps the credit card company keep you in debt—and paying interest—as long as possible. I've been there, so I know. Unfortunately, it took two experiences to set me straight. I hope you can learn your lesson the first time.

Don't despair. There is hope. Here are a few things you can do to dig yourself out of debt.

Breaking the Pattern

Your first step to reducing debt must be to break the pattern of spending that got you where you are. For most people, that means cutting up credit cards. After all, it's tough to use a credit card if you can't hand it to a cashier at the check-out counter.

Before you take out the scissors, however, read this: you don't have to cut up *all* of your credit cards. Leave yourself one or two major credit cards for emergencies like car trouble or unexpected visits to the doctor. The cards that should go are the store and gas credit cards. They can increase your debt, but they can only be used in a few places.

Here's the logic behind this strategy. If you have 15 credit cards, each with a credit limit of $2,000, you can get yourself into $30,000 of debt. The minimum monthly payment for each card may be $50. That's $750 a month in minimum credit card payments. If you have only two credit cards, each with a credit limit of $2,000, you can only get yourself into $4,000 of debt. Your monthly minimum payment may be only $100. This reduces your monthly obligation, enabling you to pay more than the minimum so you can further reduce your debt.

Shopping for Cards with Better Interest Rates

Yes, it's nice to have a credit card with your picture on it. Or one that's gold, platinum, or titanium. Or one with your college, team, club, or association name on it. A friend of mine who breeds horses showed off a new Visa card with a picture of a horse on it. She told me it was her favorite. I asked her what the interest rate was and she didn't know.

The purpose of a credit card is to purchase things on credit. When you maintain a balance on the account, you pay interest on it. The balance and interest rate determine how much it costs you to have that special picture or name on a plastic card in your wallet. Is it worth 19.8 percent a year? Or 21 percent? Not to me!

Tip   *Here's a reality check exercise: gather together all of your credit card bills for the most recent month. Now add up all the monthly finance fees and interest charges. Multiply that number by 12. The result is an approximation of what you pay in interest each year. Now imagine how nice it would be to have that money in your hands the next time you went on vacation or needed a down payment on a new car or home.*

Low-interest credit cards are widely available. Sometimes you don't even have to look for them—offers arrive in the mail all the time. They promise low rates—usually under 10 percent a year. But you must read these offers carefully before you apply for one of these cards. Most offer the low rates for a short, introductory period—usually no longer than six months. (I got one once that offered 0 percent for the first 25 days. Big deal.) Some offer the low rate only on new purchases, while others offer the low rate only on balance transfers or cash advances. Be sure to find out what the rate is after the introductory period.

Here are two strategies for using a low-interest card:

- Consolidate your debt by transferring the balances of other credit cards to the new card. For this strategy, select a card that offers a low rate (without a fee) on balance transfers. When you transfer the balances, be sure to cut up the old cards so you don't use them to add more to your debt.
- Make purchases with the low-interest card. Make the new card your emergency credit card. Be sure to cut up your old emergency card so you don't wind up using both of them.

Tip *If you really like that special picture or name on the card in your wallet, call the credit card company and ask if they can give you a better interest rate. In many instances, they can—especially when you tell them you want to close your account.*

Consolidating Your Debt

Consolidating your debt is one of the best ways to dig yourself out. By combining balances into one debt, whether through balance transfers to a single credit card or a debt consolidation loan, you're better able to pay off the balances without causing financial hardship. This is sometimes the only option when things have gotten completely out of control and you can't meet your debt obligations.

Tip *If you own a home, consider a home equity loan to consolidate your debt. The interest rate is usually lower than any credit card or debt consolidation loan and the interest may be tax-deductible. I tell you more about home equity loans in Chapter 9.*

Using Charge Cards, Not Credit Cards

There's a difference between a credit card and a charge card:

- **Credit cards** enable you to buy things on credit. If each month you pay less than what you owe, you are charged interest on your account balance. Most major "credit cards" are true credit cards. MasterCard, Visa, and Discover are three examples. Most store "charge cards" are also credit cards.
- **Charge cards** enable you to buy things on credit, too. But when the bill comes, you're expected to pay the entire balance. You don't have to pay any interest, but if you don't pay the entire balance on time, you may have to pay late fees and finance charges. American Express is an example of a charge card.

The benefit of charge cards is that they make it nearly impossible to get into debt. How can you owe the charge card company money if you must pay the balance in full every month? Using these cards prevents you from overspending. Every time you use the card to make a purchase, a little accountant in the back of your head should be adding the charge to a running total. You should stop spending when that total reaches the limit of your ability to pay.

> **Tip**   *Chapters 4 and 5 explain how you can use Quicken to track credit card balances manually or online. This includes charge cards. If you use Quicken to keep track of expenditures, you won't need that little accountant in the back of your head.*

If you don't want an American Express card (for whatever reason), use another major credit card as a charge card. Just pay the entire balance each time you get a bill. If you don't carry a balance, you won't be charged interest.

If You Can't Stop Spending, Get Help

Many people who are deeply in debt may have a spending problem. They can't resist buying that fifth pair of running shoes or that trendy new outdoor furniture. They don't need the things they buy, but they buy them anyway. There's nothing wrong with that if your income can support your spending habits, but if your net worth is less than $0, it's a real problem—one that might require counseling to resolve.

The next time you make a purchase, stop for a moment and think about what you're buying. Is it something you need? Something you can use? Something you can justify spending the money on? If you can't answer yes to any of these questions, don't buy it. If you have to buy it anyway, it's time to seek professional help.

Quicken.com's Debt Reduction Planner

The Debt Reduction Planner on Quicken.com can help you develop a plan for reducing your outstanding debt. It prompts you to enter information about your finances, including your debt and savings, then calculates how you can pay off your debt quickly, with the least amount of finance charges.

To access this feature, choose Online | To The Web | Debt Reduction Planner. If necessary, Quicken launches your Web browser and connects to the Internet. It then displays an introduction page that explains how the Debt Reduction Planner works. Click the Build Your Plan Now button to get started. The Debt Reduction Planner's Introduction window, which is illustrated in Figure 12-2, appears. Follow the instructions within it to create your debt reduction plan.

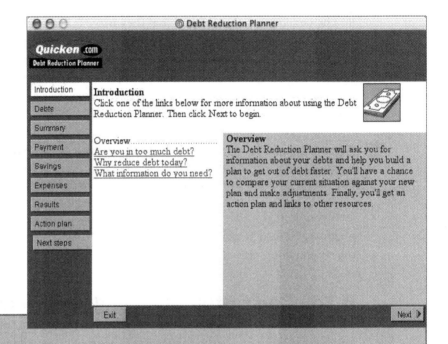

Figure 12-2 • The Debt Reduction Planner helps you create a logical, cost-saving plan for reducing your debt.

Tip   *One of the things the Debt Reduction Planner helps you do is identify and pay off high-interest debt before low-interest debt. This can save you hundreds (if not thousands) of dollars in monthly finance fees!*

Living Debt-Free

It is possible to live debt-free—and you don't have to be rich to do it. Just learn to stop relying on credit cards to make your purchases and to spend only what you can afford to.

Imagine how great it would feel to be completely debt free. It's worth a try, isn't it?

Budgeting and Forecasting

When money is tight or you're interested in meeting financial goals, it's time to create a budget and monitor your spending. But if you're serious about managing your money, you might want to create a budget before you need one. While Quicken's categories give you a clear understanding of where money comes from and where it goes, budgets enable you to set up predefined amounts for each category, thus helping you to control spending.

Budgets also make it easier to create forecasts of your future financial position. This makes it possible to see how much cash will be available at a future date—before the holidays, for summer vacation, or for the day you plan to put down a deposit on a new car.

In this part of the chapter, I tell you how to create a budget and use it to monitor your spending habits. I also explain how to create a forecast so you can glimpse your financial future.

Budgeting

The idea behind a budget is to determine expected income amounts and specify maximum amounts for expenditures. This helps prevent you from spending more than you earn. It also enables you to control your spending in certain categories. For example, say you realize that you go out for dinner a lot more often than you should. You can set a budget for the Dining category and track your spending to make sure you don't exceed the budget. You'll eat at home more often and save money.

In this section, I explain how to set up a budget and use it to keep track of your spending. I think you'll agree that budgeting is a great way to keep spending under control.

Creating a Budget

Quicken's budgeting feature enables you to create budgets for any combination of categories. You can enter budget amounts manually or tell Quicken to automatically generate a budget for you based on past transactions.

Choose Activities | Budgeting | Budget Setup to display the Create Budget window, shown next. Enter a name for the budget, then set options as desired and click Create.

Note   *If you have already created a budget, the Budget Setup window will appear (see Figure 12-3, later in the chapter) instead of the Create Budget window. To display the Create Budget window, choose New Budget from the pop-up menu in the top-left corner of the Budget Setup window.*

The first pair of radio buttons in the Create Budget window enables you to specify which categories should be included in the budget:

- **All Categories (Except Transfers)** includes all categories in the budget. Transfer accounts are not included. Selecting this option makes it easy to create a budget that includes all of your income and expenditures.

- **Selected Categories** enables you to select which categories to include. This makes it possible to create a budget for a specific purpose—for example, a budget to monitor just those expenditures that you can control, like dining, clothing, and entertainment. When you select this option, the Select Categories dialog, shown next, appears. Click to toggle check marks beside category names or click the buttons on the right side of the dialog to include or exclude specific types of categories. When you click OK, the categories that are checked will be included in the budget.

The second pair of radio buttons in the Create Budget window enables you to specify how you want to enter starting amounts for the budget:

- **Enter Zeros For All Categories** enters 0.00 for each category in the budget. You can then modify the budgeted amounts to create your budget from scratch.
- **Use QuickBudget To Enter Starting Amounts From Your Registers** enables you to create a budget based on amounts already entered in your account registers. When you select this option, the QuickBudget window, shown next, appears. Set the following options and click OK:

- **Date** is the period for which register transactions should be used for the budget. You can choose an option from the Date pop-up menu or enter beginning and ending dates in the From and Through edit boxes. For best results, choose a recent 12-month period—this ensures that you'll include both regular and seasonal income and expenses.
- **Calculate Amounts As** options specify how Quicken should fill in monthly amounts. The Monthly Average Amount option calculates an average for each month based on all the transactions in the date period. It then enters that average for each month. This is a good option if you selected a date period less than a full year or your income and expenses don't have seasonal peaks. The Actual Amount For Each Month option enters actual amounts from the registers for each month. Be sure to use this option if you do have a lot of seasonal income or expenses.
- **Round Amounts To The Nearest** enables you to choose a rounding amount from a pop-up menu: $1, $10, or $100. The amount you choose will be used to round budget entries.
- **Inflate Amounts By** enables you to enter an inflation percentage. The amount you enter is applied to each budgeted category.

Viewing a Budget

Budget information appears in the Budget Setup window (see Figure 12-3). You can open this window in a number of ways:

- Use the Create Budget window, which is discussed in the previous section, to set budget options. When you click Create, the Budget Setup window appears.
- Once a budget has been created, choose Activities | Budgeting | Budget Setup, or click the Budget button near the top of the Planning tab.

Changing the Budget View

There are a number of ways to change the way information appears in the Budget view window.

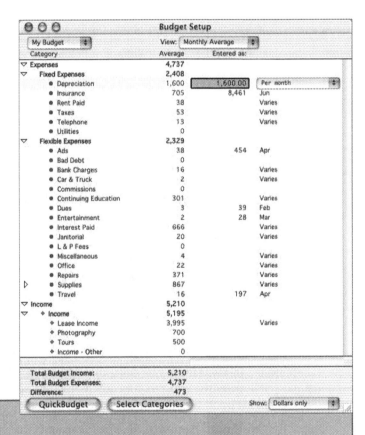

Figure 12-3 • Use the Budget Setup window to view and fine-tune a budget.

Setting the View   By default, the Budget Setup window displays your budget in Monthly Average view. You can change the view by choosing a different option from the View menu in the top of the window:

- **Monthly Average** (see Figure 12-3) displays the average amount for each month.
- **Quarterly Average** displays the average amount for each quarter.
- **Yearly Total** displays the total amount for the entire year.
- **All Months** displays the amount entered for each month (see Figure 12-4). When you choose All Months, another pop-up menu appears at the top of the window. Use it to select the first month you want to display.

Tip   *All Months view is particularly handy for modifying budgeted amounts, especially when your income or expenses vary throughout the year.*

Category	Total	January	February	March	April
▽ **Expenses**	56,847	4,606	4,577	5,350	7,380
▽ Fixed Expenses	28,899	1,600	2,190	1,607	1,621
● Depreciation	19,200	1,600.00	1,600	1,600	1,600
● Insurance	8,461	0	0	0	0
● Rent Paid	450	0	0	0	0
● Taxes	635	0	590	7	21
● Telephone	153	0	0	0	0
● Utilities	0	0	0	0	0
▽ Flexible Expenses	27,948	3,006	2,387	3,743	5,759
● Ads	454	0	0	0	454
● Bad Debt	0	0	0	0	0
● Bank Charges	189	10	25	25	27
● Car & Truck	24	0	0	14	0
● Commissions	0	0	0	0	0
● Continuing Education	3,617	599	1,000	500	1,070
● Dues	39	0	39	0	0
● Entertainment	28	0	0	28	0
● Interest Paid	7,994	1,012	1,029	995	991
● Janitorial	240	40	0	60	60
● L & P Fees	0	0	0	0	0
● Miscellaneous	50	40	0	10	0
● Office	258	0	105	153	0
● Repairs	4,452	490	0	378	770
▷ ● Supplies	10,406	815	189	1,580	2,190
● Travel	197	0	0	0	197
▽ **Income**	62,525	4,318	4,780	8,114	10,154
▷ ◆ Income	62,335	4,311	4,773	8,112	10,149
◆ Interest Earned	190	7	7	2	5
Total Budget Income:	62,525	4,318	4,780	8,114	10,154
Total Budget Expenses:	56,847	4,606	4,577	5,350	7,380
Difference:	5,678	-288	203	2,764	2,774

Figure 12-4 • You can also display individual months in the Budget Setup window.

Setting Value Options   You can also change the way values appear in the Budget Setup window. Choose an option from the Show pop-up menu at the bottom of the window. The options are self-explanatory: Dollars Only or Dollars & Cents.

Changing the Category Display   You can add or remove categories from a budget at any time. Click the Select Categories button at the bottom of the Budget Setup window. This displays the Select Categories dialog illustrated earlier in this chapter. Click to toggle check marks on or off to specify which categories should appear. When you click OK, your changes are applied to the Budget Setup window.

Rearranging Categories   Expense categories are separated into Fixed Expenses and Flexible Expenses. You can move any expense category from one area to the other. Simply drag its category line to the new position. When you release the mouse button, the category moves.

Changing Budgeted Amounts in Average or Total View

In Monthly Average, Quarterly Average, or Annual Total view, you can modify the amounts that appear in the Entered In column of the Budget Setup window (see Figure 12-3). This, in turn, will recalculate the monthly or quarterly average or annual total, thus changing your budget.

To change a budgeted amount, begin by choosing an option from the Frequency pop-up menu to the right of the amount in the Entered In column. Your options are Per Week, Every Two Weeks, Twice a Month, Every Four Weeks, Per Month, Every Two Months, Per Quarter, Twice a Year, Per Year, or Specific Months. (Another option, Varies, may appear for some categories when QuickBudget enters values for you as discussed earlier in this chapter.) Choose the option that corresponds to the frequency of the budgeted amount. If you choose Specific Months, a dialog appears, enabling you to select the months to budget.

Next, enter a value in the edit box beside the pop-up menu. The value should correspond to the amount you expect to receive or want to spend for the category for the frequency you chose.

For example, say you get paid every two weeks and want to enter your budgeted take-home pay. You'd select the Every Two Weeks option, and then enter the amount of your take-home pay in the edit box beside it. Quicken automatically calculates the average and total for the year. Here's what it might look like in the Budget Setup window:

Changing Budgeted Amounts in All Months View

Changing budgeted amounts in All Months view (see Figure 12-4) is a little more straightforward. Simply click to select the value you want to change and enter a new value. The total is automatically updated.

Tip *To copy a selected value to all months after the selected month, click the Fill Row button at the bottom of the Budget Setup window (see Figure 12-4). The value appears in all month columns to the right of the selected value for that category.*

Using QuickBudget

You also can use QuickBudget to change all the budgeted amounts for your budget. Click the QuickBudget button at the bottom of the Budget Setup window. A QuickBudget window like the one shown next appears. It offers the same basic options as the QuickBudget window discussed earlier in this chapter, along with two others:

- **Replace Already Budgeted Amounts In Budget Setup With QuickBudget Amounts** clears out the current budgeted amounts and replaces them with the result of QuickBudget calculations, as determined by the other settings in the window.

- **For Which Categories** enables you to specify whether you want All Categories or Selected categories. If you select the Selected option, the Select Categories dialog appears so you can specify which categories you want to include.

When you've finished setting QuickBudget options, click OK to apply your settings to the current budget.

Managing Multiple Budgets

Quicken enables you to have more than one budget. The pop-up menu at the top-left corner of the Budget Setup window (see Figures 12-3 and 12-4) offers options for creating and managing multiple budgets.

Creating a New Budget   To create additional budgets, choose New Budget from the pop-up menu at the top left of the Budget Setup window. This displays the Create Budget window, which I discuss earlier in this chapter. Use it to name, set options for, and create a new budget.

Switching from One Budget to Another   The name of each budget you create automatically appears on the pop-up menu at the top left of the Budget Setup window. To switch from one budget to another, simply choose a budget name from the menu. The window's contents change to reflect the information for the budget you selected.

Renaming a Budget   You can also change the name of a budget. Switch to the budget that you want to rename. Then choose Rename from the pop-up menu at the top left of the Budget Setup window. The Rename Budget window appears. Enter a new name for the budget and click the Rename button to save it.

Deleting a Budget   If you have a budget that you no longer use, you can delete it. Switch to the budget you want to delete and choose Delete from the pop-up menu at the top left of the Budget Setup window. A confirmation dialog appears, asking if you really do want to delete the budget. Click Yes. The budget's information is removed from your Quicken data file.

Viewing Budget Status

Once you have created a budget you can live with, it's a good idea to periodically compare your actual income and expenditures to budgeted amounts. Quicken lets you do this a number of different ways.

> **Tip**   *Make sure you compare budgeted amounts to actual results for the period for which you have recorded data. For example, don't view a year-to-date budget report if you began entering data into Quicken in March. Instead, customize the report to show actual transactions beginning in March.*

Budget Reports   The Reports window offers two different reports for comparing budgeted amounts to actual results:

- **Budget Month By Month** displays the actual and budgeted transactions by month.
- **Budget Summary** (see Figure 12-5) displays the total actual and budgeted transactions for the period you specify.

Note   *I tell you about creating reports, including how to customize them, in Chapter 16.*

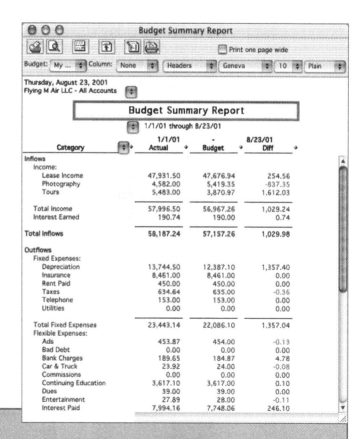

Figure 12-5 • A Budget Summary report compares actual to budgeted amounts.

Budget Graphs   The Graphs window offers two options that graphically represent a comparison of budgeted and actual results:

- **Budget Month By Month** shows the favorable and unfavorable differences between actual and budgeted income amounts.
- **Budget Variance By Category** shows the budgeted and actual values for each category.

Note   *I explain how to create graphs, including how to customize them, in Chapter 16.*

Budget Snapshot   Quicken's Insights window includes a "snapshot" you can view to keep track of your budgets. Follow the instructions in Chapter 16 to add the snapshot to your Insights window. You can then customize the snapshot by clicking the Customize This Report link in the actions area beneath it.

Using the Budget Monitoring Window

Quicken's Budget Monitoring window graphically compares budgeted to actual amounts. You select the budget you want to monitor and then set up the Budget Monitoring window so it displays the categories you want to monitor. The window uses color to tell you at a glance how you're doing.

Choose Activities | Budgeting | Budget Monitoring to display the Budget Monitoring window, shown next. Choose a budget and a period from the pop-up menus at the top of the window. Here's what it might look like for the budgeted expense items in Figures 12-3 and 12-4:

To monitor individual categories, click the Set Up Monitoring button. A dialog like the one shown next appears. It lists all the categories included in the currently selected budget. Click to toggle check marks beside each category you want to monitor and click OK.

When you click OK, the Budget Monitoring window changes to display each category you want to monitor. You can drag the Budget Monitoring window's size box (lower-right corner) to enlarge the window to show the selected categories.

Tip   *You can click a category bar in the Budget Monitoring window to learn the actual amount for the category.*

Forecasting

Forecasting uses known and estimated transactions to provide a general overview of your future financial situation. This "crystal ball" can help you spot potential cash flow problems (or surpluses) so you can prepare for them. It also makes it possible to see how much cash will be available at a future date—before the holidays, for summer vacation, or for the day you plan to put down a deposit on a new car.

Viewing the Forecast Window

Your financial forecast appears in the Forecast window (see Figure 12-6), which also offers commands and options to modify the forecast. To open this window, choose Activities | Forecast. Quicken automatically creates a forecast for you based on the upcoming transactions in the Calendar. You can use options at the bottom of the Forecast window to change the window's view.

Note   *I explain how to use the Calendar to schedule transactions in Chapter 14.*

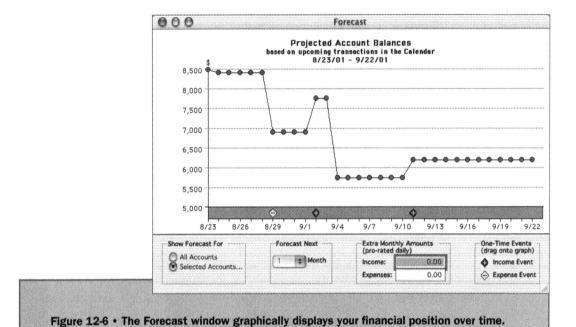

Figure 12-6 • The Forecast window graphically displays your financial position over time.

Choosing the Accounts to Forecast   The Show Forecast For area of the Forecast window offers two options for specifying which accounts should appear in the forecast:

- **All Accounts** displays all accounts in the forecast.
- **Selected Accounts** displays the accounts you select in the forecast. When you choose this option, the Select Accounts dialog, shown next, appears. Click to toggle check marks beside the accounts you want to include. Then click OK.

Tip *You may find it more meaningful to include only your most liquid accounts in a forecast. Normally, that will be bank and credit card accounts.*

Choosing the Period to Forecast The Forecast Next area offers a pop-up menu you can use to specify how many months should be included in the forecast. The options are 1, 3, 6, or 12. When you change this option, the contents of the Forecast window change accordingly.

Adding Extra Monthly Amounts

If you don't use Quicken's Calendar feature to schedule all transactions, you may find it helpful to add monthly amounts not included in the Calendar right in the Forecast window. For example, suppose you don't include your biweekly paycheck on the Calendar. You can add the monthly amount of your take-home pay as an extra monthly income amount.

To add an extra monthly amount, enter the amount you want to add in the Income or Expense edit box at the bottom of the Forecast window (see Figure 12-6) and press RETURN or ENTER. The forecast is adjusted accordingly.

Adding One-Time Events

In some instances, you may know about specific one-time income or expense events that you have not scheduled on Quicken's Calendar. You can add these events to the Forecast so Quicken includes them in its forecast calculations.

To add a one-time Income event, drag the blue diamond on the bottom-right corner of the Forecast window (see Figure 12-6) onto the Forecast graph at the appropriate date. When you release the mouse button, the Set Up Income Event dialog, which is shown next, appears. Enter the date, amount, and event name in the edit boxes and click OK. The Forecast graph is updated for your entry and a blue diamond appears on the graph's x-axis (bottom line), at the date you specified. You can see examples of two income events and one expense event in Figure 12-6.

As you probably guessed, you can add one-time expense items the same way. Just drag the yellow diamond onto the graph, enter information in the dialog that appears, and click OK.

Tip   *You can edit a one-time income or expense item by double-clicking its diamond on the graph's x-axis.*

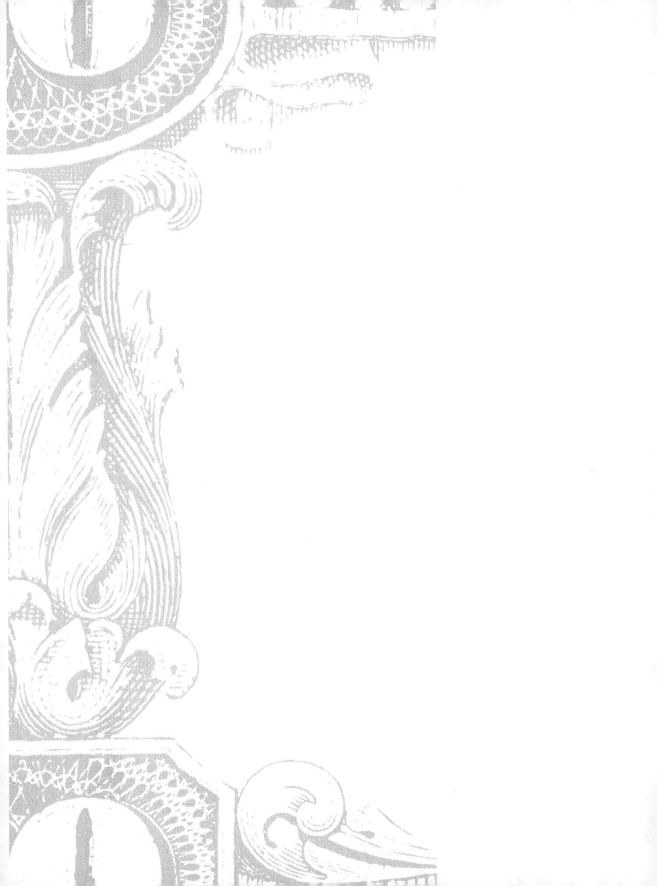

Planning for the Future

In this Chapter:

- *Planning for retirement*

- *Retirement account options*

- *Using financial calculators*

- *Quicken.com resources*

Chapter 13

To many people, the future is an unknown, a mystery. After all, who can say what will happen tomorrow, next year, or ten years from now? But if you think about your future, you can usually come up with a few events that you can plan for: your marriage, the purchase of a new home, the birth of your children (and their education years later), and your retirement. (These are just examples—everyone's life runs a slightly different course.) These events, as well as many unforeseen events, all have one thing in common: they affect your finances.

In this chapter, I tell you about planning for future events and how tools within Quicken and on Quicken.com can help. I also provide plenty of information about various retirement accounts so you can learn about your options.

Planning for Retirement

Throughout your life, you work and earn money to pay your bills, buy the things you and your family need or want, and help your kids get started with their own lives. But there comes a day when it's time to retire. Those regular paychecks stop coming and you find yourself relying on the money you put away for retirement.

Retirement planning is one of the most important financial planning jobs facing individuals and couples. In this section, I tell you about the importance of planning, and offer some planning steps and a word of advice based on personal experience.

The Importance of Planning

Retired people live on fixed incomes. That's not a problem—*if* the income is fixed high enough to support a comfortable lifestyle. You can help ensure that there's enough money to finance your retirement years by planning and saving now.

Poor retirement planning can lead to catastrophic results—imagine running out of money when you turn 75. Or having to make a lifestyle change when you're 65 just to accommodate a much lower income.

Planning is even more important these days as longevity increases. People are living longer than ever. Your retirement dollars may need to support you for 20 years or more, at a time when the cost of living will likely be much higher than it is today.

With proper planning, it's possible to properly finance your retirement years without putting a strain on your working years. By closely monitoring the status of your retirement funds and periodically adjusting your plan and acting accordingly, your retirement years can be the golden years they're supposed to be.

Planning Steps

Retirement planning is much more than deciding to put $2,000 in an IRA every year. It requires careful consideration of what you have, what you'll need, and how you can make those two numbers the same.

Tip *Quicken's Retirement Calculator and Quicken.com's Retirement Planner, which I discuss later in this chapter, can help you perform many of the calculations you need to come up with a good retirement plan.*

Assess What You Have

Take a good look at your current financial situation. What tax-deferred retirement savings do you already have? A pension? An IRA? Something else? What regular savings do you have? What taxable investments do you have? The numbers you come up with will form the basis of your final retirement funds—like a seed you'll grow.

Be sure to consider property that can be liquidated to contribute to retirement savings. For example, if you currently live in a large home to accommodate your family, you may eventually want to live in a smaller home. The proceeds from the sale of your current home may exceed the cost of your retirement home. Also consider any income-generating property that may continue to generate income in your retirement years or can be liquidated to contribute to retirement savings.

Tip *Your savings, investments, and other assets are part of your net worth. If you use Quicken to track all of your assets, you can use its reporting feature to generate a Net Worth report. I explain how to create reports in Chapter 16.*

Determine What You'll Need

What you'll need depends on many things. One simple calculation suggests you'll need 80 percent of your current gross income to maintain your current lifestyle in your retirement years. You may find a calculation like this handy if retirement is still many years in the future and you don't really know what things will cost.

Time is an important factor in calculating the total amount you should have saved by retirement day. Ask yourself two questions:

- **How long do you have to save?** Take your current age and subtract it from the age at which you plan to retire. That's the number of years you have left to save.

- **How long will you be in retirement?**   Take the age at which you plan to retire and subtract it from the current life expectancy for someone your age and gender. That's the number of years you have to save for.

When I did this math, I learned that I have only 20 years left to save for a 28-year retirement. I'm glad I've been saving!

Develop an Action Plan

Once you know how much you need, it's time to think seriously about how you can save it. This requires putting money away in one or more savings or investment accounts. I tell you about your options a little later in this chapter.

Stick to the Plan!

The most important part of any plan is sticking to it. For example, if you plan to save $5,000 a year, don't think you can just save $2,000 this year and make up the $3,000 next year. There are two reasons: first, you can't "make up" the interest lost on the $3,000 you didn't save this year. Second, you're only kidding yourself if you think you'll manage to put away $8,000 next year.

If you consider deviating from your plan, just think about the alternative: making ends meet with a burger-flipping job in the local fast food joint when you're 68 years old.

Don't Wait! Act Now!

I remember when I first began thinking about retirement. I was 30 or 31 and had been self-employed for about three years. I didn't have a pension or 401(k) plan with my former employer. I didn't have much saved. I only had $2,000 in an IRA. Up until that point, I never worried about retirement. But one day, something just clicked and retirement became something to think about.

I've done a lot of retirement planning and saving since then. While I admit that I don't have a perfect plan (yet), I've certainly come a long way in six years. But when I consider how much more I could have saved if I'd begun five years earlier, I could kick myself for waiting.

See for yourself. Table 13-1 shows how $1,000, $2,000, and $5,000 per year contributions to a tax-deferred retirement account earning 8 percent a year can grow. (These calculations do not take into consideration tax benefits or inflation.)

Savings at Age 62				
Start Age	**Years of Saving**	**$1,000/year**	**$2,000/year**	**$5,000/year**
60	2	$2,080	$4,160	$10,400
55	7	$8,923	$17,846	$44,614
50	12	$18,977	$37,954	$94,886
45	17	$33,750	$67,500	$168,751
40	22	$55,457	$110,914	$277,284
35	27	$87,351	$174,702	$436,754
30	32	$134,214	$268,427	$671,068
25	37	$203,070	$406,141	$1,015,352
20	42	$304,244	$608,487	$1,521,218

Table 13-1 • Your Savings Can Grow Over Time

Retirement Funds

There are many different kinds of retirement funds. In this section, I tell you about the most common: Social Security, pension plans, tax-deferred savings and investments, and other savings and investments.

Social Security

Social Security is the government's way of helping us fund our retirement. If you work, you make mandatory contributions to the Social Security system. When you reach age 62, you can begin to collect benefits in the form of a monthly check. (The minimum age may change in the near future.) You don't have to collect Social Security until you reach the age of 70 1/2; the longer you wait, the more your monthly benefit will be. One thing is relatively certain, however: your monthly benefit will probably not be enough to fund your retirement.

> **Tip**   *You can find out how much you'll get from Social Security when you retire by obtaining a Social Security Statement (formerly called the Personal Earnings and Benefit Estimate Statement or PEBES) from the Social Security Administration. Visit http://www.ssa.gov/ or call 800-772-1213 to request your free copy.*

Pension Plans

Pension plans are among the most common—and most traditional—methods of retirement funding. They reward loyal employees by guaranteeing benefits upon retirement. There are several types of pension plans, including company pension plans and 401(k) and 403(b) plans.

Company Pension Plan

In a company pension plan you and your employer contribute regularly to a pension fund. This is commonly referred to as a *defined benefit plan,* because the final benefit can always be calculated using a formula that usually includes your years of service, final salary, and a fixed percentage rate. Benefits are usually paid monthly starting on your retirement date and continuing for the rest of your life.

Most pension funds are insured by the Pension Benefit Guaranty Corporation (PBGC), a government agency that protects employer-sponsored defined benefit plans. That means the money will be there when you retire.

Company pension plans cannot be transferred from one employer to another. If you leave a job where you had a pension plan, your benefits stay with the plan until you turn 65, when you can start collecting benefits.

401(k) and 403(b) Plans

A 401(k) plan is a tax-deferred investment and savings plan that works like a personal pension fund for employees. It allows a company's employees to save and invest for their own retirement. The employee authorizes a pre-tax payroll deduction that is invested in one of the investment options offered by the plan. Some companies may match the employee's contribution by paying 25 percent to 100 percent into the plan.

There are two tax benefits to a 401(k) plan:

- **Reduction in taxable income**   Because the contribution comes from pre-tax earnings, it reduces the amount of taxable income, thus reducing the employee's income tax.

- **Taxes are deferred until money is withdrawn**   The contributions and earnings grow tax-deferred until withdrawal, when they are taxed as ordinary income. Because funds are normally withdrawn at retirement when the employee is in a lower tax bracket, the tax hit is reduced.

One of the benefits of a 401(k) plan over a company pension plan is portability. If you leave your job, you can take your 401(k) plan's funds to your new employer's plan or roll it over into an IRA.

A 403(b) plan is basically the same as a 401(k) plan, but it is designed for the employees of certain types of tax-exempt organizations.

Tax-Deferred Savings and Investments

You can take advantage of a number of tax-deferred savings and investments if you don't have a pension or want to supplement one. These plans all have one thing in common: they enable you to save money for retirement without paying taxes on interest or investment earnings until they are withdrawn.

IRAs

The most well-known type of tax-deferred savings is an Individual Retirement Account (IRA). An IRA is a tax-deferred investment and savings account that acts as a personal retirement fund for people with employment income. You hear a lot about these accounts around tax time because the government allows you to deduct contributions for many types of IRAs from your taxable income, thus reducing your taxes. Here's a summary of the different types of IRAs currently available:

- **IRA** contributions (up to $2,000) can be deductible or nondeductible. Earnings are tax-deferred until withdrawn after the age of 59 1/2, when they are taxed as ordinary income. There are two types of IRAs: regular and spousal. A regular IRA is designed for an individual, whereas a spousal IRA is designed for married couples in which only one person has employment income.
- **Roth IRA** contributions (up to $2,000) are not tax-deductible. The contributions and earnings, however, can be withdrawn *tax-free* after the age of 59 1/2. The idea is to provide an alternative for people who expect to be in a high tax bracket when they retire. You can contribute to a Roth IRA for as long as you like.

- **SEP-IRA, or Simplified Employee Pension IRA,** is provided by sole proprietors of small businesses to employees (including themselves). The employer can contribute up to 15 percent of the employee's compensation, up to $24,000. The SEP-IRA is subject to the same other rules as an IRA. Employees with SEP-IRAs can also contribute to regular IRAs.
- **SARSEP-IRA, or Salary Reduction SEP-IRA,** is provided by sole proprietors of businesses with fewer than 25 employees. Contributions, which can be made by both employer and employee, are tax-deductible. The SARSEP-IRA is subject to the same other rules as an IRA. New SARSEP-IRA accounts can no longer be started; this type of savings and investment plan has been replaced by the SIMPLE-IRA.
- **SIMPLE-IRA or Savings Incentive Match Plan for Employees-IRA** replaced the SARSEP-IRA in 1997. It's basically the same as the SARSEP-IRA, but can be used by companies with up to 100 employees, and allows maximum contributions of $6,000 for the employee plus the employer share. The SIMPLE-IRA is subject to the same other rules as an IRA. Employees with SIMPLE-IRAs can also contribute to regular IRAs.

Keoghs

A Keogh plan is a tax-deferred retirement plan for self-employed individuals, including sole proprietors who report income on Schedule C, and partners who report income on Schedule E. Contributions and earnings are tax-deferred until withdrawn after the age of 59 1/2. There are two kinds of Keogh plans:

- **Profit-Sharing Keogh** plans allow contributions of up to 13.04 percent of your self-employment income, with a maximum of $30,000. The contribution percentage can be adjusted annually.
- **Money-Purchase Keogh** plans allow contributions of up to 20 percent of your self-employment income, with a maximum of $30,000. The contribution percentage you select must be the same from year to year.

Tax-Deferred Annuities

A tax-deferred annuity enables you to make contributions (that are not tax-deductible) toward an investment for which the earnings are tax-deferred until withdrawal after the age of 59 1/2. Annuities are sponsored by insurance companies and other financial institutions and are commonly available through agents, banks, stockbrokers, and financial planners. There are two types of annuities:

- **Fixed annuities** have a guaranteed rate of return.
- **Variable annuities** have a rate of return that varies based on the performance of the securities in which annuity funds are invested.

Other Savings and Investments

Any type of savings or investment can be used to fund your retirement: stocks, bonds, mutual funds, savings accounts, certificates of deposit, money market accounts, and so on. I tell you about these things in Chapter 8.

Unlike the tax-deferred savings and investments discussed in this chapter, taxable savings and investments can be liquidated or withdrawn and spent at any time. This is a two-edged sword. Although the money will always be available in the event of an emergency, you may find it a tough source of funds to resist when a new car or boat is on your mind. To me, the main benefit of retirement funds is that they're almost untouchable. In my mind, my retirement funds don't even belong to me right now—I'm not tempted to spend them.

You shouldn't overlook the tax benefits of tax-deferred retirement funds, either. Your money will grow more quickly when earnings aren't taxed.

Using Quicken and Quicken.com Planning Tools

Quicken and Quicken.com offer a number of features you can use to help plan for retirement and other major life events. Here's a look at some of the ones I think you'll find most useful.

Quicken's Planning Calculators

Quicken includes two planning calculators that you can use to help yourself save money: the College Calculator and Retirement Calculator. These calculators are very similar in appearance and functionality, but each is designed for a specific purpose.

College Calculator

The College Calculator enables you to calculate savings for the cost of a college education. Choose Activities | Planning Calculators | College. The College Calculator appears:

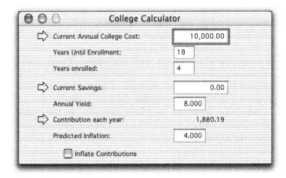

First, click one of the arrows to determine which value Quicken should calculate:

- **Current Annual College Costs** calculates the annual tuition you'll be able to afford based on the values you enter.
- **Current Savings** calculates the amount of money you should currently have saved based on the values you enter.
- **Contribution Each Year** calculates the minimum amount you should contribute to college savings based on the values you enter.

Enter or select values throughout the window. Most options are pretty straightforward and easy to understand. The Inflate Contributions check box tells Quicken to increase your contributions to keep pace with inflation. When you TAB from field to field, Quicken automatically recalculates the result.

Retirement Calculator

The Retirement Calculator can help you calculate some of the numbers you need to plan for your retirement. To open it, choose Activities | Planning Calculators | Retirement. The Retirement Calculator appears, as shown on the following page.

Begin by clicking the arrow for the value you want Quicken to calculate:

- **Current Savings** calculates the amount of money you should currently have saved based on the values you enter.

- **Contribution Each Year** calculates the minimum amount you should contribute to a retirement account based on the values you enter.
- **Retirement Income** calculates the annual amount of retirement income you'll have based on the values you enter.

Enter values and set options throughout the window. Most options are pretty straightforward and easy to understand. Tax and inflation options make complex calculations to account for the effect of taxes and inflation on your savings dollars. As you TAB from field to field, Quicken calculates the result for you.

Quicken.com Resources

The Quicken.com Web site also offers resources for retirement and life events planning. You can access some of them through Quicken's online menu; others can be found in the Retirement channel of Quicken.com.

Retirement Planner

Quicken.com's Retirement Planner (see Figure 13-1) helps you build a complete plan for funding your retirement. It walks you, step by step, through the entry of information about your financial situation, and then provides you with instructions for implementing its plan.

Figure 13-1 • **The Retirement Planner helps you build a complete plan for funding your retirement.**

To get started, choose Online | To The Web | Retirement Planner. Quicken connects to the Internet and displays the Retirement Planner's main information page in a Web browser window. Click the Build Your Plan Now button to start entering information into the planner. It takes about ten minutes to complete.

Retirement Channel

For more retirement planning tools and information, be sure to visit the Retirement channel on Quicken.com (see Figure 13-2). It offers a wealth of information for retirement planning, including investments, pensions, annuities, wills, and estates. To open the Retirement channel's home page, choose Online | To The Web | Quicken.com and then click the Retirement tab near the top of the Quicken.com home page that appears.

Note   *Like everything else on the Internet, the contents of the Quicken.com Web pages can change daily. Don't be surprised if the features you find don't match the ones shown in the figures in this chapter.*

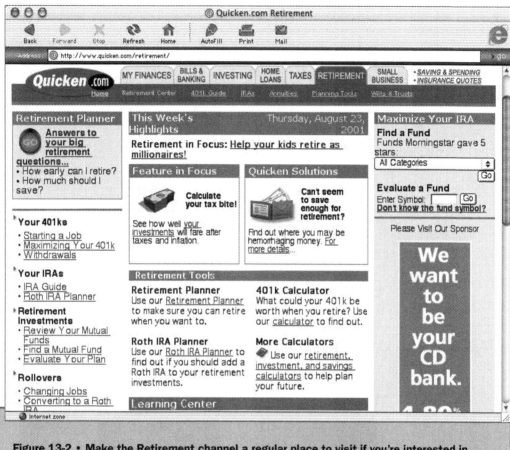

Figure 13-2 • Make the Retirement channel a regular place to visit if you're interested in planning for retirement.

Working with Quicken Data

This part of the book tells you about some of the other things you can do with the information you enter into your Quicken data file. It begins by telling you about time-saving Quicken features for automating data entry, then goes on to explain how to reconcile bank and credit card accounts and create reports and graphs.

The three chapters in this part of the book are:

Chapter 14: Automating Quicken Transactions

Chapter 15: Reconciling Accounts

Chapter 16: Insights, Reports, and Graphs

Automating Quicken Transactions

In this Chapter:

- *QuickFill*

- *Memorized transactions*

- *Bills and scheduled transactions*

- *Quicken's Calendar feature*

- *One Step Update and the PIN Vault*

Quicken includes a number of features to automate the entry of transactions. You got a glimpse of one of them, QuickFill, in Chapter 4. In this chapter, I tell you about QuickFill and the other features you can use to automate transaction entries or remind yourself when a transaction is due. I also tell you about two brand new features in Quicken 2002: One Step Update and the PIN Vault. I'm sure you'll agree that all of these features can make data entry quicker and easier.

Tip   *Before you read this chapter, make sure you have a good understanding of the data entry techniques covered in Chapter 4.*

QuickFill and Memorized Transactions

As you enter transactions, Quicken is quietly working in the background, memorizing information about each one. It creates a database of memorized transactions, organized by payee name. It then uses the memorized transactions for its QuickFill feature.

Note   *By default, Quicken is set up to automatically memorize and use transactions as discussed here. If Quicken does not function as discussed, it's probably because its options have been changed. You can set QuickFill options in the Registers preferences of the Preferences window. I tell you how to set preferences in Appendix B.*

How It Works

QuickFill works in two ways:

- When you enter the first few characters of a payee name in the Write Checks or account register window, Quicken immediately fills in the rest of the name. When you advance to the next text box or field of the entry form, Quicken fills in the rest of the transaction information based on the last transaction for that payee.
- You can select a memorized transaction in the QuickFill Transactions window and click the Use button to create an account register or Write Checks window entry for that transaction.

QuickFill entries include amounts, categories, and memos. They can also include splits and classes. For example, you might pay the cable or satellite company for television service every month. The bill is usually the same amount each month. The second time you create an entry with the company's name, the rest of the transaction is filled in automatically. You can make adjustments to the amount or other information as desired and save the transaction. It may have taken a minute or so to enter the transaction the first time. But it'll take only seconds to enter it every time after that.

Working with the QuickFill Transactions List

You can view a list of memorized transactions by displaying the QuickFill Transactions window. Choose Lists | QuickFill Transactions, or press COMMAND-T to display this window:

You can use buttons at the bottom of the window to use, modify, or delete memorized transactions:

- **Use** creates an entry based on the memorized transaction in the currently open account register or Write Checks window. Modify the entry as desired and click Record to save it.

- **Edit** displays the Edit QuickFill Transaction window for the currently selected transaction. I explain how to use this window later in this chapter.

- **Delete** removes the currently selected transaction. If you delete a memorized transaction, it is removed from the QuickFill Transactions window only—not from any register in the Quicken data file.

Tip   *You may want to periodically delete old QuickFill transactions that you no longer use. This keeps the list manageable and makes it quicker and easier to match memorized transactions when entering a name in an entry's Payee field.*

Editing QuickFill Transactions

Although you can always make minor modifications to the information entered by QuickFill, there are times when you may want to make major changes to an entry and save them as the new memorized transaction. You can do this by editing a QuickFill transaction.

In the QuickFill Transactions window, click to select the entry you want to modify. Then click Edit. The Edit QuickFill Transaction window, which is shown next, appears.

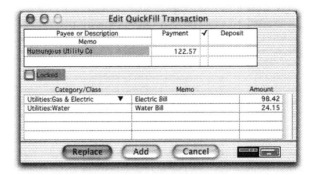

Note   *The appearance of the Edit QuickFill Transaction window will vary based on whether the memorized transaction was entered in an account register or the Write Checks window. The window shown here is for a transaction entered in an account register; the window for transactions entered in the Write Checks window looks just like the Write Checks window. You can use the buttons in the bottom-right corner of the window to switch from one view to the other.*

Modifying Transaction Information

To modify the transaction, make changes as desired in the window's fields. You can make any change to the transaction.

Locking Transaction Information

When you lock a transaction, you prevent it from being changed when it is used as a QuickFill transaction in a register entry. For example, if I locked the transaction in the previous illustration, when I used that transaction to make a payment, I would not be able to change the amounts or categories. In this example, that probably wouldn't be a good idea—utility bills vary from month to month. But if the transaction were for something that's the same every month—such as rent—locking the transaction could prevent it from being changed accidentally.

To lock a transaction, turn on the Locked check box in the Edit QuickFill Transaction window. When you save the transaction, a padlock icon appears before it in the QuickFill Transactions list to indicate that it is locked. You can always edit the transaction again to unlock it if you need to.

Note *Scheduled payment transactions for loans, which I discuss in Chapter 9, are automatically locked and cannot be either edited or deleted.*

Saving Transaction Changes
The Edit QuickFill Transaction window offers two buttons for saving the transaction:

- **Replace** saves your changes to the transaction, replacing the original transaction.
- **Add** saves your changes to the transaction by adding a new transaction to the QuickFill Transactions list. The original transaction—the one you edited—remains unchanged.

Memorizing Transactions
You can manually memorize a transaction, thus adding it to the QuickFill Transactions list. You might find this useful if, for some reason, you have set Register preferences to disable Quicken's ability to automatically add new transactions to the QuickFill list.

Open the register or Write Checks window in which the transaction you want to memorize has been recorded. Then choose Edit | Memorize or press COMMAND-Y. Quicken adds the transaction to the QuickFill Transactions window as a locked transaction. You can edit this transaction like any other QuickFill transaction if desired.

Bills and Scheduled Transactions
Many Quicken users—including me—enter information about their bills and other upcoming transactions into Quicken before they're due or paid. Then, at the time you specify, Quicken automatically enters the transaction into the appropriate account register, prepares a check, or sends an online payment instruction—or reminds you to do it. This ability to schedule transactions for future dates helps you stay on top of your finances and prevents you from forgetting bills or paying them late.

In this part of the chapter, I explain how you can schedule bills and other transactions to be entered into Quicken. I also explain how you can set up recurring transactions so Quicken can automatically enter them for you. Finally, I tell you how you can use various tools within Quicken to keep track of upcoming bills and scheduled transactions.

Entering vs. Scheduling Transactions

Before I explain how to schedule a transaction, let me make a distinction between entering and scheduling a transaction:

- When you *enter* a transaction, the transaction appears in an account register and affects the account's balance. You can enter a transaction into an account register before the transaction actually occurs.

- When you *schedule* a transaction, you enter all of the information about the transaction into Quicken, along with instructions for when and how the transaction is to be entered. The transaction is not actually entered into a register until the date you specify. Transactions must be scheduled for a future date and, in many cases, transactions are scheduled as recurring events. Bills are perfect candidates for scheduled transactions.

This chapter covers scheduling transactions. Entering transactions is discussed in Chapter 4 and elsewhere throughout the book.

Using the Scheduled Transactions List

The best way to keep track of, add, and remove scheduled transactions is with the Scheduled Transactions list. Choose Lists | Scheduled Transactions. The Scheduled Transactions tab of the Upcoming Bills and Scheduled Transactions window appears:

You can use buttons at the bottom of the window to work with transactions:

- **New** displays the Enter Transaction window (shown in the next illustration) so you can create a new scheduled transaction.
- **Edit** displays the Edit Scheduled Transaction window, which looks and works much like the Enter Transaction window, so you can edit the selected scheduled transaction.
- **Delete** enables you to delete the selected scheduled transaction.

Creating a New Scheduled Transaction

To create a new scheduled transaction, click the New button at the bottom of the Scheduled Transactions list. The Enter Transaction window appears, as shown next. It looks a lot like a register entry area, but it also has additional options for scheduling transactions. Use it to enter information about the transaction and click Record.

> **Tip** The payment type icons at the top-right corner of the window enable you to specify whether the transaction should be an online payment, register entry, or Write Checks window entry. The button you click will determine the appearance of the Enter Transaction window. The online payment button is only available if you have online payments enabled for the selected account.

If you want to schedule the transaction as a recurring transaction, choose an option from the pop-up menu in the Scheduling area. Your options are Only Once, Weekly, Every Two Weeks, Twice a Month, Every Four Weeks, Monthly, Last Day of Month, Every Two Months, Quarterly, Twice a Year, and Annually. When you select a frequency option other than Only Once, the Scheduling options in the bottom half of the window can be set.

Scheduling Options   Scheduling options include the duration or the number of payments you want to schedule. For example, if you are scheduling a transaction for monthly payments on a four-year car loan and four payments have already been made, you'd choose Monthly from the Frequency pop-up menu and enter **44** in the Stop After edit box. Selecting Unlimited in this area tells Quicken to continue making payments indefinitely.

Transaction Type   The Type options enable you to specify the type of transaction and include the following:

- **Bill** is for regularly scheduled bills.
- **Deposit** is for deposits to the account.
- **Other** is for other transactions.

Variable Amounts   If the amount of the bill is variable from month to month—as a utility bill might be—turn on the Amount Is Variable check box. This tells Quicken to prompt you for the correct amount before the entry is made.

Notification Options   Notification options are available if the Amount Is Variable check box is turned off. They enable you to specify how you want future transactions recorded.

- **Remind Me About** tells Quicken to remind you to record the transaction. It does this by displaying a dialog when you first launch Quicken on the date the reminder is due.
- **Automatically Enter** tells Quicken to automatically enter the transaction without bothering you about it.
- **Days In Advance** enables you to specify how many days before the transaction date the transaction should be entered (or you should be reminded about it). For example, you might want transactions for checks and other payments to be entered a week in advance so your account balance reflects these items before they're actually paid. This can prevent you from spending money that will be needed for future transactions.

Caution   Remember, scheduling a transaction is not the same as entering or recording it. Choosing the Automatically Enter option from the Future Transactions pop-up menu is a good way to ensure that a scheduled transaction is properly recorded.

Entering and Scheduling a Transaction at the Same Time

Take a closer look at the transaction in the previous illustration. Now imagine today's date is August 24, 2001. According to your instructions the transaction should be automatically entered three days ago, on August 21. What do you think Quicken will do?

Quicken asks you what you want to do by displaying a dialog like the one shown next. (You may recall this dialog from Chapter 9, where it was illustrated but not fully explained.) You have two options:

- **Schedule All Transactions** tells Quicken to enter the first transaction (which is due to be entered per your instructions) and schedule the others. Select this option if you have not already entered the current transaction.

- **Schedule Future Transactions Only** tells Quicken to only schedule the transactions that are not yet due to be recorded. Select this option if you have already entered the current transaction.

When you've selected the desired option, click OK. Quicken enters the transaction and records the scheduled transactions per your instructions.

Entering Scheduled Transactions

When it comes time for a scheduled transaction to be entered, one of two things will happen:

- If the transaction is set to be entered automatically by Quicken, the transaction is simply entered into the appropriate account register on the day it should be entered.

- If the transaction is set to remind you to enter it, when you launch Quicken on the day you should enter the transaction, the Upcoming Bills tab of the Upcoming Bills and Scheduled Transactions window appears as a reminder. I tell you more about this window later in this chapter.

Editing a Scheduled Transaction

How you edit a scheduled transaction depends on whether it has already been entered into Quicken.

Editing a Scheduled Transaction that Has Not Yet Been Entered

If a scheduled transaction has not yet been entered into an account register as a transaction, you can edit it from the Scheduled Transactions list. Select the transaction you want to edit and click Edit. The Edit Scheduled Transactions window, which looks and works much like the Enter Transaction window, appears. Use it to modify transaction information and click Record.

Editing a Scheduled Transaction that Has Already Been Entered

If a scheduled transaction has already been entered into Quicken, you can edit it in the account register in which the transaction appears. Chapter 4 provides the details. If the transaction is an online payment and the payment information has already been sent to your financial institution, you will have to cancel the payment instruction and re-enter the transaction. Chapter 5 explains how.

Bill Tracking

You can see what bills are coming due by checking the Upcoming Bills list. Choose Lists | Bills or press COMMAND-B to display the Upcoming Bills tab of the Upcoming Bills and Scheduled Transactions window. (This window appears automatically as a reminder when you launch Quicken when a scheduled payment is due to be entered.) It might look something like this:

You can use buttons at the bottom of the window to work with transactions:

- **Scan For Bills** uses Quicken's Bill Matching feature to find candidates for scheduling. I tell you more about this feature in a moment.
- **Edit** displays the Edit Scheduled Transaction dialog, which looks and works much like the Enter Transaction dialog, so you can edit the selected transaction.
- **Don't Pay** tells Quicken to skip the scheduled transaction. You will not be reminded again until the next time it's due.
- **Pay Now** tells Quicken to enter the transaction into the appropriate account register. If the amount of the transaction is variable, Quicken displays the Confirm Scheduled Transaction window, which might look something like the one shown next. (The appearance of this window varies depending on whether the transaction was entered in the register window, Write Checks window, or Enter Online Payment window.) Adjust the amount if necessary and click Record to enter the transaction.

Bill Matching

Quicken can automatically prompt you to record a transaction as a recurring bill if it notices that you pay it regularly. This new feature is called Bill Matching and it automates the setup of recurring payments.

Bill Matching in Action

For example, say you pay your electric bill on the first of every month. The third time you enter a transaction to pay your electric bill, Quicken will display a dialog like the one shown next, asking if you want to schedule the transaction as a recurring bill.

There are two options you can set in this dialog:

- **Exclude This Payee From Future Bill Matches** tells Quicken never to display the dialog when you enter a transaction for that payee.
- **Stop Checking For Bills** disables the Bill Matching feature.

You have three options for dismissing the dialog:

- **Cancel** dismisses the dialog and returns you to the transaction.
- **No** dismisses the dialog without creating a new recurring scheduled transaction.
- **Yes** dismisses the dialog and displays the Schedule Future Transaction window, which looks and works just like the Enter Transaction window discussed earlier in this chapter.

Scanning for Bills

The Bill Matching feature can also scan existing transactions to find patterns that indicate regular bill payments. Choose Lists | Bills or press COMMAND-B to display the Upcoming Bills list. Click the Scan For Bills button in the bottom of the window. After a moment, Quicken displays the Bill Candidates window, which might look like this:

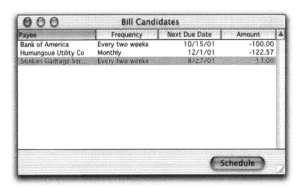

Note *If you upgraded to Quicken 2002 from version 2000 or earlier, you may have seen this feature in action. Quicken automatically scans for bills when you first launch it after upgrading and displays the Bill Candidates window if it finds any possible bills.*

To schedule one of the candidates as a bill, select it and then click the Schedule button. The Schedule Future Transaction window appears, which looks and works just like the Enter Transaction window discussed earlier in this chapter. Use it to fine-tune transaction information and click Record. The transaction is added to the Scheduled Transactions list.

Setting Bill Matching Options

You can customize the way Bill Matching works by setting options in the Missed Bills preferences of the Preferences window. You can enable or disable the Bill Matching feature, specify how far in advance bills should appear in the Upcoming Bills list, and set bill scanning sensitivity options. I tell you how to set these preferences in Appendix B.

Tip *If scanning for bills doesn't turn up any bill candidates, change the sensitivity options in the Missed Bills preferences, then try scanning again.*

Working with the Calendar

Quicken's Calendar feature keeps track of all your transactions by date. It also enables you to schedule one-time or recurring transactions for the future. To open the Calendar, choose Activities | Calendar. The Calendar window, which is shown in Figure 14-1, appears.

Tip *You can easily distinguish between scheduled transactions that have not yet been entered in a register and those that have been entered by their color. Blue transactions have not yet been entered; black transactions have been entered.*

You can create a scheduled transaction from within the Calendar window. Here are three different ways to get started:

- Click the New Transaction button in the bottom of the Calendar window.
- Choose Edit | New Transaction or press COMMAND-N.
- Double-click a date to open its Transactions window. Then click New.

Figure 14-1 • Use the Calendar window to see and schedule transactions by day.

No matter which method you choose, the Enter Transaction window or Schedule Future Transaction window, which I discussed earlier in this chapter, appears. Use it to enter information about the transaction and click Record.

Changing the Month Display

You can change which month is displayed by clicking buttons and using pop-up menus in the Calendar window's heading area:

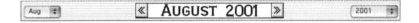

Changing the Transaction Display

The two Show Transactions For options near the bottom of the window enable you to specify which transactions are displayed on the calendar:

- **All Accounts** displays transactions for all Quicken accounts.

- **Selected Accounts** displays the Select Accounts dialog, shown next. Click to toggle the check marks beside the account names; when a check mark appears, the account will be included in the Calendar. When you've finished, click OK.

Working with Calendar Notes

You can add a note to any Calendar date. Click the date to select it, and then click the Add Note button at the bottom of the Calendar window. A Note window like the one shown next appears. Enter note text and click the window's Close box to save it.

To view the contents of a note, double-click the note icon in the Calendar window. A Note window like the one previously illustrated appears. You can modify the note's contents if desired. Click its Close box to hide it from view.

To delete a note, click to select the date on which the note's icon appears. Then click the Delete Note button in the bottom of the Calendar window—it appears in place of the Add Note button. The note is removed.

Viewing Transactions

When you double-click a calendar date, a window listing all the transactions for that date appears, as shown next. You can use buttons at the bottom of the window to work with transactions:

- **New** displays the Enter Transaction window so you can create a new transaction. I explain how to use this window a little later in this chapter.
- **Edit** displays the Edit Transaction window so you can modify the currently selected transaction. The Edit Transaction window looks and works very much like the Enter Transaction window, which I discuss later in this chapter.
- **Delete** removes the selected transaction.
- **Register** opens the account register for the selected transaction.
- **Pay Now** processes or records the selected transaction immediately. This option is only available for transactions that have not yet been processed.

One Step Update and the PIN Vault

If you take full advantage of the online features covered in Chapters 5 and 7, you may find yourself using a variety of dialogs to enter PINs and exchange information with multiple financial institutions and Quicken.com. Two new Quicken features—One Step Update and the PIN Vault—can make exchanging online information quicker and easier. This section explains how.

Using One Step Update

The idea behind One Step Update is to use one command to handle multiple online activities. This eliminates the need to exchange information via multiple dialogs throughout Quicken. One command and dialog does it all.

Setting Up the Update

Choose Online | One Step Update or click the One Step button near the top of the Banking tab. The One Step Update dialog, which is shown next, appears. It lists all of the activities you can perform online.

Click in the ✔ column to display check marks to the left of the activities you would like to perform. Then, to display an edit box for the activities requiring a PIN, click in the PIN/Password column where the gray text *<enter PIN>* appears. Enter the PIN for that account in the edit box. Repeat this process until all required PINs have been entered.

Tip   *You can use the PIN Vault to enter PINs automatically for you. I explain how later in this chapter.*

Updating Information

In the One Step Update dialog, click Update Now. Quicken connects to the Internet and exchanges information with your financial institution and/or Quicken.com per your instructions. It displays a Connection Status dialog while it works. When it's finished, it displays the One Step Update Summary window, which might look something like this:

Click OK to dismiss the window. You can then use the Download Transactions or the Download Investment Transactions window to review transactions downloaded from your financial institution, as discussed in Chapters 5 and 7.

The PIN Vault

You might find it a nuisance to have to type in each PIN when you use the One Step Update feature. This is when the PIN Vault can help.

Quicken's new PIN Vault feature enables you to store all your Quicken PINs in one central location. The PINs are then protected with a single password. When you use One Step Update, you enter just one password to access all financial institutions.

Setting Up the PIN Vault

Choose Online | PIN Vault to display the Establish PIN Vault Password dialog, shown next. Enter the same password in each edit box and click OK.

Tip   *Your password must be at least six characters long. For added security, consider including at least one number or punctuation.*

The PIN Vault dialog appears. When you first set up the PIN Vault, it's empty, as shown next. Click Add.

The Add PIN dialog, shown next, appears. Choose a financial institution from the Account pop-up menu. Then enter that financial institution's PIN twice in the two edit boxes. To display the PIN as characters instead of bullets, turn on the Show PINs In Clear Text check box, then click OK.

Back in the PIN Vault dialog, the PIN you added appears in the list:

You can use buttons along the bottom of the PIN Vault dialog to further modify the PIN Vault's contents:

- **Remove All** removes all PINs from the PIN Vault.
- **Remove** removes the currently selected PIN from the PIN Vault.
- **Edit** enables you to change the currently selected PIN.
- **Add**, as discussed earlier, enables you to add a PIN to the PIN Vault.

When you're finished working with PINs, you can click the PIN Vault dialog's Close button to dismiss it.

Using the PIN Vault

Using the PIN Vault is easy. Simply choose Online | One Step Update or click the One Step button near the top of the Banking tab. The Enter PIN Vault Password dialog, shown next, appears. Enter your PIN Vault password in the edit box and click OK.

The One Step Update dialog appears. Your PINs are automatically entered in the PIN/Password column:

Disabling the PIN Vault

You can turn off the PIN Vault by setting an option in the Preferences dialog. Choose Quicken 2002 Deluxe | Preferences (Mac OS X) or Edit | Preferences (Mac OS 9). Then click the Passwords option on the left side of the Preferences dialog, which is shown next. Turn off the Use PIN Vault For PINs check box and click OK.

Changing the PIN Vault Password

You can also use the Preferences dialog to change the PIN Vault's password. Choose
Quicken 2002 Deluxe | Preferences (Mac OS X) or Edit | Preferences (Mac OS 9)
to display the Preferences dialog. Click the Passwords option on the left side of the
dialog (refer to the previous illustration) and then click the topmost Password
button. Use the Enter PIN Vault Password dialog, which was illustrated earlier, to
enter your current PIN Vault password and click OK. Then use the Change PIN
Vault Password dialog, which is shown next, to enter your current password once
and your new password twice. When you click OK, your PIN Vault password is
changed.

Reconciling Accounts

In this Chapter:

- *The importance of reconciling accounts*

- *Starting a reconciliation*

- *Comparing transactions*

- *Making adjustments*

- *Using Auto-Reconcile*

- *Recording a credit card payment*

Chapter 15

One of the least pleasant tasks of manually maintaining a bank account is balancing or reconciling it monthly. If you're good about it, you faithfully turn over your bank statement each month and use the form your bank provides to balance the account. There's a lot of adding when it comes to totaling the outstanding checks and deposits, and the longer you wait to do the job, the more adding there is. And for some reason, it hardly ever comes out right the first time you try. Maybe you've even failed so many times that you've given up. I know someone who opens a new checking account once a year just so she can start fresh after 12 months of not being able to balance her account. That's *not* something I recommend.

In this chapter, I explain why you should reconcile your bank statements and how you can do it quickly and easily with Quicken.

The Importance of Reconciling Accounts

Reconciling your checking account is very important. It enables you to locate differences between what you think you have in the account and what the bank says you have. It can help you track down bank errors (which do happen once in a while) or personal errors (which, unfortunately, seem to happen more frequently). Completely balancing your checking account and making adjustments as necessary can prevent you from accidentally bouncing checks when you think you have more money than you really do. That can save you the cost of bank fees and a lot of embarrassment.

If you keep track of all bank account activity with Quicken, reconciling your bank accounts is easy. You don't need to use the form on the back of the bank statement. You don't even need a calculator. Just use Quicken's reconciliation feature to enter beginning and ending bank balances, check off cleared transactions, and enter the transactions you missed. You'll find you're successful a lot more often with Quicken helping you out.

Tip   *You can use Quicken's reconciliation feature to balance any Quicken banking account, including credit card accounts. Although this chapter concentrates on checking accounts, I provide additional information for reconciling credit card accounts, too.*

Reconciling an Account

Reconciling an account refers to the process of comparing transactions in your account register to transactions recorded by your bank. Transactions that match are simply checked off. Transactions that appear only in one place—your account register or the bank's records—need to be accounted for.

Normally, you reconcile an account by comparing register transactions to the paper bank statement mailed to you each month by your bank or credit card company. But if Online Account Access is enabled for your bank or credit card account, you can use Quicken 2002's new Auto-Reconcile feature to automatically reconcile the account for you.

In this section, I explain how to reconcile accounts manually and automatically with Quicken.

> **Note** Although these instructions may refer to "bank" accounts, they work for credit card accounts, too.

Manually Reconciling an Account

To manually reconcile a bank account, you must have the paper statement for the account. Bank statements usually come monthly, so you won't have to wait long.

Getting Started

With statement in hand, open the account register for the account you want to reconcile. Then click the Reconcile button at the top of the Banking tab or choose Activities | Reconcile. The Reconcile Startup window, which gathers basic statement information prior to reconciling the account, appears. Here's what it might look like completely filled in with statement information:

Note *The bottom part of the Reconcile Startup window will be empty if the account is enabled for Online Account Access. You will not have to enter bank service charges or interest manually because that information is downloaded with the rest of your transaction information. Instead, the date and amount of the last downloaded balance will appear.*

Enter balance, service charge, and interest earned information in the appropriate edit boxes—you can get all of this information from your bank statement. Then click Start to continue.

Comparing Transactions

The next step to reconciling the account is to compare transactions that have cleared on the statement with transactions in your account register. For this, Quicken displays the Reconcile window (shown in Figure 15-1), which displays all payments, checks, and deposits.

Your job is to check off the items in the window that also appear on your bank statement. While you're checking off items, be sure to check off the same items with a pen or pencil on your bank statement. Here are some of the differences you might encounter:

- An item that appears on the bank statement but not in your account register is an item that you did not enter. There are a number of reasons why you may have omitted the transaction. Perhaps it was a bank adjustment you were not informed about. Or maybe you simply forgot. In Figure 15-1, the $50 difference between the Cleared Balance and the Statement Ending Balance is due to the failure to enter an ATM transaction—something many of us forget to do! To enter an omitted transaction, click the New Transaction button to switch to the register window. Enter the transaction in the register and click Record. Then switch back to the Reconcile window and click to place a check mark in the Clr column beside the item to mark it cleared.

- An item that appears on both your account register and bank statement but has a different amount or date could be due to an error—yours or the bank's. If the error is yours, you can edit the transaction by double-clicking it in the Reconcile window. This displays the account register window with the transaction selected. Edit the transaction and click Record. Then switch back to the Reconcile window to continue the reconciliation.

- Items that appear in your account register but not on the bank statement are items that have not cleared the bank yet. These are usually transactions prepared just before the bank's closing date, but they can be older. Do not check them off. Chances are, you'll check them off the next time you complete a reconciliation.

Tip   *If, during a bank reconciliation, you discover any uncleared items that are older than two or three months, you should investigate why they have not cleared the bank. You may discover that a check (or worse yet, a deposit) was lost in transit.*

Finishing Up

When you reconcile a bank account with Quicken, your goal is to make the difference between the Cleared Balance and the Statement Ending Balance zero. You can monitor this progress at the bottom of the Reconcile window, as shown in Figure 15-1.

When the Difference Is Zero   If you correctly checked off all bank statement items and the difference is zero, you've successfully reconciled the account. Congratulations! Click the Finish button.

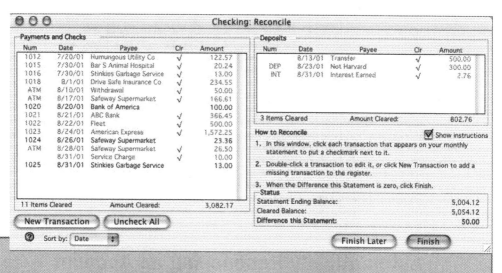

Figure 15-1 • Use the Reconcile window to compare your register transactions to your bank statement transactions.

If You Can't Get the Difference to Zero   Sometimes, try as you might, you just can't get the difference to zero. Here are a few last things to check before you give up:

- Make sure all the amounts you checked off in your account register are the same as the amounts on the bank statement.
- Make sure you included any bank charges or earned interest.
- Make sure the beginning and ending balances you entered are the same as those on the bank statement.

Creating an Adjusting Entry   If you checked and rechecked the reconciliation and still can't get the difference to zero, click Finish. Quicken displays a dialog like the one shown next that indicates the amount of the difference and offers to make an adjustment to your account register for the amount. Click Adjust Register to enter the adjustment. But next month, don't give up!

Tip   *If you mess up a reconciliation and don't realize it until after you have already clicked the Finish button to complete it, you can re-reconcile it. Simply follow the instructions earlier in this chapter to open the Reconcile Startup window and enter the beginning and ending dates and balances for the period you want to re-reconcile. Quicken will offer you a chance to re-reconcile the account. Or choose Activities | Prior Statements to display a dialog listing all of your reconciled bank statements, select the statement you want to re-reconcile, and click Reconcile Again.*

Automatically Reconciling an Account

Quicken's new Auto-Reconcile feature can automatically reconcile your online-enabled accounts to transactions and balances downloaded from your financial institution every time you review downloaded transactions. Here's how it works.

Note   *You may already have been introduced to the Auto-Reconcile feature. The first time you successfully reconcile an online-enabled account, Quicken displays a dialog offering to open the Preferences dialog so you can enable and configure the Auto-Reconcile feature.*

Enabling Auto-Reconcile

To use the Auto-Reconcile feature, you must enable it. You do this in the Preferences dialog. Choose Quicken 2002 Deluxe | Preferences (Mac OS X) or Edit | Preferences (Mac OS 9) to display the Preferences dialog. In the scrolling list on the left side, click Auto-Reconcile. The options should look like this:

Turn on the Enable Auto-reconcile check box. Then choose an account you want to automatically reconcile from the pop-up menu and set options for it:

- **Auto-Reconcile Without Reminding Me** tells Quicken to automatically reconcile the account without displaying a reminder or prompt.

- **I Reconcile My Online Account** enables you to select when you reconcile your online account. If you select the When I Receive My Paper Statement option, be sure to enter the day of the month you usually receive your account statement in the mail.

You can set options in this dialog for each online-enabled account you have set up in Quicken. Simply select a new account from the pop-up menu and click Save in the dialog that appears. When you're finished, click OK to close the Preferences dialog.

Using Auto-Reconcile

After you set up Quicken's Auto-Reconcile feature, just download and accept transactions as usual, following the instructions in Chapter 5. A dialog should appear if one of the following conditions is met:

- You set up Quicken to Auto-Reconcile every time you download, and the Auto-Reconcile Without Reminding Me check box in the Preferences dialog shown earlier is turned off.
- You set up Quicken to Auto-Reconcile when your statement arrives and the statement date has passed.

If the Reconciliation Is Successful   A dialog like the one shown next will appear. Click Auto-Reconcile to complete the reconciliation.

Note   *If you turned on the Auto-Reconcile Without Reminding Me check box in the Preferences dialog, Quicken will automatically mark all transactions as reconciled without displaying this dialog.*

If the Reconciliation Is Not Successful   A dialog like the next one will appear. Click one of the three buttons to dismiss it:

- **Skip** dismisses the dialog without completing the reconciliation.
- **Adjust** completes the reconciliation with an adjusting entry to make the balances match.
- **Reconcile** enables you to manually reconcile the account. Follow the instructions at the beginning of the chapter to complete a manual reconciliation.

Identifying Reconciled Items

As shown next, Quicken uses the Clr column in an account register to identify items that have either cleared the bank or have been reconciled:

- A *C* indicates that the item has cleared the bank. You'll see a *C* in the Clr column beside items that you have checked off during a reconciliation if you have not completed the reconciliation. You'll also see a *C* beside items downloaded and accepted using Quicken's Online Account Access and Web Connect features, which I discuss in Chapter 5.
- A bold *R* indicates that the item has been reconciled.

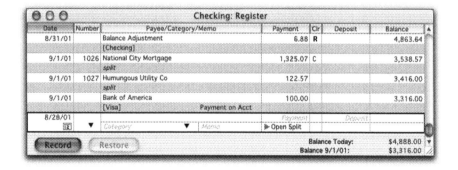

Caution   *To prevent errors in your account registers, do not edit transactions that have been reconciled.*

Insights, Reports, and Graphs

In this Chapter:

- *Quicken Insights*

- *Customizing the Insights window*

- *Creating reports and graphs*

- *Customizing reports and graphs*

- *Printing reports, graphs, and Quicken windows*

At this point, you'll probably agree that entering financial information into Quicken is a great way to organize it. But sometimes organizing information isn't enough. Sometimes you need to see concise summaries of the information you entered, in the form of balances, activity reports, and graphs.

Quicken's Insights window, reports, and graphs are three highly customizable features you can use to view and analyze your financial information. As you'll see in this chapter, they quickly and easily provide the information you need about your accounts and categories.

Quicken Insights

Quicken's Insights window provides "snapshots" of your financial information, complete with balances and graphs. It also provides useful links for accessing Quicken features and, if you have Internet access, Web pages on Quicken.com and other Internet destinations.

To open the Insights window, choose Activities | Insights or click the Insights button near the top of any tab. You'll see a window similar to the one in Figure 16-1.

Overview of the Insights Window

The Insights window combines three elements—snapshots, observations, and actions—to provide you with a centralized place for getting financial information and working with it. Here's an overview of each of these elements.

Snapshots

A *snapshot* is an up-to-the-minute view of information in your Quicken data file. Some snapshots are text-based lists, while others are charts or graphs. By default, the Insights window offers five different snapshots, each of which is illustrated in Figure 16-1.

- **Accounts** displays a list of your accounts and their balances. You can click an account's name to open its register.
- **Scheduled Transactions** lists upcoming scheduled transactions.
- **Watch List** displays the securities on your Watch List, along with their most recently entered or downloaded prices. You can click a security name to open its Security Detail window.

- **Expenses** displays a pie chart of your largest expense items for the year to date. A legend beside the chart identifies the colored slices and provides percentage information.
- **Loan Summary** lists all of your loans and provides information about the balance, rate, principal and interest paid, and number of remaining payments. You can click the name of a loan account to open its register.

Figure 16-1 • The Insights window provides information about your finances.

A number of other snapshots are available and can be added to the Insights window:

- **Bill Status** lists your overdue, due, and upcoming bills, as well as deposits and other scheduled transactions.
- **Budgets** provides information about items you have budgeted within Quicken, including the category name, budgeted and actual amounts, and the difference for the current month.
- **Credit Card Analysis** lists your credit card accounts, their balances, and your credit limits. It also displays the total amount charged on each card for the current year to date.
- **Income** lists your income categories, along with the year-to-date amounts earned.
- **Income vs. Expenses** shows a column chart of income and expenses for the year, with a pair of columns for each month.
- **Investment Accounts** displays a list of all of your investment accounts, along with their balances. You can click an account name to open its register.
- **Investment Returns** displays a column chart of your year-to-date returns, organized by investment.
- **Net Worth Graph** displays a column chart showing your assets and liabilities, on a month-by-month basis, for the current year. An overlaid line graph shows the change in your net worth.

Observations

Observations are notable pieces of information about the data in a snapshot. For example, the Observations area in the Credit Card Analysis snapshot may inform you about the total amount of interest paid to credit card companies or that one of your credit cards is getting close to its limit. These tidbits can provide valuable analysis of your financial records.

Actions

Actions are clickable links to other Quicken tasks or features related to a snapshot. For example, the Investment Accounts snapshot includes actions to add an investment, get online quotes, or view your full portfolio. Some Actions areas also include links to customize a snapshot; I tell you more about that a little later in this chapter.

Customizing the Insights Window

There are several ways to customize the Insights window: by adding, removing, or rearranging snapshots or by customizing individual snapshots.

> **Tip**   By customizing the Insights window to show the information that interests you most—in the way you want to see it—you can make it a useful analysis tool.

Adding and Removing Snapshots

In the Insights window, click the Customize button. The Customize Insights dialog appears:

Make changes as desired:

- To add an item to the Insights window, select it in the Available Items list and click Add. Its name appears in the Selected Items list.
- To remove an item from the Insights window, select it in the Selected Items list and click Remove.
- To rearrange the order of items in the Selected Items list, select an item and click the Move Up or Move Down button.

When you've finished making changes, click Done. The Insights window is redrawn to reflect your changes.

Customizing a Snapshot

Some snapshots can be customized to change the content or display. Customization options, when available, vary from one snapshot to another.

For example, you can customize the Expenses snapshot's Pie Chart by clicking the Customize This graph link in the Actions area beneath it. A dialog like the one shown next appears, enabling you to set options for the chart. Make changes as desired and click OK. Your changes take effect immediately. If you don't like what you see, don't worry. You can always customize it again.

Note *I tell you more about customizing reports and graphs in the second half of this chapter.*

Reports and Graphs

Quicken offers a variety of reports and graphs, each of which can be customized to meet your needs. I like to think of reports and graphs as the "fruits of my labor." I spend time entering data into Quicken so Quicken can crunch the numbers and create reports and graphs. I can use these documents to analyze my spending habits, find ways to save money, and submit to financial institutions when I apply for loans.

Here's a real-life example. Recently, I applied by phone for a home equity line of credit. The bank representative asked a lot of questions about my finances, including balances on my accounts and the market value of my investments. Because I track all my finances in Quicken, all the information I needed was right in front of me, in Quicken windows and reports that I could generate within seconds. The application process took less than 15 minutes and I got a preliminary approval right away.

In this section, I tell you about the types of reports and graphs Quicken offers. I also explain how you can create, customize, and print a report or graph based on the financial information in your Quicken data file.

Types of Reports and Graphs

Quicken offers essentially four kinds of reports and graphs: EasyAnswer, predefined, customized, and memorized. Here's an overview of each one.

EasyAnswer

EasyAnswer reports and graphs answer specific, predefined questions such as:

- How much did I spend during the period …?
- Where did I spend my money during the period …?
- How much did I spend during the period … compared to the period …?
- Did I meet my budget during the period …?
- What am I worth as of …?
- What are my investments worth as of …?
- How did my investment in … do in the period …?

You select a question and then provide information such as a date range, category, or account. Quicken gathers the information and generates the report or graph.

Predefined

Quicken includes a number of predefined reports and graphs. The reports are organized by topic:

- **Standard** reports include reports for your budget, categories, net worth, and taxes. Standard graphs include all categories of graphs: personal, business, and investment.
- **Business** includes reports of use to a small business owner, including accounts payable, accounts receivable, balance sheet, and income statement.
- **Investment** includes reports for capital gains, investment income, investment transactions, and investment performance.

Custom

You can create custom reports and graphs by customizing the predefined reports and graphs. This multiplies your reporting capabilities, enabling you to create reports or graphs that show exactly what you need to show.

Memorized

Memorized reports are reports you have created and customized, and then memorized to use again and again. This makes it possible to prepare frequently needed, custom reports or graphs quickly with just a few clicks of your mouse.

Creating Reports and Graphs

With Quicken, creating a report or graph is as simple as clicking a few buttons. There are several techniques: using the Reports and Graphs windows, using Shortcut commands in an account register, and clicking links in the Insights window. In this section, I explain how to use all of these techniques.

Using the Reports and Graphs Windows

The most obvious way to create a report or graph is with the Reports or Graphs window.

- To open the Reports window, choose Activities | Reports & Graphs | Report or click the Reports button near the top of the Reporting tab. It should look something like this:

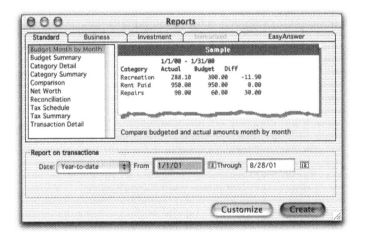

- To open the Graphs window, choose Activities | Reports & Graphs | Graphs or click the Graphs button near the top of the Reporting tab. Here's what it looks like:

To create a report or graph, begin by clicking the tab under which it is listed at the top of the Reports or Graphs window. Then click the name of the report or graph to select it and enter options in the settings area at the bottom of the window. Finally, click Create to display the report or graph. Figures 16-2 and 16-3 show examples.

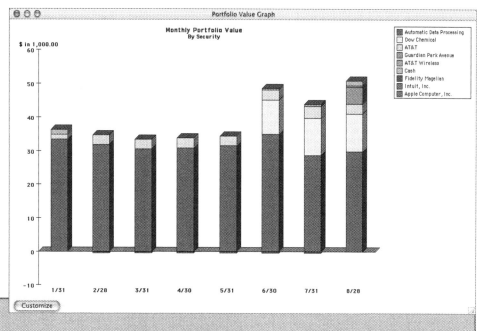

Figure 16-2 • A year-to-date Portfolio Value graph

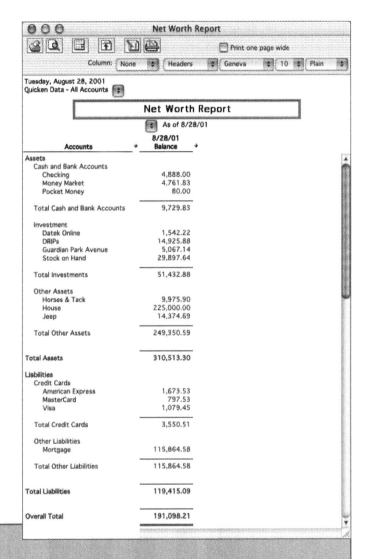

Figure 16-3 • A Net Worth report as of the current date

Note The Memorized tab in the Reports and Graphs windows is gray until you have memorized at least one report or graph.

Tip In many instances, you can double-click on part of a graph to get a new, detailed view of that part of the graph.

Using Shortcuts Commands in Register Windows

You can often use a contextual menu for the active entry in an account register to generate Transaction Detail Shortcut reports for the payee or category of the current entry. Simply hold down CONTROL while clicking on the active transaction to display the menu, as shown below. Then choose the report option you want:

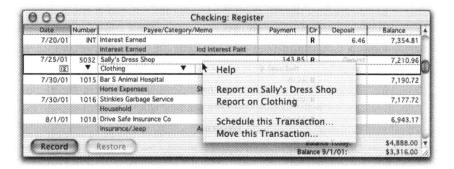

- **Report On *Payee Name*** generates a listing of year-to-date transactions for the payee or description in the entry.
- **Report On *Category Name*** generates a listing of year-to-date transactions for the category in the entry.

Clicking Links in the Insights Window

The Actions areas within the Insights window (refer to Figure 16-1) often includes clickable links for creating reports. For example, you can generate a Return on Investment report for your portfolio by clicking a link in the Actions area of the WatchList snapshot.

Customizing Reports and Graphs

You can customize just about any report or graph you create so it shows only the information you want to display. When you can customize it, however, depends on how you create it:

- When you create a report or graph using the Reports or Graphs window, you can customize it before or after you create it.
- When you create a report using Shortcuts menu options or links in the Insights window, you can only customize it after you create it.

Customization options vary from one type of report or graph to another. It's impossible to cover all variables in this chapter. I will, however, tell you about the most common options so you know what to expect. I'm sure you'll agree that Quicken's reporting feature is very flexible when you go beyond the basics.

Using the Customize Report Window

To customize a report, click the Customize button at the bottom of the Reports window (shown earlier in this chapter) or the Customize button in the report window (see Figure 16-2). The Customize Report window appears. Here's what it looks like for a Net Worth report:

The Customize Report window normally includes three tabs of options that you can set to customize the report:

- **Layout** (shown in the previous illustration) enables you to set display options for the report, such as the title, report dates, and row and column headings.

- **Content** enables you to select the transactions that should appear in the report based on entry fields such as accounts, categories, classes, payees and descriptions, memos, check numbers, and amounts. You can also specify whether Quicken should include uncleared items, cleared items, reconciled items, payments, deposits, and unprinted checks. This is a powerful feature for creating reports because of the amount of flexibility it offers; you can specify virtually any combination of options to report exactly what you need to see.

- **Organization** enables you to specify how transactions should be organized and whether account transfers should be included.

Once you have set options as desired, click OK. Quicken creates the report to your specifications. If it isn't exactly what you want, that's okay. Just click the Customize button in the report window and change settings in the Customize Report window to fine-tune the report. You can repeat this process until the report is exactly the way you want it.

Using the Customize Graph Window

To customize a graph, click the Customize button in the Graphs window or, when available, in the graph window itself. The Customize Graph window appears. Here's what it looks like for a Portfolio Value graph:

The window has two tabs for setting options:

- **Layout** (shown in the previous illustration) enables you to specify a graph title, dates, and organization.
- **Content** enables you to select the transactions that should appear in the graph based on entry fields such as accounts, categories, classes, and securities.

When you've finished setting options, click OK. Quicken creates the graph to your specifications. If it isn't exactly what you want, repeat the process to fine-tune the graph until it is the way you want it.

Using Customization Options in the Report Window

The top of the report window offers a number of buttons and pop-up menus for working with the report:

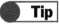 **Note** *The options that appear at the top of the report window can vary based on the report displayed, so don't expect every report to offer the same options shown here and in Figure 16-3.*

The buttons along the top of the window offer a number of options:

- **Print Report** displays the Print dialog so you can print the report. I tell you more about printing reports later in this chapter.
- **Print Preview Report** displays a preview of the report, the way it will appear when printed.
- **Add Page Break** inserts a page break above the currently selected report line. A page break appears as a dashed line across the report. Once a page break has been inserted, you can remove it by selecting the line immediately below it and clicking this button again.
- **Collapse Header** hides all report lines above the column headings. Once they are hidden, you can display them by clicking this button again.
- **Edit Columns** displays a dialog like the one shown next, which lists the report columns. Click to toggle check marks beside columns to show or hide them. When you've finished, click OK. The report changes immediately.

- **Customize** displays the Customize Report window, which you can use to set a variety of options for the report. I show and discuss the Customize Report window earlier in this chapter.

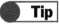 **Tip** *If you point to a button, a tiny box with the button's name appears to identify it.*

You can also use pop-up menus near the top of the report window to change the rows and columns and font formatting of a report. Simply choose options from the menus; the report changes a moment later.

Tip   *Pop-up menus within the report itself enable you to change more report options, such as report dates, accounts, and categories. The options that are offered vary from one report type to another. Don't be afraid to experiment. You can always recreate the report if you need to.*

Dragging Column Borders

You can change the width of columns on some reports by dragging the column markers. Column markers, when available, look like three-dimensional diamonds between column headings in the report window. Move the mouse pointer onto a column marker and a pair of vertical lines with two arrows appears. Press the mouse button down and drag to the right or left. When you release the mouse button, the column's width changes.

Setting Report and Graph Preferences

You can use the Preferences window to change the default settings for Reports and Graphs. Choose Quicken 2002 Deluxe | Preferences (Mac OS X) or Edit | Preferences (Mac OS 9) to display the Preferences window. Then click Reports or Graphs in the scrolling list of preference categories on the left side of the window to display appropriate preference options. I discuss these options in detail in Appendix B; consult that appendix if you need more information.

Memorizing Reports and Graphs

Often, you'll create a predefined report and customize it to create a report you want to be able to see again and again. Rather than creating and customizing the report from scratch each time you want to see it, you can memorize its settings. Then, when you want to view the report again, just select it from a list and it appears. You can do the same for graphs.

Memorizing a Report or Graph

To memorize a report or graph, start by creating and customizing one. When it looks just the way you want it, choose Edit | Memorize or press COMMAND-Y. The

Memorize Report Template dialog (shown next) or Memorize Graph Template
dialog (which looks the same) appears.

Enter a name and description for the report or graph in the appropriate edit
boxes. Then toggle the Use Current Date check box on or off as desired. With the
check box turned on, the report or graph always shows the date it is created. With
the check box turned off, Quicken uses the currently selected date option (today's
date) each time it displays the report or graph. When you've finished setting
options, click the Memorize button to memorize the report or graph.

Tip   *If you make changes to a report or graph and then close it without
memorizing it, Quicken may ask if you want to memorize it. If you click Yes, Quicken
displays the Memorize Report template so you can memorize it.*

Viewing a Memorized Report or Graph

When you memorize a report or graph, it appears in the Memorized tab of the
Reports or Graphs window. The next illustration shows what the tab might look
like with a few memorized reports. Select the report or graph you want and click
Create to display it.

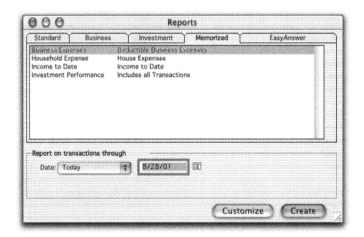

Printing Reports, Graphs, and Quicken Windows

You can print reports and graphs. This enables you to create hard copies for your paper files or for use when applying for loans or completing your tax returns. You can also print the contents of many Quicken windows to create simple reports of lists and register entries.

Note   *Before previewing or printing a report, make sure your computer is properly set up for printing. Consult the documentation that came with Mac OS or your printer for assistance if necessary.*

Tip   *When I applied for my mortgage, I was able to create and print all kinds of useful reports to include with my mortgage application forms. I don't know if it helped me get the mortgage, but it saved the time I would have spent manually duplicating needed information.*

Previewing a Report

Before you print a report, you may want to preview it to make sure it looks the way you want it to. This can save time and paper if the report isn't just right the first time you're ready to print it.

To preview a report, click Print Preview Report at the top of the report window (see Figure 16-3) or choose File | Print Preview Report. A preview window like the one in Figure 16-4 appears. Use it to see what the report will look like when you print it.

Printing a Report or Graph

To print a report or graph, choose File | Print Report or File | Print Graph, click the Print Report button at the top of the report window (see Figure 16-3), or click the Print button in the print preview window (see Figure 16-4). The Print dialog appears. Here's what it looks like for a laser printer; it may look different for your printer.

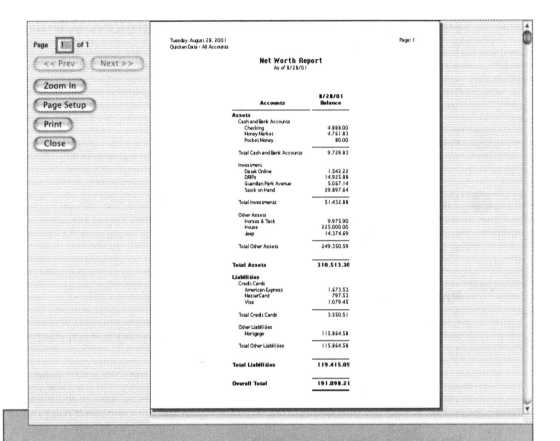

Figure 16-4 • Use a report preview window to see what a report will look like when printed.

The printing options that appear in the Print dialog within Quicken are the same as the options available in any other program, so they should be familiar to you. Set options as desired and click Print to print the report or graph.

Printing a Quicken Window

You can print the contents of many Quicken windows. Simply open the window you want to print and choose the appropriate Print command from the File menu. For example, if a register window is open, you'd choose File | Print Register to print it. If the Categories & Transfers window is open, you'd choose File | Print Categories & Transfers. The same Print dialog discussed previously appears. Set options as desired and click Print to print the window's contents.

Appendices

Managing Quicken Files

In this Appendix:

- *Creating data files*

- *Backing up and restoring data files*

- *Importing and exporting data*

- *Other file management tasks*

- *Password-protecting Quicken data*

- *Updating Quicken*

Appendix A

All the data you enter in Quicken is stored in a Quicken data file. This file includes all account and category setup information, transactions, and other data you have entered into Quicken.

Commands under Quicken's File menu enable you to perform a number of file management tasks, including creating, backing up, restoring, importing, exporting, and copying data files. In this appendix, I cover all of these tasks and explain how you can use an Internet connection to update Quicken.

Creating a Quicken Data File

Chances are, you won't need more than one Quicken data file—the one that's created as part of the New User Setup process covered in Chapter 2. But just in case you do, here's how you can create another one.

Creating the File

Start by choosing File | New File. A dialog appears, asking if you're sure you want to create a new file. Click OK. Quicken then displays the Save: Quicken Deluxe 2002 dialog illustrated next:

Enter a name for the data file in the Save As edit box and turn on the check boxes for the types of Quicken categories you want to use. You can also change the folder location for the file, but it's easier to find and back up the data file if it's in the Quicken 2002 Deluxe folder or your Documents folder. Click Save to create the file.

Quicken then displays the Set Up Account dialog, which you can use to create an account. I explain how to use this dialog to create accounts in Chapter 2. When the account has been created, you can begin working with the new Quicken data file.

Working with Multiple Files

Here are a few things to keep in mind if you have more than one Quicken data file:

- Only one Quicken data file can be opened at a time.
- When you launch Quicken by opening the Quicken application icon, it automatically opens the data file you were working with when you last quit Quicken.
- You can see which data file is open by looking at the title bar for the Accounts window—the name of the active file should appear, as shown here:

- To open a different data file, choose File | Open File and use the dialog that appears to select and open a different file.

Backing Up and Restoring Your Quicken Data File

Imagine this: you set up Quicken to track all of your finances, and you record transactions regularly so the Quicken data file is always up to date. Then one evening when you start your computer to surf the Net, you find that your hard drive has died. Not only have your plans for the evening been ruined, but your Quicken data file is also a casualty of your hard drive's untimely death.

If you back up your Quicken data as regularly as you update its information, the loss of your Quicken data file would be a minor inconvenience, rather than a catastrophe. In this section, I explain how to back up your Quicken data file and how to restore it if the original file is lost or damaged.

Backing Up

Quicken offers three backup techniques for protecting your Quicken data file:

- **Automatically back up your data file when you close it**   This can be done transparently, in the background, by Quicken. The drawback: the backup copies are made onto your hard disk, where Quicken (and probably your original data file) is stored.

- **Manually back up your data file when Quicken reminds you to**   Although this takes a bit of additional effort on your part, you can back up the file to another disk or a network drive for added security.

- **Manually back up your data file as part of your regular backup procedure**   Let's face it—your Quicken data file isn't the only one that needs to be backed up. You can copy your Quicken data file to another disk or network drive when you back up your other files.

Since everyone has (or should have) their own backup strategy, I'll concentrate on automatic backups and backup reminders.

Setting Backup Preferences

To have Quicken automatically back up your data file or remind you to back it up, you need to set options in the Preferences dialog. Choose Quicken 2002 Deluxe | Preferences (Mac OS X) or Edit | Preferences (Mac OS 9). In the left side of the Preferences dialog that appears, click the File Backup item. Data File Backup options should fill the dialog, as shown here:

There are two main options, each corresponding to a technique Quicken uses to help you keep your files backed up:

- **Automatically Back Up My Data File When Closing** enables the automatic backup feature. If you turn on this check box, you should enter values in the two edit boxes below it to specify how often Quicken should back up your data files and how many backup files it should keep.
- **Remind Me To Back Up My Data File When Closing** tells Quicken to display a backup reminder dialog when you close the data file. If you turn on this check box, you should enter a value in the edit box below it to specify how often Quicken should remind you.

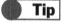 **Tip**   *You can turn on both check boxes to take advantage of both backup features.*

When you're finished setting options, click OK to save them.

Automatically Backing Up

Automatically backing up data files is easy because you don't have to do a thing. Once you set up this feature, Quicken does all the work for you.

When you quit Quicken or close your Quicken data file to open another one, Quicken automatically saves a copy of the old data file in the Backup folder inside the Quicken Essentials folder. The file is named with the number 1 at the beginning of its name. If a file with that name already existed, it is renamed with a 2 at the beginning of its name. This is done for each existing backup copy until the maximum number of backup copies is reached; then the oldest file is automatically deleted.

The benefit of this backup strategy—other than the automation, of course—is that if a file becomes corrupted, you can go back to a version before the corruption occurred.

Backing Up When Reminded

If you enabled the backup reminders feature, Quicken displays a dialog like the one shown next when it's time to remind you to back up your data file.

You have two options:

- **Skip** tells Quicken to skip the backup. The dialog disappears and you can go about your business.
- **Backup** tells Quicken to back up the data file using the settings in the dialog. You can change the name and location of the backup file if desired before you click Backup. When the backup is complete, Quicken quits or, if you told it to open a different data file, opens the file.

Tip   *Remember, if your computer's hard disk crashes, everything on it—including your backup files—will be lost. To get the most benefit of the backup reminder feature, use it to back up your data file to removable media, another hard disk, or Apple's iDisk.*

Restoring from a Backup

When disaster strikes and you need to restore your Quicken data file from a backup, you can open the backup from within Quicken. Choose File | Open Backup. A dialog like the one shown next appears. Use it to locate, select, and open the backup you want to open.

● **Caution** *Once you open and work with a backup file, all changes you make to your Quicken data are recorded to that copy of the file. If the original file still exists, it will no longer be up to date. For this reason, you may want to delete the original file and rename the backup copy you are now using with the same name as the original. You can do this in the Mac OS Finder.*

Importing and Exporting Data

Quicken supports its QIF format for importing and exporting data from other versions of Quicken to Quicken 2002, or exporting Quicken 2002 data for use with other versions of Quicken.

Importing Quicken Data

You can import data saved in Quicken QIF format into Quicken 2002 for Macintosh. You might find this useful when converting Quicken for Windows or QuickBooks files to Quicken for Macintosh format. You may also find this helpful when entering transactions downloaded from financial institutions that do not support Online Account Access or Web Connect.

● **Tip** *Quicken 2002 can automatically open files created with most versions of Quicken for Macintosh. In most cases, you don't need to use the Import command for these files; use the Open command instead.*

● **Note** *I discuss Online Account Access and Web Connect in Chapter 5.*

Before you import a QIF format file into your Quicken data file, back up the data file. Remember, Quicken automatically saves all changes to a data file. If something goes wrong with the import, your original data file could be damaged or could contain some incorrect transactions. I explain how to back up a data file earlier in this appendix.

To import a QIF format file, choose File | Import QIF. The Open dialog, which is shown next, appears. Use it to locate, select, and open the QIF file you want to import. Quicken displays a dialog while it imports the data. When it is finished, the data appears in your Quicken account(s).

Exporting Quicken Data

You can also export Quicken data to QIF format. Choose File | Export to display the Export dialog:

You have two choices:

- **Full Export** tells Quicken to export all of the data in the file.
- **Custom Export** enables you to set options for the transactions and types of information that are exported. Use pop-up menus, edit boxes, and check boxes to specify what should be exported.

When you click Export, Quicken displays a standard Save dialog. Enter a name and choose a disk location for the exported file. (You may want to include the .QIF file extension, especially if the file will be used on a Windows computer.) Then click Save to export the data.

Other File Management Tasks

Quicken's File menu and the Finder enable you to perform several other tasks with Quicken data files. Here's a quick overview of a few tasks I think you might find useful.

Copying the Current Data File

The File menu's Save A Copy command enables you to copy the current data file to a different disk or save a copy with a different name. Choose File | Save A Copy to display the tiny Save A Copy dialog, which is shown next. Enter the starting and ending date for the transactions you want to save. If desired, turn on the check box to include uncleared transactions dated before the date range's start date. Then click OK.

Next, Quicken displays a standard Save dialog. Use it to enter a name and select a disk location for the new file and click Save.

Deleting a Data File

Like any other Macintosh document, Quicken data files appear as icons in the Mac OS Finder. To delete a data file, simply locate its icon on your disk and drag it to the Trash. Emptying the Trash removes it for good.

Note *You cannot delete a data file if it is open within Quicken.*

Caution *Deleting a data file permanently removes all of the data within it.*

Renaming a Data File

You can also rename a data file within the Mac OS Finder. Locate the file's icon and click its name. (In Mac OS X, you may have to click it a second time.) An edit box appears around the file name. Enter a new name for the file and press RETURN.

Password-Protecting Quicken Data

Quicken offers two types of password protection for your data: file passwords and transaction passwords. In this section, I tell you how these options work.

Protecting a Data File

When you password-protect a data file, the file cannot be opened without the password. This is the ultimate in protection—it prevents unauthorized users from even seeing your data.

Setting Up the Password

Choose Quicken 2002 Deluxe | Preferences (Mac OS X) or Edit | Preferences (Mac OS 9). In the left side of the Preferences dialog that appears, click Passwords to display Passwords preferences:

Turn on the Require A Password To Open This Data File check box. The Establish File Password dialog, which is shown next, appears; if it does not appear automatically, click the Password button in that area of the Preferences dialog to display it. Enter the same password in each edit box and click OK. Then click OK to dismiss the Preferences dialog.

Opening a Password-Protected Data File

When you open a data file that is password-protected, the Enter File Password dialog, which is shown next, appears. Enter your password and click OK to open the file.

Protecting Existing Transactions

When you password-protect existing transactions, the transactions cannot be modified unless the password is properly entered. This prevents unauthorized or accidental alterations to data.

Setting Up the Password

Choose Quicken 2002 Deluxe | Preferences (Mac OS X) or Edit | Preferences (Mac OS 9). In the left side of the Preferences dialog that appears, click Passwords to display Passwords preferences, which was shown earlier.

Turn on the Require A Password For Transactions check box. The Establish Transaction Password dialog, which looks just like the Establish File Transaction dialog shown earlier, appears; if it does not appear automatically, click the Password button to display it. Enter the same password in each edit box and click OK. Then, back in the Preferences dialog, enter a date before which the transactions cannot be modified. Click OK to save your settings and dismiss the Preferences dialog.

Modifying a Password-Protected Transaction

When you attempt to modify a transaction that is protected with a password, the Modify Transactions Password dialog, which is shown next, appears. Enter your password and click OK to complete the transaction modification.

Password Tips

Here are a few things to keep in mind when working with passwords:

- Passwords can be up to 16 characters in length and can contain any character, including a space.
- Quicken does not distinguish between uppercase and lowercase characters.
- If you forget your password, you will not be able to access the data file. Write your password down and keep it in a safe place—but not on a sticky note attached to your computer monitor.

- You can change your password in the Password Preferences dialog, shown earlier. Simply click the Password button for the type of password you want to change and enter your current password and new password as prompted.

Remember, your data file is only as secure as you make it. Quicken's password protection can certainly help prevent unauthorized access to your data files.

Updating Quicken

If you have a connection to the Internet, you can use it to check for updates to your Quicken software. Choose File | Check For Updates to get things started. Quicken connects to the Internet and queries the Quicken server for update information. Follow the instructions that appear onscreen to install updates if they are available.

Customizing Quicken

In this Appendix:

- *Setting Quicken preferences*

- *Customizing the toolbar*

Once you've worked with Quicken for a while, you may want to fine-tune the way it looks and works to best suit your needs. Some customization options—like creating accounts and categories and setting up recurring transactions—are an integral part of using Quicken. Most of these options are discussed elsewhere in this book. Other customization options—like setting options for register window operations or adding and removing toolbar buttons—are less commonly used.

In this appendix, I explain all the customization options available for Quicken and provide cross-references to other chapters in the book where you can learn more about the features they work with.

Setting Quicken Preferences

Quicken's Preferences window offers a number of preference categories you can set to change Quicken's appearance and functionality. To open the window, choose Quicken 2002 Deluxe | Preferences (Mac OS X) or Edit | Preferences (Mac OS 9). Here's what the window looks like with General Preferences options displayed:

You can click the names of categories in the scrolling list along the left side of the window to display the various categories of options. Here's a summary of the options you can set.

Customization Preferences

The options within the Customization group enable you to customize the way Quicken's interface looks and works. The group includes the following categories of preferences: General, Auto-Reconcile, Toolbar, Registers, Reports, Graphs, QuickMath, and Country. Here's a closer look at each of them.

General

General preferences, which are shown in the previous illustration, control the fiscal year starting month. Choose a month from the pop-up menu. By default, this option is set to January.

As shown next, Mac OS 9 users can also turn on the Show Backdrop Behind Windows check box to select a textured background to appear behind all Quicken windows.

Auto-Reconcile

Auto-Reconcile preferences, which are shown next, control the Auto-Reconcile feature, which is new in Quicken 2002. (Auto-Reconcile is covered in Chapter 15.) Use the pop-up menu to choose an account for which Online Account Access is enabled. Then turn on the Enable Auto-Reconcile check box and set options as desired:

- **Auto-Reconcile Without Reminding Me** tells Quicken to automatically reconcile the account, without displaying a reminder or prompt.
- **I Reconcile My Online Account** enables you to select when you receive your online account. If you select the When I Receive My Paper Statement option, be sure to enter the day of the month you usually receive your account statement in the mail.

You can set options in this dialog for each online-enabled account you have set up in Quicken. Simply select a new account from the pop-up menu and click Save in the dialog that appears.

Toolbar

Toolbar Preferences displays the Configure Toolbar button, which you can click to customize Quicken's toolbar. I explain how to work with these options later in this appendix.

Register

Register preferences control the way account registers work. (I provide detailed instructions for using account registers and the Write Checks window in Chapter 4.) As you can see in the following illustration, there are quite a few options.

- **Pressing Return Tabs To The Next Field** tells Quicken to move from field to field when you press either the TAB or RETURN key. With this option turned off, Quicken moves to the next field when you press the TAB key only. This option is turned off by default.

- **Enter Amounts Without Decimal Point** instructs Quicken to automatically insert a decimal point two places from the right when you enter a number. For example, with this option enabled, if you enter 924, Quicken accepts it as 9.24. This option is turned off by default.

- **Request Confirmation For Changing A Transaction** tells Quicken to display a confirmation dialog each time you make a change to a previously entered transaction. By default, this option is turned off.

- **Require Category In Transactions** tells Quicken to remind you to include a category when you attempt to record a transaction without one. By default, this option is turned on.

- **Warn About Duplicate Check Numbers** tells Quicken to warn you if you attempt to record a transaction with the same check number as an existing transaction. This option is turned on by default.

- **Show Additional Note On Checks** tells Quicken to provide an additional note field in the Write Checks window. By default, this option is turned off.

- **Use QuickFill To Fill In Transactions** tells Quicken to automatically enter a transaction from the QuickFill list when you enter the beginning of the

QuickFill entry in a register. This feature can save a lot of time, as I explain in Chapter 14. By default, this option is turned on.

- **Add New Transactions To The QuickFill List** tells Quicken to automatically add each new register transaction to the QuickFill list. This option is turned on by default.

- **Auto-Open Split Transactions** tells Quicken to automatically display all line items in a split transaction when you select it. This option is turned on by default.

- **Auto-Close Split Transactions** tells Quicken to automatically hide all line items in a split transaction when you have finished working with it. This option is turned on by default.

- **Prompt For Reconcile Help On Click In Clr Field** tells Quicken to ask if you want to reconcile a transaction when you click the Clr field for a transaction. This option is turned on by default.

- **Auto-Close Other Registers When A Register Is Open** tells Quicken to automatically close open register windows when you open a different register window. This option can prevent screen clutter by keeping too many windows from being open at once, but it also prevents you from looking at more than one register at a time. By default, this option is turned off.

Reports

Reports preferences, which are illustrated next, enable you to specify default settings for creating reports. (I cover creating reports in Chapter 16.) Here are your options:

- **Show Account** enables you to choose the information that should show for each account in the report. Your options are Name And Description, Name (the default setting), and Description.

- **Show Category/Class** enables you to choose the information that should show for each category and class in the report. Your options here are also Name And Description, Name (the default setting), and Description.

- **Ask To Save Changes Before Closing A Report** tells Quicken to display a dialog asking if you want to save changes you made to a report when you close the report. By default, this option is turned on.

Formatting options can be set for each section of a report. Select the section for which you want to set formatting options, then choose options from the pop-up menus near the bottom of the window. The sample area shows what the changes look like. Do this for each report section that you want to change.

Graphs

Graphs preferences, which are shown next, look and work a lot like report preferences. (I tell you how to create graphs in Chapter 16.) Use radio buttons to select whether you want 2-Dimensional or 3-Dimensional styles (3-Dimensional is selected by default). Then set formatting options for graph sections the same way you do for report sections.

QuickMath

QuickMath preferences enable you to configure the QuickMath feature. This feature can automatically perform calculations when you enter values followed by a non-numeric keyboard key. For example, to multiply the value 5 by 0.01, you'd enter 5%. This is a predefined value for QuickMath, as shown next. You can create up to ten QuickMath functions by entering a key, operator, and value for each one.

Country

Country preferences enable you to specify whether you want to use the U.S. or Canadian version of Quicken. Select the appropriate radio button to make your selection. To complete the switch from one version to another, you'll have to click OK, and then quit and relaunch Quicken.

Bills Preferences

The Bills group of preferences controls the way Quicken handles missed bills and enables you to set up the Billminder feature. Here's a look at each category of preferences in this group.

Missed Bills

Missed Bills preferences, shown next, let you set up Quicken's new bill scanning and matching feature. This feature enables Quicken to identify bills you pay regularly and alert you when they are due. I tell you more about this new feature of Quicken 2002 in Chapter 14.

- **Check For Matching Bills On Register Entry** enables the bill scanning and matching feature. This feature is turned on by default.
- **'Upcoming' Is Defined As Due Within _n_ Days** enables you to specify how far in advance Quicken checks for upcoming bills.
- **Bill Scanning/Matching Sensitivity** options enable you to specify how likely you are to pay bills early or late or skip bill payments. By choosing one of the three options—Often, Sometimes, or Seldom Or Never—from these two pop-up menus, you can fine-tune the way the Bill Scanning and Matching feature works.

Billminder

Billminder preferences determine how Quicken's bill reminder feature works. I tell you more about this feature in Chapter 14. There are two options to set:

- **Days In Advance** enables you to specify how many days in advance Quicken should remind you about postdated checks and scheduled transactions. You can enter a value from 0 to 30 in this edit box.
- **Quicken Will Remind You When You Start Quicken** tells Quicken to remind you about postdated checks and scheduled transactions when you launch Quicken.

Internet Preferences

The Internet group of preferences enables you to configure Quicken for accessing and downloading information from the Internet. (I discuss connecting to the Internet in Chapter 3 and elsewhere in this book.) There are two categories of options: Quotes and Proxy Server. Here's a look at each.

Quotes

There's only one Quotes preference: an edit box to specify the percent at which you should be notified of a portfolio account's change when you download security prices into Quicken. By default, the value is 2%—this means if an account's value changes by 2 percent or more (either gain or loss) when you download security prices, Quicken tells you about it. I tell you about downloading stock quotes in Chapter 7.

Proxy Server

If you have a direct connection to the Internet, you can enter information about your proxy server in the Proxy Server preferences, shown next. You can get the information you need to enter from your network administrator.

⬤ **Caution**   *Do not set proxy information unless instructed by your network administrator. Doing so could prevent you from connecting to the Internet.*

Checks Preferences

Quicken can print checks for you, saving you the bother of writing them by hand. To use this feature, you must obtain Quicken-compatible check stock from Intuit or another supplier, as I discuss in Chapter 4. The Checks group of preferences offers options for setting up Quicken for check printing, as well as ordering check stock. Here is a closer look at each category of options.

Print

Print preferences enable you to set up Quicken for printing checks. The options vary slightly based on the type of printer you have. Here's what they look like with a LaserWriter 8 printer driver selected:

- **Account** enables you to select the account for which you will print checks.
- **Font** and **Size** enable you to set the typeface and typeface size to appear on checks.
- **Check Style** enables you to select one of the compatible check styles: Standard (the default selection), Voucher, or Wallet.
- **Alignment When Printing One Or Two Checks** enables you to select one of four alignment options for feeding checks. Look carefully at the pictures to

determine which one is correct for your printer. This option is not available when you have a pin-feed printer (such as an ImageWriter).

- **Print Categories On Voucher Checks** tells Quicken to print transaction category information on the voucher portion of checks. This option is turned on by default.

- **Use Today's Date When Printing Checks** tells Quicken to print the current date on checks. With this option turned off, Quicken prints the transaction date on checks.

- **CheckArt** enables you to include a graphic on your checks. Use the Copy command in your graphics program to copy an image to the Clipboard. Then switch back to Quicken, click the CheckArt button, and use the Paste command to paste the image in.

Caution   *CheckArt images may print over other check information, such as your name and address, depending on the style and layout of your checks.*

- **Positioning** enables you to fine-tune the positioning of check information on check stock. If a sample printed check indicates that adjustments are necessary, click the Positioning button to display the Adjust Positioning dialog, which is shown next. Enter values to adjust the vertical and horizontal position of various check elements and click OK to save your settings. Print another sample check to see how your adjustments affected the check printout and make additional adjustments if necessary.

> ⬤ **Caution** | *Under normal circumstances, it should not be necessary to make position adjustments. Do not make changes in this dialog unless a sample check printout indicates that an adjustment is necessary.*

Order

Order preferences, which are shown next, enable you to set check ordering reminders. This feature tells Quicken to remind you to order more checks when you get to a certain check number. This makes it impossible (or nearly impossible) to run out of check stock for any of the accounts for which you print checks with Quicken.

You can set three options:

- **Account Name** is the name of the account for which you want to be reminded to order checks.
- **Last Check Number** is the check number on the last check in your box of checks.
- **Remind Me To Reorder At Check Number** is the check number at which Quicken should remind you to order checks.

Here's how it works. Suppose you have a package of checks numbered 501 to 700. You write about five checks a week and you want to be reminded to order checks at least three weeks in advance. You'd enter 700 in the Last Check Number box and 685 in the Remind Me To Reorder At Check Number box.

To save the reminder, click the Set Reminder button. If you want to remove the reminder—perhaps because you bought checks before Quicken reminded you to—click the Remove Reminder button.

Security Preferences

The Security group of preferences enables you to set up passwords to protect online account access and your Quicken data file, as well as set up file backup options. (I tell you more about using the PIN Vault in Chapter 14 and about working with Quicken data files in Appendix A.) Here's a closer look at the two categories of preferences.

Passwords

Passwords preferences enable you to set up two different passwords for the Quicken data file:

- **Use PIN Vault For PINs** tells Quicken to use the new PIN Vault feature for online account access with financial institutions.
- **Require A Password To Open This Data File** enables you to set up a password that must be entered to open the data file. To use this option, turn on the check box, click the Password button beside it, and enter the same password twice in the dialog that appears (shown next). The characters you enter will appear as bullets. Click OK. You might find this feature useful if the computer on which your Quicken data file resides is shared by others.

- **Require A Password For Transactions** enables you to set up a password that must be entered to modify transactions made on or before a specific date. To use this option, set up the password as instructed above, then enter a date in the edit box.

Caution *If you use either of these two features, don't forget your password! If you do, you could be locked out of your data files or prevented from modifying transactions!*

File Backup

The Data File Backup preferences enable you to set options for Quicken to either automatically back up your data or remind you to back up your data:

- **Automatically Back Up My Data File When Closing** tells Quicken to back up your data file when you close it. If you turn on this check box, you can enter values in the two edit boxes below it. The first tells Quicken how often to back up the data file. The default value is 1, or every time you close your data file. The second value specifies how many backup files Quicken should keep. The default value is 6, or the last six versions of the data file. Backup files are stored with your Quicken data file.

- **Remind Me To Back Up My Data File When Closing** tells Quicken to display a backup reminder dialog when you close the data file. If you turn on this check box, you can specify how often Quicken should remind you. The default value is 1, or every single time you close the data file.

> **Tip** *Use the automatic backup feature to prevent data loss in the event of a corrupted data file. Although it doesn't happen often, it could happen. It's a lot better to have a backup copy handy than to have to rebuild a data file from scratch.*

Customizing the Toolbar

You can also customize the appearance and functionality of Quicken by making changes to the toolbar. You can show or hide any of the toolbar's elements (tabs, command buttons, and account buttons), specify which command buttons should appear on a tab, and even create your own custom tabs.

You do all this with the Configure Toolbar dialog, shown next. To display it, choose Quicken 2002 Deluxe | Preferences (Mac OS X) or Edit | Preferences (Mac OS 9) to display the Preferences dialog. Click Toolbar in the list on the left side of the dialog to display the Toolbar category of preferences and click the Configure Toolbar button that appears in the dialog.

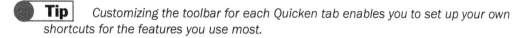 **Tip**   *Customizing the toolbar for each Quicken tab enables you to set up your own shortcuts for the features you use most.*

Toggling the Display of Toolbar Elements

Three check boxes within the Configure Toolbar dialog enable you to toggle the display of toolbar elements: Show Tabs, Show Command Buttons, and Show Account Buttons. Turn off a check box to hide the element; turn on a check box to display the element.

Modifying Tabs

You can modify tabs in a number of ways:

- To change the name of a tab, begin by clicking the tab you want to change to make it active. Then enter a new name in the Tab Name edit box. When you click Change, the tab name changes.

- To remove a tab, drag it off the toolbar. When you release the mouse button, the tab disappears.

- To create a new tab, enter a name for the tab in the Tab Name edit box, and then click the New Tab button. The tab appears at the top of the toolbar, beside the other tabs. Follow the instructions earlier in this section to customize the tab's toolbar as desired.

- To change the position of tabs, drag a tab to a new position on the toolbar. When you release the mouse button, the tab moves.

Modifying Command Buttons

Start by clicking the tab for which you want to modify command buttons. Then use one of the following techniques to make the change:

- To remove a command button from the toolbar, drag it off the toolbar. When you release the mouse button, the command button is removed.

- To add a command button to the toolbar, locate the button you want to add in the scrolling list within the Configure Toolbar dialog. Then drag the button from the list into position on the toolbar. When you release the mouse button, the command button is added.

Modifying Account Buttons

Although Quicken can automatically add account buttons to the toolbar of the tab in which you open the account, you can also specify which account buttons should appear on a tab's toolbar. First, click the tab for which you want to modify account buttons. Then use one of the following techniques to make the change:

- To remove an account button from the toolbar, drag it off the toolbar. When you release the mouse button, the account button is removed and appears in the list of accounts in the Configure Toolbar dialog.

- To add an account button to the toolbar, locate the account you want to add in the scrolling list within the Configure Toolbar dialog. Then drag the account name from the list into position on the toolbar. When you release the mouse button, the account button is added and its name is removed from the list.

- To change the position of account buttons on the toolbar, drag an account button to a new position on the toolbar. When you release the mouse button, the account button moves.

Note   *If all accounts already appear as buttons on the toolbar, the account scrolling list will be empty. In addition, if there isn't enough room on the toolbar for another account, items in the account scrolling list will appear in gray and cannot be selected or dragged.*

Restoring all Toolbars to Quicken Defaults

If you decide you don't like your changes to the toolbar, you can restore them to "factory defaults" by clicking the Revert To Default Settings button.

Saving Your Changes

To save your changes, be sure to click the Change button at the bottom of the Configure Toolbar dialog. Then click OK in the Preferences dialog to dismiss it.

Index

www.ingramcontent.com/pod-product-compliance
Lightning Source LLC
Chambersburg PA
CBHW080143060326
40689CB00018B/3837